Tireless Border Diplomacy of India with China and Pakistan

Tireless Border Diplomacy of India with China and Pakistan

Rajkumar Singh

GYAN

ISBN : 978-81-212-1325-7

Price : ₹ 950

First Published, 2016

Published by

Gyan Publishing House
5, Ansari Road
Daryaganj, New Delhi-110002
Phones: 9811692060
E-mail: books@gyanbooks.com

Printed at: G. Print Process, Delhi.

Cataloging in Publication Data—DK
Courtesy: D.K. Agencies (P) Ltd. <docinfo@dkagencies.com>

Singh, Raj Kumar, 1958- author.
Tireless border diplomacy of India with China and Pakistan/Rajkumar Singh.
pages cm
Includes bibliographical references.
ISBN 9788121213257

1. India—Boundaries—China. 2. China—Boundaries—India. 3. India—Boundaries—Pakistan. 4. Pakistan—Boundaries—India. I. Title.

DS450.C6S56 2016 DDC 327.54051 23

Dedicated to
Smt Anarsi Devi
Eldest Bhabhi

Contents

Preface 9
Acknowledgements 19
Glossary 21
Abbreviations 27

Chapter I
Initial Cooperation, Competition and Conflict with China 29

Chapter II
India-China Border Talks : Status and Strategy 59

Chapter III
Updated Border Perception and Peer Reviews 123

Chapter IV
Understanding Kashmir : Problem and Perception 153

Chapter V
Terrorism in Jammu & Kashmir : An Overview 199

Appendices on People's Republic of China 247
Bibliography 271
Index 287

Preface

Even today, foreign policy is an instrument to serve the goals and national interest of a country and managing relations with other states is a necessary activity of every state. It arises from two facts of the international situation. Firstly, that no state is an immured island but a member of a society of states, participation of which is inescapable. Secondly, in the international society power is decentralised, that is, distributed among states in unequal measure. In the situation, while formulating the principles of its foreign policy a country has to keep in mind its domestic conditions as well as the realities of the external environments. The sum total of the goals and objectives of a nation's foreign policy constitute its national interest as the nation conceives it. It is the concept of national interest that helps the nation decide the order of priorities among different objectives and goals. Although national interest, in its detail, differs from country to country, the core of national interest is the same for different countries. All countries big and small desire and continually search for national security. Security implies, at the minimum level, national independence and territorial integrity. As such, India is bound to change according to the world politics milieu and national capability. The country has moved from its tradition of pursuit of gaining power to the level of sustaining and increasing power. However, in concentrating on major international issues and regional conflicts, India will have to find ways to fulfil the requirements of national interest.

The book, ***Tireless Border Diplomacy of India with China and Pakistan*** presents before us the recognised facts of India's border diplomacy, its ups and downs along with diplomatic turn and twists, especially with the Peoples Republic of China and Pakistan. Of the strategic challenges, the most formidable enduring strategic challenge to India emanates from China and Pakistan. In the context we all are aware that the fastest growing region in the world today is Asia and not Europe or America. Now the gravity of power is shifting to Asia and China is on the top of the power hierarchy in Asia and a significant player in global politics. As a result, Beijing resents India's growing weight in the world politics and becoming more and more hostile towards India. Likewise, the peace initiative launched by Atal Bihari Vajpayee in January 2004, more than a decade ago, is continuing despite recurring terrorist attacks. Soon thereafter the UPA Government led by Manmohan Singh went a step further and formed Joint Mechanism for dealing with terrorism in Pakistan. Even this of course, has not helped India in tackling the scourge of Islamic Fundamentalism. Unfortunately, when the colonial power, Britain, withdrew from India it left a dangerous legacy of carelessly or arbitrarily drawn borders with both– China and Pakistan which are today both a cause and a symptom of endless tensions between big neighbours of South Asia. With both the neighbours– China and Pakistan India's boundary dispute is at the heart of their differences and a potential destabilising factor for their bilateral relations that also pose a danger for the region.

Sovereignty over two large and various smaller separated pieces of territory have been contested between India and China. The westernmost, Aksai Chin, is claimed by India as part of the state of Jammu and Kashmir and region of Ladakh but is controlled and administered as part of the Chinese autonomous region of Xinjiang. It is a virtually uninhabited high altitude wasteland crossed by the Xinjiang-Tibet Highway. The other large disputed territory, the easternmost, lies south of the McMahon Line. It was formerly referred to as the North East Frontier Agency (NEFA), and is now called Arunachal Pradesh. In the fight over these areas in 1962, the well-trained armed troops of the Chinese People's Liberation Army overpowered the ill-equipped Indian troops and captured most of the NEFA area in the war.

China is also in occupation of approximately 38,000 sq. kms. of India territory in Jammu and Kashmir. In addition, under the so-called China-Pakistan 'Boundary Agreement' of 1963, Pakistan ceded 5180 sq. kms. of Indian territory in Pakistan-occupied Kashmir (PoK) to China. The People's Republic of China claims approximately

90,000 sq. kms. of Indian territory in Arunachal Pradesh and about 2000 sq. kms. in the middle sector of the India-China boundary. The Arunachal Pradesh dispute is China's most intractable border issue. Because the gap between the positions of China and India is wide, it is difficult for both nations to reach consensus. The area of disputed region is three times that of Taiwan and six times that of Beijing. However, Arunachal Pradesh is the only issue which has a potential for conflict between India and China. If ever India and China go to war one day, it will be on this issue. India considers recurring Sino-India border clashes a potential threat to its security. Since the war of 1962, each side continued to improve its military and logistic capabilities in the disputed regions. China has continued its occupation of the Aksai Chin area, through which it built a strategic highway linking Xizang and Xinjiang autonomous regions. China had a vital military interest in maintaining control over this region, whereas Indian's primary interest lay in Arunachal Pradesh, its state in the northeast bordering Xizang Autonomous Region of the PRC.

The border between India and China and specifically the ill-defined Line of Actual Control (LAC), barring an armed clash at Nathu La in eastern Sikkim, had remained free of any major incidents through the 1970s and the early 1980s. While relations between the two countries remained cool, official statements from Beijing and New Delhi professed a desire to solve the border tangle peacefully through mutual consultations. Beginning in December 1981, officials from both sides held yearly/occasional talks on the border issue till date. Though lot had been done during the Sino-Indian official border talks, with number of border related CBMs put in place, the border issue remains mired in various bilateral and domestic compulsions and contradictions on both sides. Border 'encounters' between India and China are not rare and arise from the very real disagreements that exist between the two sides in demarcating the Line of Actual Control (LAC) on the ground.

In the context a recent policy shift occurred from Indian side. India after 1962 adopted a policy to not develop the border areas. The idea was that if India developed the border areas, the Chinese can easily use these facilities in the event of a war. This policy had changed by 2008. To redress the situation arising out of poor road connectivity which has hampered the operational capability of the Border Guarding

Forces deployed along the India-China border, the government has decided to undertake phase-wise construction of 27 road links totalling 608 km. in the border areas along the India-China border in the States of Jammu and Kashmir, Himachal Pradesh, Uttarakhand, Sikkim and Arunachal Pradesh. However, the two sides have differences in perception of the Line of Actual Control in the India-China border areas. Both sides carry out patrolling activity in the India-China border areas. Transgressions of the LAC are taken up through diplomatic channels and at Border Personnel Meetings/Flag Meetings. India and China seek a fair, reasonable and mutually acceptable settlement of the boundary question through peaceful consultations. Nevertheless, the potential for periodic low-level confrontations between border patrols to escalate likely will persist. Furthermore, both China and India continue to boost their militaries' capabilities on the border, adding to mutual suspicion. This has left both sides sensitive to each other's border activities and disposed toward worst-case perceptions of the other sides' intentions and activities.

Today, while dealing with China, none of these problems is new, but what is new is the new government in Delhi which assumed office in May 2014. The majority government in India– the first of its kind in two and a half decades is led by Narendra Damodar Das Modi, who is no stranger to China and travelled there when he was the Chief Minister of the State of Gujarat. Following Modi's assumption as the Prime Minister of India, in September 2014, Chinese President Xi Jinping came to India on a three-day official visit which provided the new government both an opportunity and a challenge to deal a potential/ controversial neighbour. Before Presidential visit, time and again Modi emphasised China's increasingly assertive postures and in course of his visit to Japan in August-September 2014 he said that eighteenth century mind-set of *vistaarvad* or expansionism would not work and *vikaash-vad* or peaceful development is needed for sustainable peace and tranquility in the world. In course of Xi Jinping's visit to India no progress on Sino-Indian border dispute was made even though both leaders reached agreements in various other areas. The joint statement issued at the end of the visit stressed their country's commitment to seek a fair, reasonable and mutually acceptable solution to the dispute as agreed in April 2005. Like earlier joint statements it also added, 'Pending a final resolution of the boundary question, the two sides will continue to make joint efforts to maintain peace and tranquility in the border areas'. Perhaps, the visiting President followed the declared two pillars of 'Chinese diplomacy' assertion and win-win cooperation-ignoring opinions outside China that these pillars contradict each other.

In response to Presidential visit and with a view to strengthen mutual trust and maintaining peace on their common border, Indian Prime Minister Narendra Modi paid a three-day return visit to China in May 2015. The visit yielded no breakthrough on the border row and in Modi's words, "the India-China relationship is a 'complex' one" with the two Asian giants eyeing each other with suspicion. The Indian Prime Minister, in his talks with Xi Jinping, raised India's concern on Chinese investment in China-Pakistan corridor in Pakistan and Pakistan-administered Kashmir. Earlier India and Pakistan have fought three wars over Kashmir and China's cooperation with Pakistan is an irritant in India-China relations. The Indian Prime Minister in his talks with Chinese counterpart Li Keqiang, agreed to explore a fair, reasonable and mutually acceptable resolution to the boundary issue. The overall result of even Modi's visit made in May 2015 emphasised us to conclude that a solution for a decade-long border dispute is nowhere in sight. Still, the two nations are increasingly vying for regional influence which could lead to a fresh round of tensions. In particular, over matters of strategic interest both leaders tend to adopt a nationalistic stance.

Next to China, India has also an all-weather border dispute with Pakistan. A territorial dispute is a disagreement over the possession or control of land between two or more states or over the possession or control of land, usually between a new state and the occupying power. After partition of the Indian sub-continent in August 1947 the area of the State of Jammu and Kashmir serve as the major dispute between India and Pakistan. India and Pakistan have fought three wars over Kashmir, including the Indo-Pakistani wars of 1947, 1965 and 1999. The Kashmir issue has been the main cause, whether direct or indirect of all major conflicts between the two countries. Rulers of Princely – ruled territories had the choice of joining India or Pakistan. Both India and Pakistan laid claim on Kashmir and thus it became the main point of conflict. The ruler of Kashmir, which had a Muslim majority population joined India by signing the Instrument of Accession.

The first Kashmir war started in October 1947 and ended in December 1948 with the Line of Control (LoC) dividing Kashmir into territories administered by India (Southern, central and northeastern area) and Pakistan (northern and western areas). At the time of accession Lord Mounbatten's remark and the offer made by the Government of India to conduct a plebiscite or referendum to determine the future status of Kashmir led to a dispute between India and Pakistan regarding the legality of the accession of Jammu and Kashmir to India. India claims that the accession is unconditional and final while Pakistan maintains that the accession is fraudulent.

In the context the term Line of Control (LoC) refers to the military control line between the Indian and Pakistani controlled parts of the former state of Jammu and Kashmir a line, to this day, does not constitute a legally recognised international boundary but is the de facto border. Originally known as the Ceasefire-Line, it was redesignated as the Line of Control following the Simla Agreement which was signed on 3rd July 1972. The two parts of the former princely state that are under Pakistan are known as Gilgit-Baltistan and Azad Jammu and Kashmir (AJK). Another ceasefire-line separates the Indian controlled state of Jammu and Kashmir from the Chinese-controlled area known as Aksai Chin. Lying further to the east it is known as the Line of Actual Control (LAC) and has been referred to as one of the most dangerous places in the world. Thus, the overall border is running from the Line of Control, which separates Jammu and Kashmir from Pakistan-occupied Kashmir, in the north, to Wagah, which partitioned the Indian Punjab state and Punjab Province of Pakistan, in the westward. The Zero point separates the Indian states of Gujarat and Rajasthan to Sindh province of Pakistan, in the southward. On the south side of the border of Jammu Division is Pakistan's Punjab border, and is called the 'working boundary' by Pakistan but 'international border' by India.

After the first border-related war in 1947-48, Pakistan believed that the population of Kashmir was generally discontented with Indian rule and that a resistance movement could be ignited by a few infiltrating saboteurs. Pakistan attempted to ignite the resistance movement by means of a covert infiltration, codenamed Operation Gibraltar. In fact, the Indo-Pak War of 1965 was the culmination of this game plan, designed to infiltrate forces into Jammu and Kashmir to precipitate an insurgency against rule by India. Most probably, this was launched by Pakistan believing that the Indian Army would be unable to defend itself against a quick military campaign in the disputed territory of Kashmir as the Indian military had suffered a loss to China in 1962. However, neutral assessments made during the war and thereafter agree that India had the upper hand over Pakistan when ceasefire was declared. With no surprise both before and during the war the People's Republic of China had been a major military associate of Pakistan and had invariably admonished India, with whom it had fought a war in 1962. Despite ceasefire, India was perceived as the victor due to its success in halting the Pakistan-backed insurgency in Kashmir. The *Time* magazine in its October 1965 issue assessed, 'Now it's apparent to everybody that India is going to emerge as an Asian power in its own right'. Feroz Khan, the nuclear theorist, also maintained that the 1965 war was the last conventional attempt by Pakistan to snatch Kashmir by military forces.

As at the end of first Kashmir war India controlled the most valuable parts of Kashmir, sporadic periods of violence, directly or indirectly inspired by Pakistan became a regular feature in the area but initially for a long time there was no organised insurgency movement. The 1965 war between India and Pakistan was the second conflict between the two countries over the status of the State of Jammu and Kashmir. The clash did not resolve their dispute but it did engage the United States and the Soviet Union in ways that would have important implications for subsequent superpower involvement in the region. From there onwards the international politics of the Cold War affected the nature of the conflict. After 1947 in comparison to Indo-US relations, US-Pakistani relations had been more consistent and positive. The US Government looked to Pakistan as an example of a moderate Muslim state and appreciated Pakistani assistance in holding the line against communist expansion by joining the SEATO in 1955. Pakistan's interest in this and other pacts stemmed from its desire to develop its military and defence capabilities, which were substantially weaker than that of India. Both the United States and the United Kingdom supplied arms to Pakistan in these years. One side effect of the war was deterioration of conditions in East Pakistan which, although not a border conflict, culminated in Indo-Pak War of 1971, resulting in defeat of

Pakistan and emergence of Bangladesh simultaneously. The Simla Agreement signed between the two in 1972 allowed both countries to settle all issues, including the Kashmir dispute, by peaceful means through mutual discussion within the framework of UN Charter. After 1971 war taking Kashmir from India became like a perfect revenge for Pakistan. For Pakistan, it was a complete and humiliating defeat, a psychological setback that came from a defeat at the hands of intense rival, India. On the other, India was also not serious about the gaining the State of Jammu and Kashmir back to the invader and it lost the greatest opportunity to resolve the Kashmir issue once for all by forcing defeated Pakistan to totally withdraw from the illegally occupied Indian territories of Jammu and Kashmir.

Pakistan, since its inception, has built considerable expertise in militancy and use of irregulars; on their own or as an extension of the Pak Army, for war. In line, three significant developments took place in post-1971 periods. First, the successful use of irregular forces and political legitimacy to organise and conduct *jihad* in the Afghan War. This was an extremely useful experience for Pak military. Second, the acquisition of nuclear capability by Pakistan in late 1980s, which remained covert till May 1998. This capability encouraged the Pak military to conclude that a conventional war with India was not possible. Third, loss of initiative to India in the occupation of Siachin Glacier. All these developments prompted Pakistan to make fresh attempts to annex Jammu and Kashmir through a proxy war, on the lines of Afghan War. Even during the last Kashmir war till date, in the Kargil sector in 1999, the Pakistan Army took additional step forward. Regular Army personnel shed their uniforms and dressed themselves as irregulars to intrude and fight on Indian territory. Earlier, as is well known, the Afghan War, Pak ISI siphoned off a plethora of arms, equipment and funds meant for Afghan rebels. With several million dollars of unaccounted funds, the ISI had at its disposal a large well-oiled machinery for churning out Jihad-oriented trained irregulars to be inducted into Jammu and Kashmir. As a result, a large number of young Kashmiris were covertly infiltrated to Pakistan occupied Kashmir through a porous Line of Control for arms training. The period from 1987 to 1989 saw an increase in violence and prolonged strikes in the Kashmir Valley and attacks on political leadership, police and para military forces. At Kargil, the Pak military felt confident of its success. Unfortunately, since then, there has been a renewal of effort to fuel proxy war. In fact, in Pakistan, issues like Afghanistan, Indo-Pak relations, Kashmir and nuclear capability are areas of special concern to the military. The political leadership–when there is a civilian government– is either not briefed adequately or finds it difficult to assert on such matters. This is historical, almost traditional, and is expected to continue.

The Kashmir uprising of the last three decades can perhaps be categorised into two distinct periods-discontent over Delhi's rule surfacing in the 1980s, leading to the rise of groups backed by Pakistan from the early 1990s onwards. The influence of militant groups such as Al-Badr Mujahideen, which was once very powerful in the mid-1990s, has now waned to such an extent that it is no longer considered to present, a threat. Another group that has lost power and influence is Jaish-e-Mohammad, launched in 1999 by Maulana Masood Azhar. It shot to prominence in 2000 for its role in the attack on the Red Fort in Delhi. But its activities in Kashmir failed to elicit public support, especially after a 2001 car bomb attack on the Kashmir state legislative assembly which killed more than 35 people, all civilians. However, Lashkar-e-Taiba, a Pakistan-based militant group was formed by Hafiz Mohammad Saeed in the early 1990s put the Kashmir insurgency more firmly in the hands of Pakistanis. In the late 1990s, LeT emerged as the most dangerous militant group in Kashmir, taking the fight to Indian cities outside of Kashmir including an assault on the Indian Parliament in Delhi in 2001, and the Mumbai attack in 2008 which claimed 165 lives. Despite a Pakistani ban on military activity in Kashmir in 2006, its fighters continue to attempt infiltration into Indian-administered Kashmir. Very recently in August 2015 a LeT terrorist and Pakistani citizen Mohammad Naveed was caught alive while one terrorist was killed when they attacked a Border Security Force convoy in Udhampur area of Jammu and Kashmir.

The terrorist activities in Jammu and Kashmir along with different parts of India remain a major stumbling block in smooth Indo-Pak relations. It generates cross-border activity form Pakistan, often with government backing. Terrorism makes any Indian move towards an innovative solution impossible politically, and it will take innovative thinking to get over the present impasse. Terrorist violence is more regional in nature than ever before and will not be contained without a regional solution, which requires the good faith participation of India, Pakistan and Afghanistan and possibly other South Asian states, especially Bangladesh. The US, in particular, will have to focus on promoting regional cooperation among all three countries and defusing conflict between New Delhi and Islamabad on the one hand, and Kabul and Islamabad on the other. In line, the non-event of talks scheduled in the last week of August 2015 between the National Security Advisors (NSA) of India and Pakistan, Ajit Doval and Sartaj Aziz, is a setback for our anti-terror agenda. We have lost an opportunity to highlight our terror concerns. In a nutshell, as long as the hostile elements remain influential in Pakistan, a normal state to state relationship will elude us. Pakistan's internal politics will need to change before these elements can be neutralised. In a democratic India while there is consensus on the need to have normal and peaceful relations with Pakistan, there is also a strong sentiment that Pakistan's support to terrorism against India prevents normalisation.

Rajkumar Singh

SAHARSA, Bihar
14th July 2015

Acknowledgements

I wish to thank the institutions and individuals for their encouragement, co-operation and good-wishes that I received and staff of the central libraries at New Delhi and other places where I got a lot of information and analytical/critical views of different subject experts. They all deserve cordial thanks. I am deeply grateful to several persons and colleagues.

Among teachers late Dr D.N. Mallik, Dr Kirtyanand Singh, Dr R.N. Kumar and Dr M.R. Kazami, retired professors of the University Department of Political Science, BRA Bihar University, Muzaffarpur have been constant source of guide and encouragement at every stage. Colleagues Dr Dhirendra Narayan Singh, Department of Political Science, MLT College, Saharsa, Dr Chandra Prakash Singh, Department of History, Dr Kumar Jyotivardhan and Dr Usha Sinha, Department of Hindi, Dr Ram Naresh Singh, Department of Maithili, West Campus P.G. Centre, Saharsa and departmental colleagues, Dr Bijay Kumar Verma and Dr Pawan Kumar are thankful for their co-operation and good-wishes. Eldest brother, the late Suryanath Singh, elder brother Bhuvneshwar Prasad Singh, father-in-law Ramanand Singh, retired Professor and Head, University Department of Physics, BRA Bihar University, Muzaffarpur, and Smt Lalmani Devi deserve deep sense of gratitude for their sincere good-wishes. I am no less thankful to colleagues and staff of the B.N. Mandal University, West Campus, P.G. Centre, Saharsa.

I would be failing in my duty if I do not record my honest good-wishes and gratitude to the family members including my wife Dr Hemlata Singh, son, Aditya Priyadarshi and Apurv Adarsh in the completion of the book.

Glossary

Ahmadis	Followers of Mirza Ghulam Ahmed Qadiani; a religious minority in Pakistan.
Ahimsa	Non-violence.
Alim	Religious scholar.
Amir	A person holding authority, a ruler, head of an organisation.
Arms race	A competition between nations in which each side attempts to achieve or maintain military superiority.
Arms trade	The international selling of armaments for profit, which is carried on by governments and private contractors around the world.
Authority	Power that is attached to a position that others perceive as legitimate.
Autocratic rule	Rule by a specific leader who concentrates power in his own hands.
Balance of power	The theory that military conflict can be avoided if both sides have roughly equivalent military power.
Beliefs	Shared ideas held by a collective of people within a socio-cultural system.
Bioterrorism	The threat or the actual dispersal of biological or chemical agents to cause widespread disease or death in order to further a group's political, economic or social agenda.
Bureaucracy	A way of organising the activity of any institution so that it functions efficiently and impersonally.

Cabinet	Name for the small body of senior politicians responsible for directing the administration of a country.
Cabinet Government	A collective government by a committee of individuals who are theoretically equal and bound by their collective decisions.
Capitalism	An economic system based on the private ownership of the means and distribution in which the goal is to produce profit.
Centralisation	Power and authority concentrated in a few offices.
Census	A count of the population, often including a detailed profile of that population.
Charisma	A personal quality attributed to leaders who arouse fervent popular support and enthusiasm.
Civil defence	Any systematic attempts or plans by governments to limit civil casualties and damage to civil property during a war.
Class	Socio-economic differences between groups of individuals that create differences in their life chances and power.
Coalition	Groupings of rival political units in the face of a common enemy.
Cold war	The state of extreme hostility between the super-powers, associated with arms race, diplomatic conflict and hostile measures of every kind.
Conventional war	War waged only with non-nuclear weaponary.
Deobandi	Belonging to the Muslim religious seminary of Deoband, India; an orthodox sect which abhors superstitions attributed to the Brelavi sect.
Dharma	Appropriate form of moral and religious obligations in Hinduism.
Dictatorship	A form of government in which one person exercises supreme power and authority.
Fatwa	A ruling by a jurist on the legality or otherwise of an action.

Fidayeen	An action suicide.
Globalisation	The development of extensive worldwide patterns of economic, social, or political relationships between nations.
Government	Formal institutional structures of the nation-state whose purpose is to regulate internal and external relations.
Gross domestic product	The total value of all goods and services produced within the boundaries of a particular country in any given year.
Guerilla movement	The organised efforts of a non-government military organisation in resisting the legally established government.
Hudood	Plural of hadd, punishments under Islamic Law.
Ideology	Shared ideas or beliefs that serve to justify and support the interests of a particular groups or organisations.
Imam	Faith.
Islamiat	Islamic religious studies.
Jihad	Striving for perfection; spiritual endeavour; holy war.
Kafir	One who refuses to believe in the unity of God, infidel.
Karma	Action or deed; theory of future births being based on quality of actions in the present or previous lives.
Lashkars	Armies.
Leadership	The ability of a person or a group of persons to persuade others to act according to one's proposed course of action.
Limited war	Warfare fought principally by a relatively small numbers of soldiers to reach specific and politically limited objectives.
Maulana	Title given to Muslim religious scholar.
Maulvi	Title given to Muslim religious leader.
Madrassas	Religious schools.

Majlis-i-Shoora Consultative council.

Middle class A social class broadly defined occupationally as those working in white-collar and lower managerial occupations.

Muhajir Muslim migrant.

Mujahid One who participates in Jihad.

Mujahideen Plural of mujahid.

Nawab Title given to a nobleman or a king.

Nizam Rule or ruler.

Pakhtun or Pushtun People of the Afghan race inhabiting mostly the North–West Frontier Province in Pakistan.

Personality The consistent pattern of attitudes and beliefs that an individual projects to the social world.

Politics Attempts to influence government activities.

Power The ability to achieve aims or further the interests that one holds even when opposed by others.

Qazi A judge; judge of Shariah Court.

Quaid–i–Azam The great leader, a title used for the founder of Pakistan, Mohammad Ali Jinnah.

Religion A set of beliefs involving symbols regarded as sacred together with ritual practices in which members of the community engage.

Revolution A violent and total change in a political system.

Secular state A secular state is one which has no official ties to any religion.

Sharia Literally 'a clear path' set of moral injunctions constituting Islamic law.

Socialism A politico-economic system where the state controls the basic means of production.

State A given territory ruled by government institutions whose authority is backed by law and the ability to use force.

Sufi Muslim mystic; the word 'sufi' comes from the coarse woollen garment, 'suf', worn by the early mystics of Islam.

Sunnah	Tradition of the Prophet.
Tanzeem	Organisation.
Terrorism	The use of violence or the threat of violence to achieve political, social or economic ends.
Ulama	Learned authorities on Islam.

Abbreviations

AJK	:	Azad Jammu and Kashmir
APMSO	:	All Pakistan Mohajir Student's Organisation
APHC	:	All Parties Hurriyat Conference
BJP	:	Bharatiya Janata Party
BSF	:	Border Security Force
CBMs	:	Confidence Building Measures
CENTO	:	Central Treaty Organisation
CFA	:	Cease Fire Agreement
CIA	:	Central Intelligence Agency
CPM	:	Communist Party Marxist
FDLs	:	Forward Defence Lines
G-B	:	Gilgit-Baltistan
HM	:	Hizb-ul-Mujahideen
HuJI	:	Harkat-ul-Jehad Islami
IB	:	Intelligence Bureau
IM	:	Indian Mujahideen
ISI	:	Inter-Services Intelligence
JEG	:	Joint Expert's Group
JeM	:	Jaish-e-Mohammad
JI	:	Jamaat-i-Islami
JKLF	:	Jammu and Kashmir Liberation Front
JWG	:	Joint Working Group
LeT	:	Lashkar-e-Toiba

LAC	:	Line of Actual Control
LoC	:	Line of Control
MUF	:	Muslim United Front
NAM	:	Non-Aligned Movement
NC	:	National Conference
NCTC	:	National Counter Terrorism Center
NDA	:	National Democratic Alliance
NEFA	:	North East Frontier Agency
NFZ	:	No-Fire Zone
PLA	:	Peoples Liberation Army
PML	:	Pakistan Muslim League
PoK	:	Pak-occupied Kashmir
PPP	:	Pakistan People's Party/ Public-Private Partnership
PRC	:	People's Republic of China
SAARC	:	South Asian Association for Regional Cooperation
SEATO	:	South East Asian Treaty Organisation
TTP	:	Tehrik-e-Taliban Pakistan
UNGA	:	United Nations General Assembly
UNMOGIP	:	United Nations Observer Group in India and Pakistan
UNO	:	United Nations Organisation
UNSC	:	United Nations Security Council
UPA	:	United Progressive Alliance
USA	:	United States of America
USSR	:	Union of Soviet Socialist Republic
WMD	:	Weapons of Mass Destruction
WoT	:	War on Terror
WTC	:	World Trade Centre

Chapter I

Initial Cooperation, Competition and Conflict with China

1.1 India and China with Panchsheel in Asia

The famous five principles of Panchsheel or peaceful co-existence-mutual respect for each other's territorial integrity and sovereignty, non-aggression, non-intervention in other's domestic affairs, mutual benefit and equality and peaceful co-existence were first incorporated in the Sino-Indian Agreement on Tibet in April 1954. In succeeding years it occupied the form of a norm in the world community. It became a general principle of right conduct to which a community expects all its members to conform which shape the very structure of international relations. Alongside the five principles various other codes of a similar nature can be found in the constituent charters of such bodies as the United Nations, the Non-aligned Movement, the Organisation of African Unity and so on.[1] But for India and China these principles remained more than a declaration. China elevated the five principles as the cornerstone of its foreign relations with all states. It continues to stress peaceful co-existence in current pronouncements of foreign policy. India too has made strenuous and successful attempts to have these principles accepted by the non-aligned movement and incorporated as 'basic principles of international law' through the Declaration on Friendly Relations passed by the UN General Assembly.

When the principles of Panchsheel were recognised by India and China it was the honeymoon phase of Sino-Indian relations. At this point they espoused common principles on international security and international relations. Coming out of their own anti-colonial struggles, both countries adopted different systems of statehood, but they shared a common antipathy to western global hegemony. The change in the geopolitical situation today has been accompanied by the rapid rise of India, and especially China, as the economic powerhouse of the future. In the circumstances China's biggest worry is American unilateralism and the avowal of George Bush to convert the world into an American dream of democracy. Similarly, India, with its adherence to Nehruvian non-alignment also opposes American unilateralism.[2] Prevailing situation needs friendly ties with India and China. It is this common goal that allows both countries once again to espouse common security principles, based on the old ideals mooted in Panchsheel.

The origin of the essence of this peace ideology can be traced back to the fourth-fifth century AD's work of Buddhaghosha, *Visuddhimaggo* which mentions the five principles that a Buddhist follower has to follow. Before its enshrinment in the India-China Treaty on Tibet, these five principles were first proposed by Dr Surkarno as Pantja Sila in Indonesia, a Buddhist country, on 1st June 1945. In Indonesian context these were nationalism, humanism, freedom, social justice and faith in God.[3] There is no doubt in the fact that this ancient principle belongs to the Indian tradition, it was considered by the signatory of the treaty differently. While Chinese emphasised the Asianness of the doctrine of Panchsheel by using it in their dealings with Afro-Asian states and rarely in their dealings with the managers of the world system, that is western states, India laid stress on its global and modern relevance by relating it to the UN Charter.[4] However, they did not hesitate in calling Panchsheel an Asian value. The Chinese, in particular, gave the concept a cultural dimension.

Superpower Rivalry in Asia

In the post-World War II period the world was divided into military and ideological blocs, each trying to bring within its orbit as many countries as it could. The United States of America abandoned her traditional policy of isolationism and established firm partnership with the peoples of Europe, Asia, Africa and Middle East. Soon it established bilateral and multi-lateral security arrangements with more than forty countries. On the other was the Soviet Union, its arch rival, whose leaders openly affirmed their faith in the doctrines of Marx and Lenin and exhorted the people to make preparation for the inevitable conflict with the capitalist countries. It pushed Bulgaria, Hungary, Rumania, Yugoslavia, Albania, Czechoslovakia, Poland and East Germany into the Communist orbit. Going a step further the USSR also took the first major step in consolidating the solidarity of the communist states by setting up the Communist Information Bureau (Cominform) of the major European communist parties.[5] The relations between the two superpowers were marked by an undercurrent of mutual distrust and jealousy. Perkins and Duesen called these differences as inevitable because "their objectives were widely different, on one side was the idea of free society, on the other an iron despotism; on one side was an economic system which put the major emphasis on the ingenuity and enterprise of the individual, on the other an economic system the state controlled virtually the whole economy; on one side was the hope of tranquality and orderly development, on the other the hope of revolution and of the coming of a new order, on one side was a reluctance to use force, on the other a disposition to invoke force whenever and wherever it could be done without undue risk. In such a situation neither side could do justice to the motives of the other."[6]

In one way or the other hegemony was considered to be the maximum goal of superpowers in Asia. The perception of the two powers and their interests in Asia, in the developing countries, and in the world in general, has for most of the time been fairly divergent. At the minimum, the basic national interest of the United States, as in case of any nation, has been its national security- the protection of territorial integrity and political independence. In case of the US, the changing milieu of international environment have pushed the security principle from the national boundaries to the whole Western Hemisphere and transcending finally to the preservation of power equilibrium in Europe and Asia. Later the concept has widened to the effect of equating any communist advance in world politics- territorial, political, economic, cultural or military, with threat to American security. This led the United States to speak and act in the name of the so-called free world or free nations not excluding feudal-monarchial, unpopular, authoritarian and corrupt regimes of the time. Western leaders and Americans, in particular, consistently argued that their actions were in support of nationalism, the freedom of choice of new governments, and orderly processes of political change.[7] The United States' government also made it clear that it would not permit changes to take place which compromised its security or that of its allies.

In the background of US relations with the countries of Asia, the Soviets embarked on the course of competitive co-existence in the hope that it would lead to the ultimate triumph of proletarian internationalism. In general the main objectives of the foreign policy were- strengthening and developing the world socialist system, the unity and cohesion of the socialist countries and their friendship and fraternity; giving an all-out support to the national liberation movements and fostering solidarity and with the independent Asian, African and Latin American countries, and promoting peaceful co-existence.[8] The range of goals of Soviet policy in Asia was meant to have maximum and minimum objectives. At the high end of the scale must inevitably be the desire to exert hegemony over Asia- either as an expression of Russian power or of communist ideology. Hegemony can be thought of in various ways; a total communisation of Asia along the Soviet model is the extreme case and is unlikely to achieve. But attainable would be a situation in which the other Asian states have no strong and reliable external support and none of them would be strong enough to resist Soviet domination.

The USSR under Stalin was concerned with Asia- it had to adjust to the existence of a Communist regime in China and had to take a position vis-à-vis the rash of Communist revolts in the South East Asia at the end of the 1940's. But the efforts applied in Asia was extremely small. The Soviets had only limited resources and these were overwhelmingly committed to Europe where the Soviets perceived the greater danger and more hopeful prospects. By the beginning of the Khrushchev era the basis of a change in Soviet Policy towards Asia was evident because the situation in Europe had stabilised and China refused to become another Soviet satellite like Mongolia. In fact, Moscow approached Asia not as a target for Communist revolutionary activity but as a collection of nations with whom it was possible and often profitable to deal on a state-to-state basis. Since many Asian countries were glad to reciprocate the relationship, the USSR became an acceptable player in the Asian balance-of-power game. However, the importance of both the nations was never undermined and even in that period there was much talk in Washington as well as in Moscow that the future of Asia would be determined by the competition between India and China.

Position of India and China in Asia

So far as the position of Asia in world politics is concerned in post-1945 phase it has been swept by political and social revolutions. It has released the forces which have subsequently changed the face of Asia and fundamentally altered its role in world affairs. The colonial and traditional regimes that existed earlier have been replaced by a wide variety of new states. Powerful new forces of the time-nationalism, Communism, the drive for self-determination and demands for social change have shaped the development of the region. New elite groups and political leaders had emerged in every Asian state, and they all were dedicated to political, economic, and social change. Apart from the leaders in Communist China and its small Communist neighbours, a majority of the new leaders in Asia professed belief in some form of parliamentary democracy comparable to that in the West.[9] In the early 1950's despite conflicting interests of many sorts to divide the states in the region, a powerful slogan of "Asian Solidarity" came which found its expression in Sino-Indian Treaty on Tibet in 1954. Later on several developments had marred its prospect in this part of the world.

The signatory nations of the principles of Panchsheel- India and China are the two giants of Asia. In population, human resources, and potential they far outstrip any other country of Asia or even many of them combined. In spite of their differing social and political systems, both had been exploited by western imperialism and colonialism. Both had ancient cultures that had survived many internal upheavals and external onslaughts. And lastly they both had just emerged from foreign domination as proud, nationalist entities. Additionally, China also enjoyed a certain natural advantage in geopolitics. It virtually looked down upon the hills and plains of India from its higher mountain tops in Tibet and Sinkiang.[10] Even before the establishment of Communist rule in China, Jawaharlal Nehru strongly advocated friendship with the country whose culture he admired. He sincerely believed that if India and China stood together they would be a pillar of strength and add a voice of reason and maturity to international affairs.

In consolidating Asia and preserving its unity India was far ahead of China. Nehru looked at the Indian situation in the wider perspective of western domination over the whole of Asia. The latent feeling of "Asianism" in Nehru found expression in a new form, in a sort of pride in Asia, in the need for finding Asian solutions to Asian problems in Asia and not in the courts and chancelleries of Europe.[11] India took initiative in organising two conferences at New Delhi in 1947 and 1949 respectively. Inaugurating the Asian Relations Conference in New Delhi on 23 March 1947 Nehru said, "In this crisis in the world history, Asia will necessarily play a vital role. The countries of Asia can no longer be used as pawns by others, they are bound to have their own politics in world affairs. In this atomic age, Asia will have to function effectively in the maintenance of peace. Indeed, there can be no peace unless Asia plays her part. Emergence of Asia in the world affairs will be a powerful influence on world peace."[12] As a true well wisher of Asia Nehru convened a Conference on Indonesia in January 1949 when the Dutch launched a second invasion on that country.[13] India had been taking special interest in the liberation struggle of the Indonesian people and it was one of those countries which raised the issue of Dutch aggression against Indonesia in the United Nations. India regarded herself as the moral conscience keeper of Asia. India's voice echoed the feelings of the other parts of Asia, Africa and the world. As more and more countries became independent, India tried to widen this area of "Peace and Protest" in Asia.

The year 1949 witnessed the end of Chinese civil war and establishment of a Communist rule. In the affairs of China India kept herself non-partisan and Nehru, in his note to the then Ambassador of China suggested 'The situation is difficult because of the civil war that is going on. While maintaining close and friendly relations with Chiang Kai-shek's Government, should not allow himself to become a partisan in the civil conflict.'[14] However, turning China red and the dramatic events were hardly a favourable sign for India because they had not only skewed the Asian balance of power in favour of the apparently monolithic Communist world, but had, with the Chinese occupation of Tibet, brought a dynamic and an unfriendly Communist state to the very doors of India. The situation became more delicate as a formal alliance with the West was excluded in view of the forthright decision of the government to make non-alignment its article of faith. An alliance with the Communist world was equally impossible due to the profound ideological and political gap that separated those who were in power in India from those who were the decision-makers in Communist countries.[15] In response to the need there arose a broad consensus among the Indian decision-makers to deploy different efforts to face the new situation.

To meet the new threat India adopted a two-pronged policy, on the one hand it decided to bring about a modest improvement in country's defences and advocated a way of befriending the Chinese, on the other. In pursuance of its first strategy new treaties were negotiated with the Himalayan states of Bhutan (1949), Sikkim (1950) and Nepal (1951). Discreet steps were taken to improve communications throughout the mountainous tribal areas, to increase the number of check-posts in the middle sector, and to extend the rudiments of effective administration in the North-East Frontier Agency right up to the McMahon line.[16] Most of these steps were primarily diplomatic, administrative and police and aimed to bring about an improvement in India's defence system.

The above defence-related steps proved unable in satisfying the minds of Indian people at large and there appeared a general consensus among the decision-makers that political rapprochement with the Communist world was really the only rational substitute for any military confrontation. It was in this background that a diplomatic offensive was launched to seek some normalisation with the Communist countries. China, being geographically and spiritually nearer to India became the first objective of Indian diplomacy. Nehru cherished hopes of making friendship with China. His faith in a resurgent Asia, free from the domination of Europe and America was strong. He demanded the admission of Peking into the United Nations, insisted on the return of Formosa to the People's Republic, and declined to accept the invitation of the United States to go to San Francisco to sign the Japanese Peace treaty only because the China had refused to accept the American draft treaty. Very soon the single minded policy began to pay off and it became increasingly evident that Peking was slowly abandoning its belligerent line. But India's refusal to sign the Japanese peace treaty was welcomed by the Chinese press editorially which expressed the view that such an action proved 'that the age was past when imperialist governments can do whatever they please.'[17] Peking also appreciated India's determination to adopt an independent line on many controversial issues concerning China in international affairs.

Modern People's Republic of China emerged as a result of the civil war between Ideologist as well as the Nationalist forces of the country. In the period of internal clash to rule over China the nationalist forces were supported by the United States of America, a group which stood opposite to the Communist party. Several fact-finding missions and experts were sent to China by the US, who, despite admitted corrupt practices in the Chinese National Government of Kuomintang pleaded in favour of supporting them politically, morally and financially. They suggested, 'it is highly preferable that the United States have a free, though immoral Government in China than to have a hostile Government- no matter how pure and moral- dominated by Communist influences.' The Nationalists gained a good deal of military successes practically till the end of the first half of 1948, but by spring 1949 the Communists strengthened their rural mass base and were in full control of North China. Mao Tse-tung, the supreme leader of the Communist Party of China appeared confident, of establishing the People's Republic. He declared after the Communists convened the people's political Consultative Conference in September 1949, 'our nation will never again be an insulted nation. We have stood up.'[18] On 1, October 1949, 'People's Government started its affairs and Chiang Kai-shek took his Government to the island of Formosa (Taiwan) to survive as the so-called legitimate government of China under the American patronage and protection.

To the surprise of none the new regime of China was aimed to spread Maoist radicalism in the non-communist countries and it necessitated apposition to the West and the US in particular. As the new dispensation owed some differences on several issues with the USSR, it required co-existence with numerous middle powers on the basis of expediency. Chinese aid was given principally to Peking - oriented parties which were expected to remain faithful to Maoist principles of strategy and accept Peking's guidance.[19] According to the steps already decided the advanced capitalist states, especially the US, were alleged to express their class character by pursuing aggressive policies against China and the Asian Communist movements. Peking was happy to counter US and its interventionist activities and by increasing China's own armed strength to make it a more significant deterrent. On the other with a view to cultivate intimate relations with the neutral countries of Asia, Africa and Latin America Peking signed treaties of mutual non-aggression or friendship with Burma, Nepal, Afghanistan, Guinea, Combodia, Indonesia etc. and settled outstanding differences with them through diplomatic channels. As a supplement China also strengthened its cultural relations with a large number of foreign countries and used economic weapon to further its interests.

Basically Chinese leaders believed in Marxian-Leninist ideology and stood for proletarian internationalism. For the attainment of this objective they thought it desirable to establish intimate relations with other Communist powers, especially the Soviet Union. In this period China tried to maintain her revolutionary fervour in internal and external affairs and propounded the new doctrines of 'the inevitability of war' and 'permanent revolution'. The importance of the Sino-Soviet cooperation was acknowledged by different Chinese leaders who asserted that the unity of the two could play an extremely important role in the unity of peoples of the world.[20] Thus, when the Chinese Communist leaders began to build up a Socialist system in early years, they were evidently agreed that the Soviet Union should be accepted as a model.

Death of Stalin in 1953 witnessed some ideological dilution in Soviet policy which included "revisionism" and "peaceful co-existence". Chinese viewed these concepts as basic change in Soviet policy. They considered it grave and fundamental danger and total hostility towards the USSR was viewed as the only correct response. As a result in sphere of ideology Peking decided to work as effectively as possible against the Soviet diplomacy in the developing areas which allegedly seek to advance Moscow's great power aims at the expense of the national Communist movements. Chinese associated the struggle against revisionism as their duty in order to establish friendship and cooperation with other Socialist states that evidenced the intensity of Chinese hostility towards the USSR.

"Peaceful Co-existence" as Chinese consider, is a line of diplomacy that facilitates expedient compromises and settlements with the imperialists and their allies. The diplomacy itself carries formal commitment to certain principles which concern the regime's dealings with other governments and there is no justification of another peaceful co-existence if the theme of diplomacy is taken into account. Thus, in the post-1953 period Chinese leaders were evidently unwilling to recognise that Stalin's ideological authority had passed to the USSR's unstable collective leadership.They disapproved Khrushchev's liberalisation in the USSR and his new foreign policy which stressed co-existence with the West and the promotion of Communism in the Third World by peaceful methods. In spite of public respect for Moscow's leadership China's government accelerated extraordinary new programme of Socialist economic development, apparently in the hope of demonstrating that the regime had a superior dynamism with a view to give great inspiration to Communist movements in Asia and elsewhere.

Wide Reactions

India's thrust for Asia, its refusal to be a part of any post-war alliance and China's stiff attitude towards the USA along with ideological differences with USSR culminated in the signing of a treaty between the two on Tibet in April 1954. It was the high time for Asian solidarity that symbolised in the five principles of Panchsheel. These principles were included in the preamble of the treaty under which Tibet was referred as the Tibetan Region of China and India was permitted certain reciprocal facilities of trade and pilgrimage in relation to Tibet. Further China tried to befriend the non-aligned and the developing countries and signed the Bandung Declaration of the Afro-Asian Heads of Government held in April 1955. The Conference provided a real golden diplomatic opportunity to the People's Republic of China to carve out a major diplomatic entry for itself in the region along with several other regions of Asia.

Signing of the treaty by the two Asian giants– India and China on the basis of five principles was not liked by the USA while the USSR was less than happy. In reference to country's hostility with PRC and mistrust of non-aligned India, the US had stiffened her opposition to Communist China's entry into the UN and created difficulties for India by arming Pakistan. The USSR welcomed it hoping that it would hasten the entry of India into the socialist camp but at the same time also wondered why India was getting closer to China than to them. Most Asian countries including the nations of South East –Vietnam, Cambodia, Laos and Indonesia heartily welcomed it except Pakistan who was jealous of India and closely aligned with the USA and the West. The Non-aligned world, in general, became ease that the two Asian nations were trying to solve their mutual problems peacefully and bilaterally without third-party intervention.[21]

India was overwhelmed with joy and Nehru tried his best to develop a *modus vivendi* through this treaty with China. He believed that peace in Asia could not be maintained or would not endure without India and China having an understanding about each other's policies and cooperation. Hope in India was natural that the treaty would create and enlarge the area of peace in Asia as a whole and especially in South and South-East Asia. Beyond doubt the treaty was not an arrangement to divide Asia into segments of spheres of influence, but it was an instrument to solve the problems of Asia in Asia through Asians. However, interpretation of the treaty was different from China's points of view. For Peking, it was an undoubted gain in as much as it gave her greater respect and credibility in Asia, Africa and the Third World. It did not consider that the treaty solved all the problems pending between her and India. In fact, Nehru and his advisor had overlooked small but important proviso in the Tibet Trade discussions, that it did not cover "pending, unresolved issues between the two countries," and the Sino- Indian border was one such issue. One error led to another followed by a disaster in 1962.

Most of us consider today after 50 years of Panchsheel that these principles need some rethinking in context of developments and globalisation. Politically too, the world at large revolves round the United States. A close look at recent foreign policy pronouncements emanating from both countries highlight three issues which China and India share a common interest. These are opposing US unilateralism, support for multilateral organisations and diversification of trade. Things can change for the better if countries of the region stand together and do not allow the powers of the world to dominate them. Strength lies in unity and cooperation and not in becoming pawns on the chess board of big powers.

1.2 National Security of India in Post – 1962

Theoretical Components

Conceptually, defence is entirely a sub-arena of national security and is therefore possible to direct the defence effort to serve national security much more pointedly than efforts in other areas. For its realisation in practice the relationship between national security and defence should be appropriately structured at the stages of making and implementing policies.[22] In more detail even the concept of security is not static. Human nature being dynamic, society is also ever-changing and so is the concept of security which has to be adjusted in order to promote human development. The concept of security has undergone a change.[23] It is no longer confined to the military or territorial threats to a state but also considers non-military threats. The emphasis has now shifted on the internal source of threats emanating from within the boundaries of the state. The contemporary approach to security takes into consideration the non-military threats, such as, coercive diplomacy, economic and psychological warfare, political subversion, defamatory propaganda, terrorism and political violence.[24] All citizens are protected through it from major disasters such as foreign occupation, civil wars and famines.

Thus, in a broadened view, the first traditional concept of security is security against external threats. Generally this is perceived to be the primordial goal of all nations. Even those nations, which do not have a recognisable adversary and, therefore, do not any reason to fear any external aggression, place this goal in the forefront. In comparison to the first, second aspect is more recent and relates to internal dimension. The increasing fear of domestic socio-political destabilisation has brought to the fore this aspect of national security. In many countries it has become even more important than the traditional external menace. The third is the strategic environment in which nations live. For countries that are dimensional in size, endemic political instability on the periphery or the undue presence of other adversial powers in the neighbouring countries may be considered a security threat.[25] These three components of national security have driven many nations to increase their military strength and neither India nor China is exception to this.

In the last five decades both India and China have developed their largest system of conventional weapon's programme in terms of capital assets, spread, workforce and products. From the late forties these two nations of Asia were wedded as much to the idea of economic construction along with national security. External adversaries, like US-aided Pakistan in case of India and the US itself in case of China, made defence industrialisation important for both countries. Procurement of weapons or weapon technologies is generally made either through import from foreign countries or through defence industries. Since procurement from foreign countries is dependent on the vagaries of the international strategic environment, both India and China preferred to acquire the same through internal resources, that is through the establishment of defence industries,[26] though it undergone a drastic change in both the nations, partly as a result of external threats posed to these countries, as well as due to the internal technological and economic considerations. In the absence of any major technological sustenance from the western countries, both India and China looked forward largely to the Soviet model of industrialisation, particularly in the defence sector.

Actualisation of India's Defence Policy

Despite the fact that all the above aspect of national security apply to India, originally, it was only the external threat that was perceived as real. For a country who had historically been the target of innumerable aggressions, invasions emanating from the outside it became a focal point in the concept of national security. After withdrawal of the British from the Indian subcontinent the emergence of new political leaders at the helm of affairs did not improve matters. In fact they had no defence policy to speak of and keeping in view the problems of India in consideration they decided to get the goal of national security mainly through diplomacy. In the beginning the creation of a hostile Pakistan within the sub-continent and the extension of effective Chinese power to the Tibet Plateau fundamentally altered the country's security circumstances. On her western flank, the new India had now to face an unfriendly and suspicious Pakistan with whom difficulties had surged over Kashmir- difficulties that had finally exploded into a military conflict only a year after the independence.

On the other front was China, the largest state of Asia, which shares a 1500-mile border with India and the Himalayan border states. It remained a constant puzzle to the Indians who have never satisfactorily defined the terms of their relationship with the People's Republic of China. In the 1949-52 period, India's friendly overtures to Communist China were treated with considerable suspicion by Peking, and New Delhi's bona fides as a non-aligned power were questioned. From 1953-58, Chinese policy towards India shifted drastically, and Nehru played a leading role in Peking's efforts to establish relations with the Afro-Asian world on the basis of the principles of "peaceful coexistence."[27] Later on boundary dispute between the two arose in 1954 and assumed increasingly serious proportions in the context of Tibetan revolt of 1959. India's boundary dispute with China led ultimately to former's humiliating defeat in October 1962.

As India-China war of 1962 came in the wake of Sino-Soviet split, the event served as a lesson for both-India and the USSR. India had learnt, what she did not fully realise, that subscription to the Five Principles, backed by two thousand years of friendship, was no guarantee against aggression. The USSR has learnt, what she had long suspected but would not admit, that a common ideology was no bar to the play of national egoism.[28]

The war of 1962 falsified the notion of Indian leaders that India's goal of national security could be met effectively only through political means. In fact, Nehru was caught between the dilemmas of the time but he had no doubt about the importance of defence policy and industry as well. Citing the success of the American forces in the World War by utilising its defence industry and scientific research, he said, ———

far more than the army and navy and air force, defence means industry and production...you have to have the production of all essentials of warfare...If you are industrially strong, you can build up your army and navy and air force at short notice. If you depend on buying your warships and everything else in a foreign country and that source dries up, it is quite useless to have only a few thousand men shouting about war. So, in the ultimate analysis, even the business of war brings you back to production and the growth of industries, small and big.[29]

The defeat of India at the hands of China was a compensatory factor as it acted as a catalyst and generated a new-mood of re-evaluating India's concept of national security. The pre-war phase was characterised by three notable failures: the failure to develop a modern security and defence decision-making system, the failure to build up a military capability against China, and the failure to factor realism into the defence self-reliance effort.

Lapses in Indian defence system were admitted by Nehru himself in September 1963 that enough resources for the modernisation of the armed forces had not been diverted from the beginning. He said that after our Independence, there was the general background of our not spending too much on the army. Of course, we wanted to keep a competent army without increasing it- and we actually reduced it, but later we had to increase it. Secondly, although we tried to modernise it the process was rather slow, because of the cost involved. We thought of modernising it to the extent that we ourselves were producing the things we needed; some things we did import.[30] The new situation resulted in the orchestration of a dual strategy of upgrading the armed and of seeking a military alliance with the Soviet Union. It was a major departure from the original Nehruvian concept of national security that India followed immediately after independence.

A major breakthrough in India's defence system occurred in the 1963-64 when the Ministry of Defence, in its report, formulated the following policy objectives:

- Expansion in the modernisation of the army;
- Modernisation of the air force;
- Creation of an adequate production base;
- Improvement and expansion in the means of communication and transport;
- Replacement of overage ships of the navy and making it a balanced force.[31]

Earlier in November 1962 the Department of Defence Production was established for furthering the cause of indigenous defence production of arms, ammunition and equipment and accordingly, a five-year Defence Plan (1964-69) was formulated. On the guidelines of the ministry, production of self-loading rifles, light and long-range mortars, mountain guns, medium and light-tanks, standardisation of small arms on a single calibre; and the addition of Seahawk jet fighters to the recently commissioned aircraft carrier INS Vikrant were promoted.[32] The ministry had argued that greater emphasis should be laid on research, and development of modern equipment to suit our own requirements.[33] As this time's five-year defence plan was not based on long-term requirements of services it was revised and rephrased to cover the period 1966-71. In 1970, with a view to update the plan every year the concept of 'roll-on' was adopted.

The period between 1962-71 saw India fight three major wars. It witnessed the military developing skills and sinews at the operational level, although higher level decision-making capability continued its downward slide. The most notable failure of this period was the shying away from developing a nuclear capability. China had carried out its first test in 1964 and India had achieved plutonium reprocessing capability in 1965. Despite India's unwillingness on nuclear issue in the broader aspects of its foreign policy, it had much better reason to be satisfied with its regional policy. The last war India fought with Pakistan was on Bangladesh and it improved India's power status in South Asia. The real gap in military strength and capacity between India and Pakistan for instance, was probably greater than a decade ago. The substantial Chinese military presence in Tibet had also been largely neutralised, at least in terms of major operations south of the Himalayan crest. It enhanced India's pre-eminence influences in the Himalayan border states.

But India was not fully satisfied with its defence position. After the Bangladesh war in 1971, to counter the still patchy and clouded strategic environment in Asia, the Defence Ministry adopted policy of a 'credible capability to protect our vulnerable areas in all times to deal adequately with developments that might escalate into open hostilities.[34] Accordingly, a plan for the period 1974-79 was drawn up but was modified in the light of the West Asian War in October 1973. Specific programmes mentioned in this period were aeronautics, electronics, avionics, and so on. Interdependence of the defence industry and the civilian sector of the economy soon became the watchword.[35] In line, the Ministry of Defence, in its annual report of 1976-77, mentioned the following thrust areas in defence planning :

- indigenous design and development of the major weapon systems and equipment requirements of the three services;

- increase in the pace of indigenous production of complete weapon systems, equipment, ammunition and connected items, based on indigenous development effort or, where necessary, on licensed production;
- indigenisation of spares and connected items of major equipment, which have to be necessarily imported from abroad, so that dependence on foreign sources could be reduced to the minimum; and
- speedy disposal of accumulated surpluses.[36]

These objectives continued to dominate the successive defence plans. The first objective clearly was the politics of accelerating the strategy of increasing India's military clout. The external aid that Mrs Indira Gandhi sought and the internal resources she mobilised to expand and restructure India's military might had become one of the main preoccupations of successive governments. Though attempts had already been made to upgrade India's military strength in the sixties, its efforts became much more conspicuous in the seventies. From then on there was no going back, no questions asked, and no doubts raised regarding the priority and urgency of improving India's military clout.

China's Early Defence Preparations

The emergence of the Chinese People's Republic in October 1949 changed the politics of the Asiatic continent. The new Chinese leaders and Mao-Tse-tung in particular, believed in Marxian-Leninist ideology and stood for proletarian internationalism. For the attainment of this objective they thought it desirable to establish intimate relations with other Communist powers, especially Russia.[37] As to Asia, Chinese aims are clear. She wants to establish hegemony in the region adjoining her borders, and in the rest of the Asiatic continent. For this she has been opposed to the establishment of either US or Soviet influence in the area. She hopes to establish her influence not only in Asia, but also in distant Africa and Latin America.[38] However, the United States of America was the single power who opposed Chinese designs in pre- and post-revolution phase. After its war in Korea the US had evolved a policy of pressure and diplomatic isolation directed against Peking and the main elements of this policy include non-recognition of the Chinese Communist regime, opposition to its seating in the United

Nations, an embargo on all American trade with mainland China and opposition to other contacts with the PRC. [39] In World War-II phase cold war between the Communist and non-Communist nations has already begun in Europe and its dark shadows were reaching to the region.

Chinese and especially Mao have also peculiar image of human nature and social process. Mao-Tse-tung's image of human nature was more Roussean-like than Hobbesian, for he believed that conflicts were inherent in the social process itself rather than in the biological or psychic make-up of man. According to him, 'the concept of man lacks content, it lacks the specificity of male and female, adult and child, Chinese and foreign, revolutionary and counter-revolutionary. The only thing left is the vague features differentiating man from beast.'[40] As to the Chinese concept of foreigners, wrote Lu Hsun, who is regarded as the Chinese Gorki, 'Throughout the ages the Chinese have had only two ways of looking at foreigners: up to them as superior beings or down on them as wild animals. They have never been able to treat them as friends, to consider them as people like ourselves.[41] This accounts for such expressions as "foreign devils" and "outer barbarians" which are still current in common Chinese parlance.

With these images and attitudes China, in 1949, inherited a far more dangerous external security environment than India had, acquiring an implacable enemy in the sole superpower of that time- the United States. The country tackled the situation with a well thought out security strategy. Earlier Mao-Tse-tung has personally directed the Red army, as it fought its way across western China during the Long March (1934-36), and later the Eighth Route and the 18th Group armies when they fought against the Japanese during 1937-45. Drawing strength from its war hardened Peoples' Liberation Army and the ideological-cum-nationalist fervour it ignited in the masses.[42] Though India and China started off in the late forties in similar social and economic positions the growth in the defence industry of China has been, relatively speaking faster.

In 1950, China's Peoples Liberation Army was numerically about six times as big as India's armed forces but its organisation, training and equipment were markedly inferior. But soon with the help of Chinese international isolation in the sixties, they made a virtue out of necessity by concentrating on the principle of self-sufficiency in defence industrialisation process. Caught between advocates of a 'needs-oriented' policy and a 'speciality-oriented approach, the Chinese government in the early years veered towards the policy of upholding the pressing economic and defence needs of the country, rather than investing in special, high-tech projects.[43] However, China's participation in the Korean War resulted in a massive Soviet assistance to the conventional weapons programme. A large number of factories were established with the Soviet assistance, helped China modernise its armies, substantially.

Now onwards, China moved towards the military strength. Rapid advances in nuclear arms programmes dating from the 1950s have made possible the production of a modest stock of hydrogen weapons and possibly one hundred 20 KT atomic bombs, short, middle range and intercontinental missile delivery systems were being developed. The ground forces, at that time, comprised principally 115 line divisions and 20 artillery divisions were adequately supplied with light and medium weapons. The navy and the air force were developing significantly.

China from its own experiences as well as of the Korean war that took place in early years of the fifties the country had learnt the importance of expanding defence industry. Mao-Tse-tung underlined its significance in 1953 while addressing the gathering of the establishment of the Institute of Military Engineering and said :.......... in order to build a modernised national defence, our army, air force, and navy must all possess fully mechanised equipment and ornaments, and none of this can be achieved without complex specialised technology. What we direly need today is a large number of people who are capable of managing and steering the direction of technological advancement and to see to it that our technology may improve and make progress uninterrupted.[44]

In pursuance of the policy already announced the First Five Year Plan from 1953 included 44 new big mainstay 'engineering projects in aviation, radio, ordance and shipbuilding and 51 medium to big' projects for the reconstruction and repair of old factories. It followed the launching of a long-term Science and Technology Programme

(1956-67) which was aimed to fill the gap in comparison to world's most advanced countries as quickly as possible in sphere of science where Chinese needs were most urgent and to plan for research on the basis of what has been achieved in the world. The plan for the period 1956-57 as to the conventional weapons programme, concentrated on light-weight and high mobile tanks and artillery, jet engineers submarines, defensive tactile missiles and rockets, electronics, etc. Initially nearly 30 per cent of the total expenditure in the state budget was for defence but at the close of the fifties it was reduced by 8.2 per cent to achieve greater and faster growth in economic construction.

Withdrawal of Soviet assistance in 1960 caused a severe setback to China's efforts at technology upgrading. As a result, except in the field of nuclear weapons and long range missiles, where the country put in massive focussed effort, China stayed with 1950s technologies for the next decades. Break with Moscow was completed in 1964 but earlier having a negative signal several policy shifts were effected in China that included.

- Initiation of a new-year plan between 1963 and 1972 as the previous twelve year plan projects were completed before time;
- Commencement of the third-line defence industries in Sichuan, Shaanxi, Guangxi, Yunnan and other interior provinces;
- 1966- policy of 'foreseeing three moves in the game of scientific research', that is simultaneous work on design, testing and trial production; making blue prints; and exploration; and
- Prohibition of the Red Guard in interfering with the work of the defence projects.

1.3 Sino-Pak Nexus Against India

China's Transfer of Technology to Pakistan

In the initial years China's relations with Pakistan were not so cordial as with India, although the latter was one of the first Muslim countries to accord recognition to the Red Government of China.

Diplomatic relation between the two was established in 1951 and it was strengthened further due to Pakistani decision to join the Western dominated military alliance named SEATO in 1954. Pakistani attitude at the moment was praised by Zhou Enlai who declared at the Bandung Conference that the two countries had achieved a mutual understanding. He also defended Pakistan by saying that it 'had no other motivation in joining the pacts' than protecting herself against any Indian attack.[45]

But soon Sino-Pakistan relations had been converted into a strategic link between the two. Pakistan required China's military equipment, technology, and political support to deny India's dominance of the South Asian System. This converged with China's interests of rivalry with India. Even earlier Pakistan, despite its intimate relations with the Western military powers, continued to assure the Chinese leaders that they had no enmity against the Communist regime of China. At the moment China also realised that Pakistan nourished enmity towards India and would naturally like to come closer to China. However, relations between the two took a turn for the worse when President Ayub assumed power in Pakistan in 1958 and Islamabad, as a precautionary step, concluded a treaty with the US in 1959 to resist communist aggression.

Relations between the two visualised a silver line for itself during 1961-62 when tension between the US and USSR subsided and the Sino-Soviet schism took a formal shape. Further Sino-Indian war of October 1962 and ascent of President Kennedy in favour of India paved the way for cordial relations. In the war Pakistan side itself with China and branded openly India as an aggressor. It exhibited partly, Pakistan's expression of her anti-Indian policy as well as a move to placate the Chinese. China, understanding Pakistan's policy and attitude concluded a number of economic and cultural agreements with it, signed a border agreement and supported the latter on the issue of Kashmir by declaring that the fate of Kashmir should be decided by the people of Kashmir themselves.[46] Thus, a convenient environment was provided to their relations in the early years of the sixties. If recalled the whole set of relations was based on statement made in 1959 by the then Chinese ambassador to the Indian Foreign Secretary face-to-face, 'China dislikes to be concerned about the US and China coming together'. He added in plain language of blackmail: 'Friend it seems to us that you too can not afford to open two fronts. This is a point which our two sides should be able to appreciate, as our apprehensions in this context are similar.'[47] It was a hint rather explicitly that India could face dangers if China were to build Pakistan up militarily. Since then, China's military assistance to Pakistan has become a reality.

The decade of the sixties made China's relations with Pakistan solid from the viewpoints of mutual interest, regional strategy and international milieu as well. China's links with Pakistan were directed against India and obliquely, against the US and USSR. The association with Islamabad became very active and close after China's defeat of India in the Himalayan war of 1962. As a result of the war Sino-Indian relations deteriorated and China in the aftermath went a step further by offering military protection to Pakistan in the event of an Indian attack. It became more clear when in July 1963, Z.A. Bhutto declared : An attack by India on Pakistan would also involve the territorial integrity and security of the largest State in Asia. This new factor that has arisen is a very important one. I would not, at this stage, wish to eluciate it any further. It would suffice it to say that the national interests of another State would be involved in an Indian attack on Pakistan because the State and other States know about India's aggressive intentions and know that India is capable of embarking on aggression on other country.[48]

It was the starting-point of what we call "Sino-Pakistan collusion" but Islamabad was more than conscious at the time and despite turning to China it was also normalising its relationship with the Soviet Union as if to proclaim to the world the end of its alignment with the United States. Ayub Khan, the then President of Pakistan, in his memoirs called this diplomacy as one of 'walking a triangular tightrope'. Since no great power was wholly reliable and since each great power could be useful to Pakistan, it was necessary to cultivate good relations with all. The United States was necessary for continues economic and military assistance; China was useful as source of strategic support that had the function of deterring the Indians from major military action towards Pakistan; and the Soviet Union could possibly be useful if Pakistan could normalise relations and exert some influence on Moscow to reduce its level of support for India, or, conversely, increase support for Pakistan.

The Sino-Pakistan Collusion which took a definite shape in the sixties has two parts - China's arms supply to Pakistan and development of latter's nuclear capability. In fact, process of arms transfer began with the conclusion of the first military agreement in July 1966 and has continued to this day. The magnitude of Chinese aid can be viewed from the fact that by 1970 'the tanks supplied by China constituted 25 per cent of the entire tank force of Pakistan's disposal. The aircraft supplied by China constituted 31 per cent of Pakistan's air force : 65 per cent of all interceptor bombers and 99 per cent of its modern fighter planes'. It also left far behind in supplying arms to Pakistan. The total Chinese military sales to Pakistan constituted 31 per cent of the 1,079 million dollar arms procurement programmes of Pakistan, whereas the US contribution was only one per cent.[49] The importance of this aid was evident from the fact that it has greatly contributed to the narrowing of the gap that had begun to develop in the late eighties between the Pakistani forces and the Indian forces deployed on the Pakistani front.[50] However, this ongoing Sino-Pakistan military cooperation failed to have any effect on Indian military behaviour in the war of 1965 and 1971 in any way.

Apart from common hostility against India, another factor that contributed towards building a close linkage between China and Pakistan was the Soviet threat to South Asia, which was highlighted by the Soviet intervention in Afghanistan in 1979. Consequently, until the withdrawal of Soviet forces from Afghanistan, China and Pakistan, along with the United States; maintained a triangular strategic and military relationship in South Asia. By the time Pakistan also became the largest recipient of Chinese economic aid. [51] Mohammed Khan Junejo, the Prime Minister of Pakistan, expressed his country's gratitude while welcomed Zhang Aping, Chinese Defence Minister, in July 1985 and said, 'Pakistan today stands self-reliant in many of its defence requirements only because China had so generously transferred its technology and knowhow. It was with the PRC's assistance that the Heavy Mechanical Complex at Taxila, the backbone for other major industrial projects, was set up. The factory at Taxila to rebuild tanks, the Heavy Forge and Foundary, the Aeronautical Complex at Karma and the textile machinery manufacturing units' were all monuments to Chinese aid.[52]

Sino-Pakistan cooperation in sphere of arms supply and development of missile programmes continued to be intimate in the nineties. In afterwards, Islamabad had started production of Main Battle Tank (MBT), Al-Khalid with Chinese assistance after a formal agreement in this regard which was signed between high ranking Chinese officials and the Chairman of Heavy Industries Taxila. For Al-Khalid research and development had started in 1990 and was considered to be one of the most modern MBT's, and was comparable to contemporary tanks. It was amounted with a 125-mm smoothbore gun equipped with a dynamic muzzle reference system that was capable of firing all types of ammunition, including Armour Piercing, Fin-Stabilised. Discarding Sabot and High-Explosive Anti-Tank and High Explosive shells, it was also capable of firing-anti-tank and anti-helicopter missiles.[53] Beijing had established a deep relationship with Pakistan that had nothing to do with ideology or revolution.

The US think-tank report conducted in the wake of nuclear explosion by India and Pakistan in 1998, held China responsible for the situations in South Asia. It noted, 'China bears some responsibility for the situation in South Asia, given its own nuclear and missile programme that concern India and the assistance it has provided over the years to Pakistan's nuclear and missile programme.[54] According to a *'Newyork Times'* report the American Intelligence agencies had told Clinton Administration and Congress in July 2000 that China continued to aid Pakistan build long range missiles capable of carrying nuclear payloads. It described how China stepped up the shipment of speciality steels, guidance systems and technical expertise to Pakistan.[55] Despite China trying to allay concern over aid to Pakistan that its support to Pakistani Missile development was not directed towards India, New Delhi has been quite apprehensive of its long-term effects on its relations with both China and Pakistan.

China's Nuclear Assistance to Pakistan

The nuclear programme of Pakistan has an independent origin dated back in 1953 with the establishment of Atomic Energy Council (AEC), under the chairmanship of Dr Nazir Ahmed and which was upgraded to the Pakistani Atomic Energy Commission (PAEC) in 1956. Initially the nature of Pakistani nuclear development activities carried out during the regimes of Ayub Khan and Yahya Khan clearly pointed to the direction of peaceful use of nuclear energy.[56] Zulfikar Ali Bhutto, in fact, was the chief architect of Pakistan's nuclear policy and its nuclear programme. Under him, Islamabad's nuclear thinking underwent a significant change related to the non-peaceful uses of atomic energy.

So far as the Sino-Pakistan nuclear cooperation is concerned it is traced back to 30 June 1966 when an agreement to this effect was concluded. The credit for this must go to Z. A. Bhutto who signed two agreements with Beijing for scientific and military cooperation in the nuclear sector. In Asia, China was first to explode nuclear devices in 1964 followed by India in May 1974. To meet the challenge, arising out of India's nuclear blast chairman of the Pakistan Atomic Commission said that "he will do his duty" implying that Pakistan would soon explode a nuclear device too and build up a nuclear arsenal.[57] Bhutto also took the opportunity to write to the Chinese Premier Chou En-lai seeking nuclear technological aid. In response Chou agreed to sharing Chinese nuclear knowhow with Pakistan on condition that Pakistan would exert to develop its own independent technology side by side. In December 1974, a Chinese delegation of scientists visited Pakistan when a special committee to develop nuclear science was set up and the Chinese assured "all possible help" to enable Rawalpindi to go nuclear. The Indian leaders despite their military superiority to Pakistan continue to harbour fears that a Pakistan assisted actively by China could pose severe threats to India's security and integrity.

In May 1976, Z. A. Bhutto visited Peking and in course of the visit a secret pact was made between the two countries in which China agreed to help Islamabad produce nuclear arms. From all indications emanating from the United States cooperation between the two countries had developed in plutonium reprocessing and uranium enrichment through the centrifuge method by 1978. By 1984, Pakistan had received the technical information for the actual designing of nuclear weapons. Since 1987, Pakistan had developed and deployed nuclear weapons. Dr A. Q. Khan, in early 1987, informed an Indian journalist that Pakistan had enriched uranium to 90 per cent for weapons purpose. Benazir Bhutto also once stated in an interview that 'Pakistan has acquired the requisite capability for making an atom bomb. As per the estimates, by 1992, Pakistan had enriched uranium sufficient for 6 to 10 bombs.[58]

In the nineties, Pakistan became a missile capable country with overt and covert Chinese assistance. Keeping its geopolitical strategy for the region in mind China sold the M-l1 series missiles to Pakistan and helped them on guidance and control systems, solid fuel and work on various M-l1 missile variants. During the period 1992-94, China had exported 50 M-ll missiles to Pakistan. It successfully raised nuclear industry with the guiding support of China, who distributed the nuclear technology. One explanation for Islamabad acquiring nuclear capability with the active assistance and advice of China and others is that it is part of a calculated projection of a "threat" from India. Chinese help continued even after the former signed the NPT in 1992 and gave assurance to US in 1995 that it had stopped transfer of technology to Pakistan. Reports of such transfer have emerged even after China provided written assurances in October 1997 of stopping supplies.

On 6 April 1998 Pakistan successfully test-fired its Intermediate Range Ballistic Missile (IRBM), Ghauri, capable of carrying nuclear warheads. It was a surface to surface missile with a range of 1,500 km and a payload of 700 kg, was the most powerful weapon in the country's defence armoury. George Fernandes, the then Defence Minister of India, had named China as the "mother of Ghauri". China has been supplying missile technology to Pakistan despite having given an understanding to the United States to do no such thing.' It is widely believed that Beijing has collaborated with Pakistan in the full range of missile development activity from transfer of sub-systems, technologies for propellant production and initial guidance system, related to the Hatf programme to the outright supply of M-ll missiles. And in response to Indian explosion on 11 and 13 May 1998, Pakistan too exploded its nuclear devices on 28 and 30 May 1998. According to a study conducted in September 2000 by the Centre for Non-Proliferation Studies at the Monterey Institute of International Studies 'Beijing has been a constant supplier of a variety of nuclear products and services to Pakistan ranging from uranium enrichment technology to research and power reactors.[59] In comparison, Tibet and the issue of Dalai Lama on the part of China and border dispute along with Chinese transfer of arms and technology to Pakistan, on the part of India, continued to remain a serious security-related problem for both the nations.

References

1. Raymond Cohen, *International Politics, the Rules of the Game* (New York: Longman, 1981), p. 93.
2. *The Hindustan Times* (Patna), January 28, 2005.
3. G.H. Jansen, *Afro-Asia and Non-Alignment*, (London: Faber and Faber, 1966), p.127.
4. G.P. Deshpande, 'Verbalities and Realities of Foreign Policy' in G.P. Deshpande and Alka Acharya, *eds.* 50 Years of India-China-Crossing a Bridge of Dream (New Delhi: Tulika, 2002), p. 387.
5. Deva Narayan Mallik, *Postwar International Politics- A Ouadripartite Survey* (Muzaffarpur: Veena Mandir, 1973), p.183.
6. Dexter Perkins and Glyndon G.Van Deusen, *The United States of America – A History,* Vol.II, pp. 666-67, as cited in H.K.Chhabra, *Foreign Policies of Major Countries*, Vol. III (Delhi: Surjeet, 1980), p. 256.
7. Wayne Wilcox, Leo E.Rose and Gavin Boyd eds; *Asia and the International System* (Massachusetts: Cambridge, 1972), p. 256.
8. V.M. Khostov and L.N. Kutakov, 'The Foreign policy of the Union of Soviet Socialist Republic' Black and Thompson eds., *Foreign Policies in a World of Change* (New York: 1963), pp. 256-77.
9. Johna, Garraty and Peter Gay eds., *The Columbia History of the World* (New York : Harper and Row, 1972), pp.1117-34.
10. V.P. Dutt, *India's Foreign Policy* (New Delhi: Vani Educational, 1984), p. 277.
11. T.N. Kaul, *India, China and Indo-China* (New Delhi : Allied, 1980), p. 8.
12. Jawaharlal Nehru,s Speeches September 1946-May 1949, Vol. 1 (New Delhi: Publication Division, Government of India, 1983), p. 251.
13. *Ibid.*, p. 253.
14. K.P.S. Menon, Many World's Revisited-An Autobiography (Bombay: Bharatiya Vidya Bhavan, 1981), p. 230.
15. Harish Kapur, 'India and the Soviet Union', in K.P. Misra ed., *Foreign Policy of India- A Book of Readings* (New Delhi: Thomson Press, 1977), pp. 245-46.
16. Lorne J. Kavic, *India's Quest for Security : Defence Policies; 1947-65* (Berkeley : 1967), pp. 46-61.
17. *People's Daily* (Peking), September 16, 1951.
18. Clande A. Buss, *Asia in the Modern World* (New York: Macmillan, 1964), pp. 538-45.

19. Lin Piao, *Long Live the Victory of People's War* (Peking: Foreign Languages Press, 1967), p. 37.
20. H.K. Chhabra, Foreign Policies of Major Countries (Delhi: Surjeet Publications, 1983), pp. 100-103.
21. T.N. Kaul, India, China and Indo-China, pp.12-14
22. Verghese Koithara, *Society, State & Security-The Indian Experience* (New Delhi : Sage Publications, 1999), pp. 394-95.
23. Rajkumar Singh, *Less Tasty Indo-Nepal Political Relations 1947-1997* (Patna : Novelty & Co., 1998), p. 205.
24. R.S. Sharma, 'Process for Formulation and Execution of National Security and Defence Policies in the 1990,' in Kouser J. Azam (ed.), *India's Defence Policy for the 1990s* (New Delhi; 1992), p. 27.
25. Harish Kapur, *India's Foreign Policy 1947-1992-Shadows and Substance* (New Delhi : Sage Publications, 1994), pp. 17-18.
26. Jasjit Singh, 'Defence Industry : Towards Greater Self-Reliance,' in Army-Industry Partnership 1995; *Proceedings, Indian Army and Confederation of Indian Industry* (New Delhi : 1995), pp. IX-XII.
27. Wayne Wilcox, Leo E. Rose and Gavin Boyd (eds.), *Asia and the International System* (Cambridge : Winthrop Publishers, 1972), pp. 80-81.
28. K.P.S. Menon, *Many World's Revisited – An Autobiography,* pp. 301-02.
29. For Nehru's Speeches see, *Jawaharlal Nehru's Speeches, September 1946–May 1949*, Vol. 1, pp. 91-102.
30. *Ibid*, Vol. V, March 1963-May 1964, p. 193.
31. *Annual Report*, 1963-64, p. 3.
32. K. Srikanth, 'Policies and Programmes of Conventional Weapons Development,' in G.P. Deshpande and Alka Acharya (eds.), *50 Years of India-China-Crossing a Bridge of Dream* (New Delhi : Tulika, 2002), p. 343.
33. *Ibid.*
34. *Annual Report,* 1972-73, pp. 8 and 10.
35. *Ibid.*, p. 11.
36. K. Srikanth, 'Policies and Programmes of Conventional Weapons Development,' p. 345.
37. R.S. Gupta, *History of Modern China* (New Delhi : Sterling Publishers, 1987), pp. 454-62.
38. H.K. Chhabra, *Foreign Policy of Major Countries*, p. 100.
39. John A. Garraty and Peter Gay (eds.), *The Columbia History of the World* (New York : Harper and Row Publishers, 1981), p. 1124.
40. Samuel S. Kim, *China, the United Nations and World Order* (New Jersey : Princeton University Press, 1979), p. 59.

41. K.P.S. Menon, *Many World's Revisited-An Autobiography*, p. 349.
42. Verghese Koithara, *Society, State & Security-The Indian Experience*, pp.134-35.
43. K. Srikanth, 'Policies and Programmes of Conventional Weapons Development', p. 346.
44. Michael Y. M. Kau and John K. Leung (eds.), *The Writings of Mao Zedong 1949-76*, Vol.1, September 1949–December 1955 (New York: M. E. Sharpe, 1986), pp. 378-79.
45. *The Pakistan Times*, 11 April 1963.
46. H.K. Chhabra, *Foreign Policies of Major Countries*, pp. 107-108.
47. S.K. Singh, 'Slow Cranes Flying', *The Hindustan Times*, 9 July 2003.
48. *The Dawn*, 20 July 1963.
49. Harish Kapur, *India's Foreign Policy 1947-1992 Shadows and Substance*, p. 112.
50. K. Subrahmanyam, 'Our Security Future', *The Hindustan Times,* November 1990.
51. Yakov Bertzbarger, *China's South-Western Strategy* (New York: Prager publishers, 1985), pp. 94-99.
52. *The Pakistan Times*, 7 July 1985.
53. Rajkumar Singh, *Indo-Pak Nuclear Tension* 1974-1998 (New Delhi : Samiksha Prakashan, 2001), p. 151.
54. *Ibid*, p. 194.
55. *The Hindustan Times*, 4 July 2000.
56. Dr Aftab Alam, 'Pakistan's Nuclear Development and Capability', *Third Concept,* April-May 1998 (New Delhi:1998), pp. 13-14.
57. *Opinion Weekly*, 9 July 1974.
58. Dr Aftab Alam, 'Pakistan's Nuclear Development and Capability,' pp. 16-17.
59. *The Hindustan Times*, 7 September 2000.

Chapter II

India-China Border Talks : Status and Strategy

2.1 Essentials of Border Dispute

The border dispute between India and China persisted due to divergence of approach on the issue. They are the only known neighbours not to be separated even by a mutually defined line of control leaving their entire 4,057 kilometer frontier in question. While China appears to fit well with the status quo as it keeps India under strategic pressure, Indian diplomacy is neither guided by the past nor by the cardinal principles of reciprocity, leverage and pragmatism. After the debacle of 1962 they resumed their border talks in 1981 but the Line of Actual Control is yet to be demarcated. The first requisite to good – neighbourly relations is a defined front line as the famous proverb goes, 'good fences make good neighbours.'

Delineation of Boundary

The entire India – China border can be generally divided into three areas; the border to the east of Bhutan, the central or middle border across Uttar Pradesh, Punjab and Himachal Pradesh and the border separating Jammu and Kashmir from Chinese territories of Sinkiang and Tibet. The boundary of Kashmir with Sinkiang and Tibet is about 1,100 miles of which the frontier of Ladakh forms nearly two-thirds. Traditionally, at least from the tenth century, important points on the present alignment were recognised as the limits of Ladakh on the one hand and Tibet on the other. This whole area of the Aksai Chin plateau and the Lingsi Tang plains was administered by the Government of Ladakh and Kashmir and utilised for grazing by the people of Ladakh. A regular sequence of official records, stretching over many years provides testimony on such matters as revenue assessment, police jurisdiction, public works' projects, census returns, control of trade routes and survey and mapping operations. The boundary of middle sector lies along the major watersheds; and its delimitation secured confirmation in the treaty of 1954 between India and the People's Republic of China. The eastern sector has the trijunction of India, Burma and China and it also follows the major watersheds.[1]

Before conclusion of the agreement and demarcation of McMahon line, in 1890, British rulers of India made a treaty with China that delineated the Indo-Tibetan border. The treaty was rejected by Tibetan rulers and Russia's interference appeared imminent in country's affairs. In order to check Russian influence Lord Curzon, the then Governor-General of India, sent British Indian troops in 1904 under the command of Young Husband that resulted in a treaty in 1906 with China whereby Britain accepted Chinese suzerainty over Tibet. It also provided that a British Agent would be posted in Lhasa and India would construct postal system there. By this treaty India also acquired the right to maintain troops in Tibet for the protection of trade routes. Anglo-Russian differences relating to Tibet were sorted out by an Entente signed in 1907 whereby both accepted Chinese suzerainty in Tibet. They also agreed to deal with Tibet only through China. This privileged position of China in Tibet was challenged after the Chinese revolution of 1911, led by Dr Sun Yat-sen, when Tibet forced the Chinese troops to leave the plateau. Even subsequent attempts on the part of China failed to re-establish its authority and it warranted a situation leading to the meeting at Simla in 1914.

Thus, the international alignment in this area, along the highest watershed ranges, was formalised at the initiation of the then Chinese regime. The Simla negotiations of 1913-14, and the McMahon line delineating the border of North Eastern Frontier Agency that emerged from it, had been a British response to China's attempt to assert control in Tibet.[2] The conference was held to sort out border differences between Nepal, Bhutan, Sikkim and Tibet, though it was represented by British India, Tibet and China. Arthur Henry McMahon, the then

Secretary of State for India, participated in the conference as a representative of British India. In the meeting an agreement was concluded which confirmed the Chinese suzerainty, but divided Tibet into two parts– Outer Tibet and Inner Tibet. The autonomy of outer Tibet was accepted and China agreed not to interfere in its internal affairs, nor give it representation in Chinese Parliament, nor station its troops, nor appoint its civil servants, nor to turn it into a Chinese colony.[3] At the same time another boundary between outer Tibet and India was demarcated at the high mountain which divided the two countries at the watershed. Since the line dividing India and Tibet was drawn on the suggestion of McMahon, who himself drew a line by a red pen on the map, it came to be known as the McMahon Line. This demarcation passes through Tibet plateau in the north and Indian hills in the South. The map was signed by representatives of British India, Tibet and China.

From 1914 till the date of independence India's policy towards Tibet and Sinkiang was conducted by the British. The Chinese, however, refused to ratify the agreement, the then Government of India also failed to take it seriously. Because China, torn by civil wars, was not in a position to assert herself it was considered an opportunity for India to dominate. Several British officers including Olaf Caroe, one of Deputy Secretaries, had realised that the north-east frontier might one day become as live as the north-west, and pressed for the extension of the rudiments of administration, civil and military, into the areas abutting the McMahon line. In this period our relations with Tibet were conducted through a Political Officer in Sikkim, who was also in charge of our relations with Bhutan. Sir Charles Bell, a close friend of Dalai Lama, remained there for years and so long as he was incharge, it was unnecessary to keep any troops on the north-east frontier.

In Sinkiang, on the pattern of Tibet, Philip Macartney, who went to Kashgar, the remotest post of the Indian empire, was made permanent officer to look after the affairs of Sinkiang. The Government of India's policy in Sinkiang was seemingly inconsistent with their policy towards Tibet. In Tibet they did all they could to repudiate Chinese sovereignty; in Sinkiang, they did all they could to affirm it. The reason was to prevent Sinkiang from falling a prey to what then seemed a greater menace, Russia.[4] When in the middle of the thirties Chinese control over Sinkiang weakened and the Tungans had risen in revolt against the provincial Government, first, the Government of Sinkiang appealed the Chinese and having failed, turned to Russia for support. Russia was happy to intervene and Sinkiang passed on to Russian hegemony. From there onwards the Indian Government began to support Chinese sovereignty in Sinkiang. The discrepancy that we found in British India's policy towards Tibet and Sinkiang was, ultimately aimed to prevent the approach of any other strong power towards India. Throughout the nineteenth century, British foreign policy in Asia was dominated by the 'Russian bogey'. In other words, India's relations with Sinkiang and Tibet in British days were based on a mistrust of her neighbour, China and Russia and a recognition of the game of power politics.

Assertiveness of China

Earlier the British Government of India had undertaken to support the independence of Tibet, subject to the suzerainty of China. Independent India had, in a sense, inherited this commitment with a sea change in circumstances. As long as China was weak and ever since the Revolution of 1911 she had been in the throes of civil war, it was easy for Tibet to assert its independence and for India to support it.[5] When India in 1947, and China after two years in 1949, emerged into the international stage, neither of them at the time of their establishment inherited a defined space and there was considerable ambiguity about the extent of the territorial limits of the new sovereign state. In fact, the alignment of these frontiers had never been properly surveyed or delimited. In the north the Himalayan hill states of Bhutan, Sikkim, Nepal, and even Tibet, had been brought within the fluid frontiers of British India through a variety of separate arrangements. For India the problem was aggravated because it was the British in Delhi or London, who had conducted surveys, negotiations and even war on border matters. In general, Indians lacked experience and acquaintance with border affairs as they had never been involved with decision or policy-making.

On the other hand, the People's Republic of China had come into existence on October 1, 1949, as a consequence of the Chinese civil war. After its proclamation China took hard decisions regarding its imperial heritance of far-flung frontiers and tributary states. The process for this was started even earlier and in 1939, in a seminal essay, Mao Zedong had described the territorial limits of his envisaged new China as being less extensive than those of imperial China because they excluded the tributary states of the region. Accordingly the new state recognised erstwhile frontier states like Mongolia, Nepal, Vietnam and Korea as sovereign states but at the same time laid its claim to Tibet, Hong Kong, Macao and Taiwan by virtue of legal and treaty rights, as parts of its integral space. Thus, in 1949 the frontiers or limits of PRC's, sovereignty had been clearly defined and it had taken concrete steps in this regard.

From strategic and security considerations the emergence of a strong and stable PRC posed a new challenge to the Indian Policy-makers. Jawaharlal Nehru, in a letter to K.M. Panikkar, the then India's Ambassador to China, had said that whenever China had a strong government, it had tended to expand beyond its frontiers. He viewed the happenings in China not a palace revolution, but a grass root revolution and later told the parliament while presenting the budget demand for the Ministry of External Affairs on March 17, 1950, "It was a basic revolution involving millions and millions of human beings. It is not a question of approving or disapproving; it is a question of recognising a major event in history, of appreciating it and dealing with it."[6] While dealing with China, as most of us viewed, the only area where our interests overlapped, was in Tibet.

As expected the newly established Government of the People's Republic of China announced on January 1, 1950 that one of the basic tasks of People's Liberation Army would be to 'liberate' Tibet. When determination of the Chinese leaders found expression, K.M. Panikkar met Chinese Premier Chou En lai in which the latter had assured the Indian ambassador that though the liberation of Tibet was a sacred duty of China his government would seek this goal through negotiation and not by military action. However, despite assurance China launched a full scale invasion on Tibet in October 1950. With the use of force by China in Tibet it became apparent that the event would alter the geo-politics of the region. It made India and China immediate geographical neighbours for the first time in history and gave rise to such security concerns for India as was previously unknown.[7] More important, it raised the vital question of where the territorial limits of a partitioned and weak Indian state lay.

Regarding Tibet, India was interested in preserving its autonomy that it was maintaining for decades. On number of occasions Jawaharlal Nehru had made it clear that India had no territorial or political ambition in regard to Tibet and our relations were cultural and commercial. He also made it clear that we did not challenge or deny the suzerainty of China over Tibet.[8] In fact, after the establishment of strong government in China there was a physical limit to what the Government of India could do to support the independence of Tibet. The most, India could do was to protest against the use of force and to insist that the autonomy of Tibet should be respected. In dealing with the crisis the Government of India had not only to take into account the practical possibilities of the situation, but the long-range results of any policy which they might adopt.

The occupation of Tibet by force not only brought China to India's very doors but made India anxious and its anxiety became all the more acute in view of its awareness of its own military weaknesses against China.[9] Following Chinese action in Tibet Sardar Patel, the Deputy Prime Minister of India, in a letter drew Pandit Nehru's attention to the problems of India's security in the north and suggested measures to strengthen them. He expressed the apprehension that the Chinese and the Russians would not miss any opportunity of exploiting weak spots in the north.[10] Nehru himself was not unmindful of India's northern frontier and responding to the changed situation declared that the McMahon Line would be India's non-negotiable border in the north-east 'map or no-map',[11] but significantly made no statement regarding the frontier in Ladakh. In line, Nehru decided further to draw the Indian security perimeter along the Himalayan range, taking in Nepal, Bhutan, and Sikkim and to warn that any breach of the Himalayas would be regarded as a threat to India. Years following the occupation of Tibet, India did not want to start their relations on the wrong foot and supported China on several international issues including latter's support when the United States of America intervened in Korea and advocated PRC's place in the United Nations. This led to the warming of the Sino-Indian relations, culminating in signing of a trade treaty with China in April 1954 whose preamble incorporated the much trumpeted five principles of peaceful co-existence.

Signing of Panchsheel was the last laugh for India in its relations with the PRC. In spite of the fact that Tibet had been referred as the 'Region of China' in this treaty, the PRC had accused India of being influenced by the imperialist power. After the signing of a treaty between China and Tibet on May 23, 1951, Dalai Lama left Tibet and then made unsuccessful attempts to raise the issue of its autonomy at the UN. Dalai Lama's mobilisation of world opinion in Tibet's favour was considered by China as an imperialist design and it held India responsible for it partially, if not wholly. On the other friendship with China was the cornerstone of the entire edifice of Nehru's worldview and structure of policy, and he placed his trust on the 'Chineseness' of communist China, on its national pride and its 'Asianness.'[12] Despite strong domestic pressures and fears following the extension of Chinese sovereignty to Tibet and the harsh Soviet and Chinese criticism of him, non-alignment and India, Nehru took deliberate measures to avoid confrontation. However, in years to come the question of frontiers and borders became alive and immediate issue for both which it had not been in 1950.

In post-Panchsheel phase, though in a mild tone, India and China began to warm up the issue of territorial delimitation. Basing himself on the view that India's northern frontier was a traditional one and that there was no doubt as to where it lay, Nehru had decided in September 1954 that the whole boundary should be shown on maps as a continuous line and no reference need to be made to undemarcated areas. But unfortunately, no map on a larger scale could be issued. In the meantime, China had been issuing maps of varying scale showing boundary alignments which were never the same but included Aksai Chin, NEFA and various little pockets of Indian territory within China. When India objected to this they simply said that they were merely following Kuomintang maps and it did not satisfy India. Later on, nature of the border dispute enlarged and the Government of China stated that they had not as yet undertaken a survey of their boundary nor consulted with the countries concerned and they would not make changed on their own.[13] Thus, for the first time they virtually repudiated the traditional alignment shown on Indian maps and implied that the boundary was an open issue which should be the subject of discussion. In response Nehru wrote a letter directly to Zhou expressing his surprise at Chinese attitude which was contrary to what he had been since 1949 and what he had repeatedly said in parliament.

Realistically speaking, the reassurances of China and the apparent relaxation in tension between the two did not, in substance, mean more than a mere temporary postponement of more vital issues whose seriousness came to be realised only afterwards. Minor border incidents and incursions took place before 1955 that might be considered as insignificant, they however, began to take a large amount of Indian territories in following years. In 1955 and 1956 the incident of border crossing happened and on several occasions Chinese troops were found on the Indian side of Shipki La. At about the same time major incursions began with full knowledge of the Chinese authorities where India delineated the limits of her territories, started levelling a caravan route across the inhibited plateau of Aksai Chin. From Sinkiang to Tibet, this road was meant to open Western Tibet to Chinese immigrants and to divert its trade from its traditional southward direction into Western China and the Soviet Union. It was completed in about two years and simultaneously Chinese patrols were also regularly visiting southern Demchok, a village in Kashmir near the Tibetan boundary; and a party of Chinese soldiers was seen in 1956 in the Nilang area in Uttar Pradesh. The Chinese Government also asserted their claims to Bara Hoti, two miles south of Tun Jun La.

In the circumstances Chou En-lai, the Chinese premier, visited India in December 1956 and assured that although China had never recognised the McMahon Line, his country felt, they should recognise it because it was an accomplished fact and because of their friendly relations with India. When Nehru suggested that the two sides should agree on some principles which bases the minor boundary disputes, the visiting guest only said that the question could be solved or should be settled early. This oral commitment and word strengthened Nehru's faith in premier's friendship. The period of patch up of differences appeared to have gone some way in consolidating their friendship which contained seeds of future trouble.[14] Further China alleged that "The American Chiang Kai-shek clique with fugitive reactionaries from Tibet" had for sometime been active in the Indian town of Kalimpong.

Divergence of Approach Deepened

From the start Indian and Chinese approaches to the territorial issue remained poles apart. While for Nehru the question of the territorial definition of India continued to be as an ex-colonial modern state and he failed to make it a priority goal of foreign policy. Mao regarded the territorial formation of the PRC with utmost seriousness and took hard decisions in this regard. Now the basic policy defects of India began to impart dividends and from 1958 divergence of approach to the territorial issue surfaced. Incidents occurred at Bara Hoti inspite of the renewal of the understanding as well as agreement not to send armed personnel to the area. In July 1958, the Government of India received information about the intrusion by Chinese troops into the Ladakh region of Kashmir and occupation by them of India's Khurnak Fort. About at the same time the news of Chinese troops crossing into the Lohit Division of NEFA and establishment of outposts at Lapthal and Sangch Malla along the Indo-Tibetan border came to which India dispatched protest notes. Height of the event was on 14th December 1958 when Nehru personally wrote to Chou En-lai rebutting the Chinese claims. India was shocked when in his reply the Chinese premier said that "the Sino-Indian boundary has never been formally delimited" and that the so-called "McMahon Line was a product of British policy of aggression against the Tibet region of China." Obviously by that time China's borders with its neighbouring states in the Himalayan region except India, had been finally settled and its troops had been posted all along the Sino-Indian border. Complaints and counter-complaints were pushed in the background as Sino-Indian border conflict took a serious turn causing great anxiety.

However, fluctuating Chinese instance could easily be attached to the developments in Tibet. In general Nehru sought to work out a policy which would harmonise our seemingly conflicting objectives : to help the Tibetans while maintaining friendship with China and to ensure the security of India in a new context without casting off the anchor of non-alignment.[15] The background of Tibetan revolt of March 1959 was prepared by the Khampa who raised a voice against China in 1956. Initially its centre was east of Tibet province and this unrest now spread to Tibet itself. In this phase of downward slide in Sino-Indian relations even the decision of the Government of India to prevent armed Khampas from crossing the border and, in case of those who managed to cross over, to disarm them and send them back to Tibet did not help to stem the steady decline. Further the Chinese authorities charged that this revolt was engineered by the privileged class of the old social order. These elements were encouraged by foreign vested interest and imperialist.

The last event that destroyed Sino-Indian border understanding was the revolt of Tibet in the middle of March 1959. This sudden uprising in Lhasa, the capital of Tibet, led to the outbreak of hostilities between the Tibetans and the Chinese forces. A proclamation declaring independence of Tibet was issued by the Tibetan cabinet and the Seventeen Point Agreement, made between Tibet and China in 1951, was also declared null and void. As the situation worsened the Preparatory Committee for the Tibetan Autonomous Region set up by the Chinese was recognised with Pancham Lama as chairman. The revolt was put down by the People's Liberation Army of China with a heavy hand and it entrenched itself well across the borders of India. At the end of March 1959, the Indian Government granted asylum to Dalai Lama and admitted several thousand Tibetan refugees who accompanied them. The flight of Dalai Lama and his arrival in India placed the already brittle relations a heavy strain from which they never recovered.

Before and even after the outbreak of the Tibetan revolt India adopted cautious and correct approach, deliberately framed to please the Chinese. From January this year India was faced with the problem of numbers of Tibetan refugees is thing to cross over. Nehru, maintaining a correct position, ordered that no Tibetan should be permitted into India. Again when he received reports of fighting in Lhasa, refused to give any general commitment that refugees would be let in. He was quite clear about the future of Tibet and India's policy thereof. Nehru's meeting with Dalai Lama on 24 April 1959, made the latter known 'Let us face the facts. The whole world can not bring freedom to Tibet unless the whole fabric of the Chinese state is destroyed. Only a world war, an atomic war, could perhaps make that possible. In the same vein he was clear in regard to India's Tibet policy and said 'There was no question of India intervening in Tibet; the most that India could do in helping the Tibetans to have a square deal, was to assist a situation gradually to develop which would induce the Chinese Government to moderate their policy in Tibet. India's policy side approach was appreciated by the Chinese Government.

What vitiated the atmosphere was the other side of the coin. Particularly in case of political asylum to Dalai Lama India was guided by reasons more than one. Nehru's decision to grant asylum to Dalai Lama had the near-unanimous support of public opinion in India. This humanitarian act suited the guest as he was respected in India as a high priest of Buddhism.[16] There was also wide-spread sympathy for Tibet because of the 'cultural kinship'. Despite being affirmative in 1954 when Panikkar said about the asylum of the Government of India if Dalai Lama had ever sought, this time in 1959 China regarded the grant of asylum as an unfriendly act. It condemned India's attitudes and actions as inconsistent with the Panch Sheela and charged India 'expansionist' withholding the Dalai Lama 'under duress'. Later it was also charged India with encouraging the rebels and interfering in China's internal affairs.[17] In the meantime the Prime Ministers of the two countries met in April 1960 but failed to cut much ice. In fact, the summit was the last real opportunity for arriving at a common approach to the border problem – weakened the prospect of a negotiated settlement. Even three meetings of the officials of the two countries held in Peking, New Delhi and Rangoon respectively in 1960 failed to find any solution rather they made perceptions even more obvious. Simultaneously relations between the two went on deteriorating and border incursions becoming more frequent they assumed more menancing dimension.

Earlier at the close of the year 1959 pressed by Chinese advances and strong public sentiment Nehru decided to pursue the 'Forward Policy' with a view to exercise effective control upto its borders. The sole purpose of this decision was to establish checkposts and despatch patrols, wherever possible, up to the boundary and to constitute a special board to complete the building of roads in the border areas within two years to make clear that any further Chinese advance was obvious aggression. This step of the Indian government was necessitated as the Chinese had been steadily moving southward into Ladakh and a parallel Indian position became essential. This might halt the flow of Chinese encroachment and help to create a climate where good sense would prevail and negotiations could begin.[18] By the end of 1961, about 50 posts were established by Indian forces all along the border. Meanwhile, the PRC improved its relations with Nepal, Ceylon and Pakistan.

The early months of 1962 saw a continued exchange of diplomatic notes with China protesting at the patrolling and the establishment of border posts by India. In March and April 1962 some posts were established by India on the Depsang plains and one post twelve miles north-east of Daulat Beg Oldi. These posts were intended to affirm Indian sovereignty over these border areas rather than to withstand Chinese attack but it was misinterpreted by China and the latter had resorted to aggressive tactics. Intense Chinese activity was reported in the western sector, especially in the Chip Chap, Chang Chenmo and Pangong regions, but many protests were lodged by India when there was confrontation or firing. Expressing readiness for talks, disappointed Nehru remarked on 3rd October 1962 when B.M. Kaul, India's Chief of the General Staff, met him, 'India had tolerated Chinese incursions into her territory for far too long and a stage has come when she should take-or appear to take-a strong stand irrespective of consequences.'[19]

The climax of India-China border dispute came on September 8, 1962, when Chinese troops crossed the McMahon Line in NEFA in the eastern sector and occupied a good part of Indian territory. Pressed by political compulsions Nehru told the media on October 13, 1962 that his Government had asked the army to throw the Chinese out of our territory. Many people in the country including B.M. Kaul were surprised and acknowledged that this might have provoked the Chinese to launch a massive attack on October 20, 1962.[20] By October 25, Chinese were inside India about 16 miles south of McMahon Line. Further the Chinese began attack on a very large scale on November 15 in both NEFA and Ladakh sectors. The victorious Chinese reached a spot in Assam overlooking river Brahmaputra, plains of Assam and the Bay of Bengal in the eastern sector. Suddenly on November 25, 1962, the Chinese announced unilateral cease-fire. Timely help by Britain and the US perhaps compelled China to cease-fire and withdraw to the point chosen by them.[21] The Indian armies abided by the cease-fire and did not impede the Chinese withdrawal in the eastern sector, although this meant that the Chinese would remain in possession of about 2,500 square miles recently occupied in the western sector. While the Chinese asserted that they would withdraw to the 'line of actual control' as on 7th November 1959, they also let slip that, in fact, to do so would mean withdrawal from about 6,000 square miles of territory which they had occupied.

1962 enabled China to establish an international identity ideologically and political distinct from that of the Soviet Union. Its military victory and its unilateral withdrawal enhanced its image and standing in the third world. It paved the way for China to play an independent role in world affairs. By contrast, for India, the year proved a trauma. The collapse of India-China amity effectively destroyed the structure of Nehru's foreign policy. It did more : it shook the foundation of his worldview. After 1962 the two concerns became most pressing for it. The one was territorial definition and consolidation which became the core problem in its relationship with all neighbours, especially China and Pakistan. The other was an active search for security vis-à-vis China. In the aftermath of the war Nehru, perhaps as his last brave act, attempted to moderate the mood of the Parliament and advised it not to shut the door to the possibility of future talks with China, and not to cast China as an 'enemy'. It, however, was a definite end to a more expectant past and a new beginning for India and China in almost every aspect of state life.

Today the map-marked McMahon line is the on-the-ground divide in the east except for China's occupation of the Thagla ridge and some area in the vicinity of Longju. The Sino-Indian boundary is still undemarcated and China has not foreclosed its claim that include nearly the whole of Arunachal Pradesh and some areas on the Indian side of Karakoram range in the north-west. China signalled its ascension to great power status in post-1962 period by becoming a ballistic missile-armed, thermo-nuclear power the border, however, remained peaceful with India effectively accepting China's occupation of Aksai Chin and China not contesting India's return to the NEFA following the war.

2.2 Dynamics of India-China Border Talks

The border line difference between India and China despite being in existence took an alarming proportion with the developments in Tibet at the close of 1950s and it resulted in a declared war in October 1962 with India's humiliating defeat, which sealed the fate of India-China relations in all spheres for the long fourteen years. In 1962, while China was ready for massive aggression on India, the later think the disaster either physically or mentally and no one who lived in India through the winter months of the year can forget the deep humiliation felt by all Indians, irrespective of party. However, even after the border conflict New Delhi did not close its option of a negotiated settlement of all outstanding problems and sought a realistic co-existence with Beijing, yet adverse relationship between the two by and large, operated at stabilised level and sometimes became more intense on account of open Chinese support to Pakistan in its 1965 and 1971 war with India. It was only from the mid 1970s that both sides began to feel the need of mutual cooperation and keeping in view the aspirations, they responded positively which suggested the winds of change in their relations. In line India-China talks on border problem began in December 1981 and passed on from normal border talk to Joint Working Group (JWG) to meeting of Special Representatives. Till today, in all along the period above 40 round of talks have been conducted but the problem is nowhere near in its solution. Although over the years, India's relations with the People's Republic of China have, no doubt, improved largely in economic sphere, in particular, the continuation of the vexed border problem between them tells us sufficiently about their mutual deficit of trust and sympathy in each other's perception and pursuit.

Background of Initiation of Border Talks

The unresolved border issue, a legacy of the India-China war of October 1962 cast a long and deep dark shadow on areas of engagement in the post-war period. Although ambassadorial level relations between them was restored in April 1976 the first positive development on the part of China came when greeting the Indian diplomat in 1970 said that India is a great country and that India and China should be friends again.[22] The border issue between them was intensified after administering a blistering defeat in 1962 war, the Chinese forces withdrew 20 Kilometers behind the Mc Mahon Line, which China called "the 1959 line of actual control" in the eastern sector and 20 Kilometers behind the line of its latest position in Ladakh, which was further identified with the "1959 line of actual control in the western sector. This left China in possession of 23,200 square kilometer of territory in Ladakh. India asked for status quo-ex-ante as of September 8, 1962 in all sectors, which China rejected. It resulted in a stalemate on the boundary dispute."[23] The Indian suggestion of status quo was further refuted in December 1964 by Chou Enlai while speaking to the National People's Congress in Beijing he called the suggestion of restoration of the status quo as of September 8, 1962 "an unreasonable Indian pre-condition". He declared on the occasion that China would never dismantle its posts and reminded India that China had not relinquished its claim to an additional 90,000 square kilometer south of the McMahon Line. This territorial demand was in addition to the 23,200 square kilometer in Ladakh that was already with China.[24] Thus, the bigger border issue, if made central to further development of Sino-Indian relations, would effectively freeze any progress towards entente.

In fact, the conflict left a trail of bitterness whose traces are still present in their relations. For many years to come their mutual hostility determined their foreign policy. There were no ambassadors in each other's capital for many years and there was virtual absence of contact. There is nothing worse for a country's image than defeat, as the prestige and image of a nation gets tarnished. Its capacity to influence other nations gets seriously affected. As J. F. Kennedy aptly put it: 'Victory has many fathers, defeat is an orphan'.[25] Internationally, they traded abuses and generally adopted opposite standpoints. Peking was engaged in a full-scale campaign against India, a chief purpose of which was to carry conviction that India was no longer non-aligned but was firmly in the American camp.[26] With Chinese propaganda and its alliances against India, now the later was deeply suspicious about Chinese motives and designs. India believed that China wanted to dominate Asia as Lal Bahadur Shastri, the then Prime Minister of India, said in Parliament, 'To justify its aggressive attitude, China is pretending to be a guardian of Asian countries, who, according to China are being bullied by India. The basic objective of China is to claim for itself a position of dominance in Asia, which no self-respecting nation in Asia is prepared to recognise.'[27] The annual report of the Ministry of External Affairs for the year 1964-65 spelt-out India's perception of Chinese motivations. After a long period of hostility and strife from the mid-1970s the two countries felt the need to normalise their relations and accordingly they moved in this direction, although slowly. In line, China participated in the 33rd Table Tennis Championship at Calcutta in February 1975. Peking began to respond to the earlier Indian initiatives.

The relations between India and China were stepping further and the two were talking quietly about the normalisation of relations which was culminated in sudden announcement of restoring diplomatic relations. Y. B. Chavan, the Foreign Minister of India, declared in the Lok Sabha on 15th April 1975 that New Delhi has decided to sent an ambassador to China and designated K. R. Narayanan for the post. Earlier the Chinese had taken the view that since India had recalled its ambassador first, she should take the initiative in sending one back. Following India's announcement Peking declared its decision to appoint an ambassador in New Delhi. Relations improved gradually since 1976 when diplomatic relations were restored at ambassadorial level.[28] This exchange of ambassadors did not by itself signify a detente but it had come to represent an important political step for a return to normalisation. Since then, the cultural exchanges between the two countries were also on rise.

Major change of guard took place almost simultaneously in India and China. As a result of general election held in early 1977, for the first time since country's independence in 1947, a non-Congress Government of Janata Party coalition, under the leadership of Morarji Desai, assumed the office of Prime Minister. The Chinese confidently expected that the Janata government would considerably distance itself from the Soviet Union and move towards new bonds with Washington and Peking. The change of Government was welcomed in Peking and as reported in *The Times* (London), it expressed the hope that the new Indian Government would bring changes in the hitherto pro-Soviet policy of the Government of India.[29] The new Government and Atal Bihari Vajpayee, its Minister for External Affairs, assured the Chinese Government by reiterating that India considered Tibet as a part of China[30] and normal relations maintained in the period with exchange of delegations from both sides, it however, made clear to the Chinese authorities that border issue between the two is central to normal relations when Wang Ping Non-visited India in March 1978 as the leader of a goodwill delegation and emphasised that the bitterness that had developed between the two countries as a result of the border conflict sixteen years ago was a thing of the past.[31] From the Government of India's points of view complete friendship with China will be possible only after the return of its territory.[32]

Morarji Desai, the Prime Minister of India, also told the Rajya Sabha that there was no possibility of having full friendship with China-border solution first amity after.[33] Thus, the question in India was seen as a precondition to the normalisation of relations between the two countries.

In the context the first rapproachment in diplomatic relations commenced more than a decade ago in 1967 when Congress Party won the elections and return to power with shrunken majority at the Centre. Tense situation at the Actual Line of Control (LAC), deadlock in Sino-Indian relations at diplomatic level, forced the leader of the ruling Party to visualise the importance of China. Owing to this situation, Government of India realised that it would be in New Delhi's interest to give up its rigid insistence on the Colombo Proposal and inject some flexibility in the situation. On 1st January 1969, Indira Gandhi at a press conference disclosed that the government was prepared "to try and find" a way out of solving the dispute with China without insisting on its acceptance of Colombo Plan as a precondition.[34] On being both sides slight positive towards normalisation of relations India although refused to participate in Afro-Asian Table Tennis Tournament to be held in November 1971 at Peking, as a gesture of goodwill it removed the Police post maintained outside the Chinese Embassy. On 25th October 1971, the United Nations' Organisation (UNO) granted admission to China.[35] India congratulated and expressed the hope that cooperation between India and China in the world body would lead to peace and progress in Asia. The progress in understanding had softened Chinese attitude towards the Indo-Pak war of 1971 in comparison to 1965 war. Thus, India's efforts in the direction of improving relations with China were not in vain because the later was responding slowly and steadly towards normalisation.

In China too the post-Mao regime realised the importance of maintaining relations with India. They started reassessing its foreign policy of Maoist era. The Foreign Minister of China Huang Hua attained the Republic Day celebration function for the first time and expressed the desire for improving relations between the two countries. In fact, between 1970 to 1980, "the regional events" and "politics" compelled China to change her foreign policy, be a good neighbour and co-exist in peace with all. USSR's intervention in Afghanistan in 1979 indeed disturbed the strategic balance in South Asian region, along with Iranian revolution, Vietnamese intervention, Vietnamese intervention in Kampuchea (Combodia), which China perceived as a threat in the form of an encirclement by the Soviet Union. In the region US started arms supply to Pakistan and India started to justify USSR's presence in Afghanistan. Further, an agreement was also signed between the Soviet Union and India for supply of military hardware. All these political developments and the situation in general demanded that China should develop friendly relations with India for two reasons: (i) for its security and (ii) to safeguard its interest in India. In addition, domestic compulsions, Tibetan problem and her dream to become well progressed industrial nation compelled China to normalise relations with India.

At the time the Janata Government took over there were two good reasons for India for improving relations with the People's Republic of China. Strained relations with China distorted India's priorities by imposing on it unduly heavy defense burden. Secondly, unless India improved its relations with the PRC, New Delhi could not safely assume that Pakistan would not reverse its policy of reconciliation with India and revert to its old stance.[36] The rule of Janata Party was replaced by the Congress Party's Government under Indira Gandhi in January 1980. In her first mandate what India really attempted was to become militarily strong by investing in research and development, and by buying sophisticated arms abroad. The objective was to become a hegemonic power in South Asia by playing a much more assertive role than she has ever done before; keep the nuclear option open by conducting an underground nuclear explosion in May 1974; and by blasting, in July 1980, India's own satellite SLV-3. At the juncture, the principal thrust of India's foreign policy was more power and region oriented than one of seeking out a new global role for herself. In her tenure of second mandate Indira Gandhi sought out a more international role. Now that India had attained the status of a regional power, and was internationally recognised as such.

Equally important, India wanted to improve relations with China and stressed its role in the non-aligned movement. China, too was interested in improving relations with India after developments in Afghanistan. China tried to facilitate normal relations with India by avoiding the Kampuchean issue where both nations were pursuing altogether different policies. With Indira Gandhi's government China was psychologically prepared to carry on the dialogue, perhaps with greater realisation that the nexus between national interests and foreign policy, in India as in other countries, could not be conducive to cyclonic changes in foreign relations. Indeed the two countries accepted each other's possibilities and assumptions and tried to enhance the greater chances for a durable peace in the region. The positive thread was picked up in May 1980 when Indian Prime Minister Indira Gandhi and her Chinese counterpart Hua Kuo-feng met in Belgrade to attend the funeral of President Tito. This was the first meeting at the Prime Ministerial level since 1961 when Chou En-lai visited India. In their meeting they agreed to persist the process of resolving issues and improving relations.[37] Thereafter, the Chinese leader Deng Xiaoping reiterated in June 1980 and April 1981 that neither India nor China pose any threat to each other and repeated Chinese desire for developing friendly relations with India. The Indian Prime Minister Indira Gandhi too on her part, reiterated India's desire to further normalise and improve Sino-Indian relations during Brezhnev's visit to New Delhi in December 1980 but at the same time assured the visiting guest that India's relations with any other country would not affect her relations with Soviet Union.[38] These apart, on 29th May 1981 Indira Gandhi sent a passionate condolence message stating the memorable moments of India's freedom struggle on passing away of Song Qingling, the widow of Sun yat-sen. The griefing message not only represented profound friendship between the people of India and China but also paved the way for Huang Hua's path-breaking visit to India in June 1981 which broke the long deadlock on border issue between the two.

As a major breakthrough Huang Hua, Deputy Premier and Foreign Minister of China, visited India in the last week of June 1981. However, prior to Huang's India visit, China sent Zhao Ziyang, Premier of China, on a state visit to Pakistan, Bangladesh and Nepal. By this Peking's new policy in the region had become more transparent. Now it wished to upgrade relations with India but without having to concede too many concessions and without impairing in any way the relationship, in some cases special and in some others if not special then very close and cordial, with Pakistan, Nepal and Bangladesh along with other neighbours of India. New Delhi-Peking relationship, like the New Delhi-Islamabad had been characterised by ups and downs, though not in the same way and not to the same extent. In particular, Chinese Premier's visit in the region was aimed at reinforcing Pakistan's confidence in China that any Sino-Indian rapproachment should not be viewed as abandonment of Pakistan by China.

In course of his visit Hua met Narasimha Rao, Foreign Minister of India, on 27 and 28 June and both the foreign ministers held talks on different national and international issues of mutual concern. On 28 June the visiting guest held talks with Indira Gandhi and was also called on Indian President Neelam Sanjeeva Reddy and Vice - President Hidayatullah. By this visit and discussions thereof the relations between the two moved positively forward. The visit of China's Deputy Premier and Foreign Minister opened a new chapter in Sino-Indian relations, as both sides agreed to the establishment of an annual dialogue at the level of vice-ministers alternatively in Beijing and New Delhi. Although these meetings did not achieve any significant breakthrough but they did help build confidence between India and China, and push forward exchanges in the fields of culture, science and technology, academics and sports. Significantly in their discussions, both sides refrained from touching the issues on which there were disagreements. Both the countries deemed it important to not let the differences of opinion become an obstacle in the normalisation and improvement of Sino-Indian relations.

On the border issue too Huang Hua reiterated that the two sides must adopt an "attitude of treating each other on an equal footing, mutual understanding and mutual accommodation and seek through negotiations a reasonable and fair overall settlement of the problem, taking into consideration the historical background and the present actualities as well as the national feelings of the people of both countries.[39] He added further that pending a settlement, the two sides should maintain the status quo on the borders and maintain tranquility in the border areas. However, the status quo position on border was hardly acceptable to India as the indefinite continuance of the position was also not regarded by New Delhi in her interest. Nor was India greatly attracted by the package deal as mentioned by Deng Xiaoping to Indian media persons which would give contractual, legal sanction to the existing situation, a kind of "you-keep-what-you-have and We-retain what-we-possess."[40] Without significant gains on the border issue, a deadlock had been broken with slow serpantine movement of adjustment and accommodation. China agreed in the discussions that the border issue was a vital problem that had to be resolved and could just not be shelved. The two sides were also determined that the officials of the two countries should take up the problems and seek settlement through periodic and ongoing discussions. At least, Hua's visit prepared the sufficient ground and understanding for initiating the border talks between the two countries. Their understanding was further enhanced when Indian Prime Minister Indira Gandhi met Chinese Premier, Zhao Ziyang at Cancun in Mexico on 28th October 1981 at the sidelines of North-South Conference on Cooperation and Development. The occasion provided the two Prime Ministers held friendly talks and prompted to start border talks between them in December 1981.

Initiation of Border Talks 1981-1988

In the period 1981-1988 total eight round of border talks held between India and China in pursuance of the understanding reached between the two during the New Delhi visit of Huang Hua, Chinese Deputy Premier and Foreign Minister in December 1981. Although the new Chinese policy originated in 1970s, it gathered rapid momentum which culminated with the Indian Premier Rajiv Gandhi's historic visit to China in December 1988. The changes that occurred in Chinese foreign policy in the 1980s were to great extent a result of the emergence of a new leadership under Deng Xiaoping who helped to steer Chinese foreign policy away from communist idealism and towards socialist pragmatism.[41] The decade 1980s saw the promulgation of an 'independent' foreign policy by China. At the 12th Party Congress in 1982, the Secretary of the CCP Hu Yaobang announced: 'Our adherence to an independent foreign policy accords with the discharge of our lofty international duty to safeguard world peace and promote human progress.[42] As part of its new policy China began closely identifying itself with the Third World, and strongly supported the cause of the Non-Aligned Movement (NAM) and the efforts to promote South-South cooperation.[43] In the opinion of China, the strength of both superpowers was on the decline and the world was witnessing the gradual emergence of a multipolar world in which the role of Third World would be enhanced. In the situation China's positive response to the border problem was met with an equally enthusiastic response from India, which gave hope for an eventual settlement of the most irksome issue between the two countries. Even under the Janata government, efforts were made by China and India to reach an amicable settlement of the border problem, showed that the change of government in India would not adversely affect the warming up of Sino-Indian relations.[44] In line China also valued the correct policy pursued by India towards Tibet that Tibet is a part of China and India will not interfere in China's internal affairs. Of the eight border talks five were held during Indira Gandhi's régime and three in the period of Rajiv Gandhi's Premiership.

The *first* official level talks on border problem between India and China were held in Beijing from 10th to 14th December 1981. Eric Gonsalves Foreign Secretary in India's Ministry of External Affairs led Indian delegation and Chinese side was represented by Han Nialong, the Vice Minister of Foreign Affairs. During the discussion India proposed that the Colombo proposals should be the basis of negotiation, which China summarily rejected and put forward its own proposal of "mutual understanding and accommodation" and "package deal" that was not acceptable to India. In the meeting India stressed "sector-wise examination as against the Chinese proposal. Thereafter, Beijing suggested that the border issue be frozen and progress can be made in the fields of science and technology, trade, socio-cultural exchanges etc. India accepted the suggestion on condition that while proceeding towards cooperation, at the sametime an attempt should also be made for settling the border problem.[45] India on its side rejected the offer of keeping the crucial border issue being "frozen" but suggested China to recognise the McMahon Line as it was apprehensive that once the legality of McMahon Line was ascertained, China would make further concessions in the Western Sector. In the circumstances the first official level talks failed to yield an acceptable solution but they both were determined to sign an agreement and in the hope they decided to continue their efforts to resolve their differences on the boundary issue.

However, despite unyielding attitude from both the sides they, in course of discussions, adopted positive gestures and their leaders were hopeful of finding an acceptable solution of the issue. Reporting the matter, the Chinese official news Agency *Xinhua* quoting Huang Hua stated, 'the talks that Chinese and the Indian officials are now holding on the boundary and other questions will surely have a positive influence on furtherance of friendly and cooperative relations between the two countries.[46] It was Hua's first public statement on the recent nature of Sino-Indian relations. On the other Narasimha Rao, India's Minister for External Affairs too became positive and addressing the members of the Parliamentary Consultative Committee for External Affairs he stated, 'There are wide differences on the border issue, but it continues to be the take off point. The improvement of Sino-Indian relations is not only the common desire of the two peoples but it is beneficial to the strengthening of peace and stability in Asia and the world.[47] This first round of border talks between the two witnessed throughout an air of frank and friendly exchange of views on boundary question without any hesitation from either side.

Second round of India-China official level talks on border issue was held at New Delhi from 12th to 20th May 1982 in which Indian delegation was led by Eric Gonsalves, Secretary in the Ministry of External Affairs and Fu Hao, an advisor in the Chinese Ministry of Foreign Affairs from the Chinese side. During the talks China proposed that they were willing to accept the present Line of Actual Control (LAC) as a solution to the border issue. India rejected it calling the reiteration of package deal in different language. In the discussion the Chinese side appeared very serious and sincerely expressed their desire to resolve the border question at the earliest. As such they both, India and China suggested a set of guiding principles as a basis for Sino-Indian dialogue. In the context China put forward five principles:—

- Equality.
- Friendly consultation.
- A fair and reasonable settlement.
- Mutual understanding and accommodation.
- A comprehensive solution.

As against the Chinese proposal India suggested a set of six principle which included:—

- A early solution of the border problem.
- A just solution taking into account the legitimate interests of both the sides.

- A common approach and a basis for discussion.
- Consideration of each other's proposal.
- Steps to create an appropriate climate.
- Efforts to settle the border issue in each sector.

Although in the talks no breakthrough was achieved, the two sides tried to narrow down their differences on the issue. The India-China relations had become a complex issue in regional and global context as stated by Eric Gonsalves, leader of the Indian delegation, 'India-China relations were imposed by the logic of our being neighbours, by the interest of our two people and by the challenge we face in the region and in the world of today.[48] However, in the discussions both sides emphasised to broaden exchange in other areas. Following this exchange of experts in various spheres took place from both sides. Among others, in the third week of October 1982 a delegation of the Indian Council of Social Science Research (ICSSR) led by G. Parthasarthi visited China and Deng Xiaoping talked with them on 22nd October in which he expressed the Chinese view on border issue and remarked, 'The border problem between India and China is not really a big issue, India does not pose any threat to China, and neither does China pose any threat to India, there is nothing but a boundary problem between us. Both sides must do something to restore the friendship of 1950s. As long as both sides adopt a fair and reasonable method, 'I believe', it is not difficult to resolve the boundary question.[49] On the occasion he also added that if it cannot be solved immediately, we can put it aside, we can do many things in the areas such as trade, economy and culture, increase bilateral exchanges, promote understanding and friendship, we still have very broad prospects for bilateral cooperation. However, these sentiments apart, when it came to the situation on ground both sides protested against each other's moves, a reminder to the fact that boundary problem was the biggest irritant in the improvement of relations.

The *third* round of official level talks on border problem between India and China was held from 28th January to 2nd February 1983 in Beijing led by K.S. Bajpai, Secretary in the Ministry of Foreign Affairs and Fa Hao from Chinese side. In the discussion both sides repeated earlier and known positions. For example, India raised the plan of

Colombo proposal to counter the Chinese five principles which they suggested in earlier round of talks. India wanted to discuss the legality of the case as the legal position of the two sides had been fairly well documented in the official reports of 1960. At the end of the talks it was said that both sides were positive in their attitude in negotiation on the boundary issue and the air was friendly.[50] But in other domains, the bilateral exchange continued unhindered. Exchange of trade delegation and other goodwill missions continued as earlier that showed that the border question should not be a hindrance in developing relations in other areas.

In the same year the *fourth* round of talks was held in New Delhi from 24-30th October 1983 in which China was represented by Gong Dafei, Deputy Foreign Minister of China. While from the Indian side was K.S. Bajpai, Foreign Secretary. In the meeting the China proposed some commonalities that might be defined for the basis of discussions. It propounded four-points: (i) Adherence to the Five Principles of Peaceful Co-existence; (ii) The desire for an early settlement through consultations in a spirit of friendship and equality; (iii) The need to consider the history, existing conditions and national sentiments of each country; and (iv) The maintenance of peace on the boundary before a settlement is reached.[51] Indian delegation liked the Chinese proposal and termed the approach positive and constructive. Significantly this time India adopted a new approach and decided to proceed with normalisation in other spheres without permitting the border dispute to obstruct the process of normalisation. As such this round of talks enhanced the exchange in the field of media, arts, science and trade sectors. They agreed that both sides will refrain from using force in the settlement of this issue. An attempt was also made to bridge the gap that separated the basic negotiating positions of two sides.[52] In comparison to earlier three rounds, this round proved fruitful and indicated a measure of compromise on both sides, more so on part of China. The earlier meetings, although unproductive, were at best an exercise in testing the political behaviour of both sides. The two Asian giants were determined to bring a "new era" in their relations through scientific, socio-culture and trade exchanges. Thus, the first four rounds certainly proved a good beginning and pragmatic approach in their relationships. Better understanding has been created by these four rounds of border talks and as a result China accepted the Indian proposal of sector-wise examination and discussion. They also came to the conclusion that they would refrain from using force in settlement of the border dispute.

From 17th to 22nd September, 1984 the *fifth* round of border talks at official level were held at Beijing and K. Natwar Singh, India's Foreign Secretary represented Indian side; while Gong Dafei led the Chinese delegation. The talks were held in a frank and friendly atmosphere and Indian side mooted six-point principles for the resolution of boundary issue. These included: (i) finding a speedy method for the resolution of border issue; (ii) the method should be fair and look into the legitimate rights and interest of each side; (iii) both sides should seek a common plan and basis for discussion; (iv) due consideration should be given to the method proposed for the resolution of this problem by any side; (v) some measures must be adopted so as to create a conducive atmosphere for the resolution of the problem; and (vi) a sector to sector approach should be adopted as each sector had different situation. Although China found nothing new in these proposals but both sides further elaborated their respective positions and endeavoured to narrow the differences and broaden the commonalities. In this round of talks China was ready to settle dispute along the McMahon Line in the Eastern Sector with minor concessions by India and discussed in detail the modalities but subsequently domestic politics led to an abandonment of this proposal as Indira Gandhi was concerned about the forthcoming elections in 1985. She did not wish to give an impression of India bargaining from a position of weakness.[53] Thus, India lost an opportunity to settle her crucial border dispute with minor adjustment with China on account of political prestige.

Soon after the conclusion of fifth round of border talks, Indira Gandhi, the Prime Minister of India, was assassinated by her own body guards in Delhi on 31th October 1984. On the same day her eldest son Rajiv Gandhi took the oath of India's sixth Prime Minister. After taking over as Prime Minister of India, Rajiv Gandhi started to fashion his China policy with a renewed enthusiasm. China too showed interest in improving Sino-Indian relations with the new leadership and in a long congratulatory cable on the occasion of 35th anniversary of the establishment of Sino-Indian diplomatic relations mentioned the history of profound feelings and long friendship. Through this message sent on 30th March 1985 China hoped that in coming years Sino-Indian relations would continue to grow and strengthen in fields of polity, economy, culture and science and technology; the unresolved problems between the two countries will certainly be resolved.[54] In reply Rajiv Gandhi wrote, 'We sincerely hope that with our common efforts, we will be able to resolve the unsettled issues on the basis of Five Principles of Peaceful Co-existence and restore and strengthen the historic relationship that existed between our two countries.[55] In coming years the regime got a major breakthrough in its relations with China when Rajiv Gandhi visited Beijing in December 1988.

The *sixth* round of talks on border problem were held at New Delhi from 4th to 10th November 1985. Liu Shuqing, Deputy Foreign Minister of China led the Chinese delegation. This round of border talks proved a negative turning point in many ways. Adopting a sector by sector approach both sides explained their respective positions on the Eastern Sector. The Chinese side studied their historical claims South of the McMahon Line on the basis of the Chang dynasty records and they became more vocal about their claims in the Eastern Sector. In this talk China introduced a new element by demanding for territorial concessions by India in the Eastern Sector but showed no flexibility in the western sector from her side. It declared that the Eastern Sector is the biggest disputed territory and the Indians are in occupation of as much as 90,000 square miles of Chinese territory.[56] Many analysts viewed that the stiffening of the Chinese attitude was resulted from the Russian rapprochement with China. Beijing was interested to strike a deal with India as her main objective was to break the Indo-Soviet encirclement of China. Thus, instead of expecting progress, it brought both the sides back to square one. Chinese strategy led to intrusion in an area known as Sumdorong Chu Valley (Tawang District) in Arunachal Pradesh of India.

In a tense atmosphere the *seventh* round of border talks was held in Beijing from 21st to 23rd July 1986. Indian Foreign Secretary Venkateswarn represented the Indian side and Liu Shuqing led on behalf of China. Before the beginning of the talk while receiving the Indian delegates, the Chinese Foreign Minister Wu Xueqian told them that boundary problem was left over by the history, the atmosphere in which previous rounds of talks were held was very good, however, it is not that good at this time. On the other hand Venkateswarn pointed out that there has been some true and some untrue reporting in the Indian newspapers. The resolution of Sino-Indian boundary problem is the cornerstone of the friendship that both countries desire to build. The official statement in Beijing also highlighted the difference of approach between the two which stated, 'the two sides enhanced their mutual understanding but made no headway, China laid claim to 90,000 square kilometers territory in the Eastern Sector in Arunachal Pradesh. India reaffirmed its claim to 38,000 square kilometer in the Western Sector in Aksai-Chin and 2,000 square kilometer in the Middle Sector. The Indian side noted a hardening of the Chinese stand, the Chinese pointed out that India was demanding only one side to make concession.[57] *The Beijing Review* also declared that disputes exist in the eastern, central and western sectors of the border, but the biggest dispute is in the eastern sector.[58] Consequent upon the developments the Indian Government prompted to enact a bill in the Parliament in December 1986 and on 20 February 1987, Arunachal was granted full statehood. The Chinese Foreign Ministry made a statement and slammed India of "violating Chinese territorial sovereignty" and "gravely injuring feelings of the Chinese people." Constitutional incorporation of Arunachal as a state meant that it would be difficult for any government to cede this territory.

Despite differences on border crisis in Eastern Sector, India and China continued their talks was a positive development from both the sides. Obviously, desire for a peaceful settlement of the border issue, domestic, political and economic changes in both the countries, and relaxation in the tense international situation contributed greatly to such an understanding. In the encouraging environment *eighth* round of talks were held in New Delhi from 16th to 18th November 1987 in which K. P. S. Menon, India's Foreign Secretary and Liu Shuqing from Chinese side headed their respective delegations. Keeping in view their earlier background both sides avoided confrontation of any kind and discussed;

- Both the sides restressed the urgency to prevent military confrontation.

- Issues regarding economic cooperation and trade were discussed.
- Border issues including maintenance of peace and tranquility at the border.

In the talks both the sides realised that the border issue could not be settled at the bureaucratic level and that it requires certain political direction and atmosphere. After completion of the eighth round of talks, the Indian political commentator stated in brief: 'what seems to have been achieved is the awareness of the need for a political initiative. At present time, there has been an understanding on the steps to de-escalate armed confrontation on ground, a move which will be facilitated in this season of heavy snow in the concerned areas. It is also agreed by both sides that conscious effort need to be made for stepping up trade and economic cooperation while more activity in the field of cultural cooperation will certainly help better understanding at the popular mass level.[59] This was perhaps a policy change under Rajiv Gandhi. Indira Gandhi had attached the resolution of boundary issue to the development of relation in other domains. Rajiv's government now deviated from this position and emphasised that the improvement and strengthening of relations in other spheres such as trade and commerce, science and technology and culture should not be held hostage to the border issue.[60] Probably it was the genuine desire for the improvement of bilateral relations.

After breaking the deadlock between India and China in the first phase eight rounds of border talks were held in the years 1981-1987 but unfortunately it failed to yield an acceptable solution because of differing views, opinions and stands towards the settlement of border issue. In the talks both India and China represented their viewpoints different to each other. On the border issue China is of the view that it could be solved on a "give and take" basis or in other words, by a "package deal". China would like to give formal recognition to the Mc Mahon Line and in return India should leave her national claim on Aksai Chin. China wanted to cede less strategic areas of occupied Ladakh and in return, India would have to withdraw from "Tawang". In addition, the Chinese mainly emphasised on "demarcation". In the context they use the term "formalisation" which in practice means, actual demarcation of the boundary on the ground. But this view is possible only when both sides agree where the boundary really lies on the ground.

In contrast to the Chinese views, India is of the opinion that boundary between the two has been recognised by tradition and customs for centuries and therefore India treats it as formally settled by the historical demarcation. As to the Arunachal Pradesh and the Aksai-Chin India considered that legally and historically the area belongs to India but China has grabbed the Indian territory in both the areas by force. The border problem solved on the basis of equality and mutuality means that the Chinese should give up some territory in western sector (Ladakh) besides recognising the McMahon Line in the Eastern Sector. In this connection India is in favour of solving the issue by a sector-wise examination on the basis of maps, historical usages, records, old and legal claims and actual position of the armed forces on the ground. The Chinese side disliked this and remained interested only in improving her relations with India by expanding areas of cooperation and to continue only negotiations for negotiation's sake. It amply showed China's status quoist attitude on the border. Thus, all the eight rounds of talks were held with frequent gestures of friendship and it aroused a false hope of a settlement of this crucial question, in practice the search for settled seemed endless as both the countries proved "tough bargainers" on the border dispute.

In course of the deliberations on border issue between India and China the Participates from both the sides concluded that the problem could not be settled at the bureaucratic level and therefore, direct talks by the political leaders are inevitable. In this direction India took first initiative and Rajiv Gandhi paid an official visit to China from 19th to 23rd December 1988. His visit was a major landmark in improving India-China relations. However, between 1962 and 1987, much water had flown under the bridges of Ganga and Huaanghe. The old guard in both the countries was gone. With Nehru's departure faded his idealism and to some extent the role of nonalignment in international politics. Likewise with Mao's departure from the Chinese political scene, gone was the idea of "exporting revolution" by assisting people's revolutionary wars. China's doors were opened to outside world and emphasis was laid on economic construction and peaceful co-existence with neighbours and international community rather than armed co-existence of Mao.[61] With Mao, also departed the rhetoric of "imperialism", "reactionaries", "revisionism" and hence the vitriolic propaganda against India.

On the Indian political stage too, four Prime Ministers shaped India's internal and external policies. Among these the years of Indira Gandhi were extremely important. She broked the ice with China and fashioned the course of Sino-Indian relations. During her time, five rounds of talks on border were held in Beijing and New Delhi alternatively. Though no breakthrough was achieved, it nevertheless engaged the two estranged neighbours in meaningful talks that on its sidelines facilitated exchange in other fields. Indira Gandhi had also in mind the special relationship between Pakistan and China. Her instant approval for Operation Falcon in the Eastern Sector and simultaneous talks to China points to her reversal of Nehru idealism in favour of combining diplomacy and military in statecraft. She must have turned a leaf from the history of Sino-Indian relations and learned this lesson from Mao and Zhou, if not from the Arthshastra of Chanakya.[62] After her assassination Rajiv Gandhi picked up the threads of Indira Gandhi's China policy, modified in the face of rapid changes in India and China in particular and in international arena in general.

Joint Working Group Level (JWG), 1989-2003

Rajiv Gandhi's visit to China was indeed a turning point in the history of Sino-Indian interaction. It was a true beginning directed to mitigate mutual fear and distrust, and enhance mutual understanding between the peoples of two countries. In course of the visit as a major breakthrough the leaders of India and China agreed to set up a "Joint Working Group" to evolve consensus on border issue between the two countries. The Joint Working Group was also bound with a time frame of two to three years. This attempt was perhaps the most serious one to resolve the border dispute on the principle of mutual understanding and accommodation which would be acceptable to the people of both the countries in terms of mutual interest and benefits.[63] As agreed the Joint Working Group was to be represented by the Foreign Secretary on the Indian side and the Deputy Foreign Minister from the Chinese side. The leaders of the two countries were determined that JWG will meet at stipulated intervals and make recommendations to their respective governments. Also it was expected to include military officers, and surveyors, governors and generals from both the sides. In a nutshell there were three main objectives of establishing the JWG :-

- Make concrete recommendations for an overall solution to the boundary question within a definite time frame. That solution must be acceptable to the parties which would be in their mutual interests and mutual benefits.
- Ensure the peace and tranquility in the border area, until the final settlement is arrived at.
- The working group conceived as a joint undertaking involves institutions like foreign minister, military experts, surveyors, communications experts and legal bodies on both the sides.[64]

The *first* meeting of Joint Working Group was held in Beijing from 30th June to 4th July 1989. The Indian delegation was led by S. K. Singh, Foreign Secretary and Lin Shu Quien, Vice Foreign Minister, headed the Chinese team. In the meeting "general lines" on which the future work should progress in the further meetings of the group were discussed intensively and it was agreed that emphasis should be laid on look forward into the future in a practical, realistic and workman like manner. Regarding maintaining of peace and tranquility on the border, both sides recognised that there was a need for confidence building arrangements. In addition, they were also determined to take concrete steps to diversify and expand trade, culture, scientific and technical exchanges.[65] The main outcome of this talk was the realisation of both sides the urgency of maintaining peace and tranquility in the border area. The discussions were held in a friendly atmosphere.

The *second* round talk of Joint Working Group was held at New Delhi on 30th and 31st August, 1990. The Chinese delegation was led by Qi Huai Yuan; Vice Foreign Minister and the Indian side by Muchkund Dubey, Foreign Secretary. In the talks the two sides enhanced significantly their understanding of each other's approach to the solution of the boundary problem. All efforts were made to adopt a practical and realistic approach and look towards the future. The two sides were also determined to establish contacts between the military personnel of both the countries.[66] The main achievement of this second round of JWG meeting, was that the "mechanism introduced between two countries was that their military personnel will meet from time to time at an appropriate level, with a view to maintaining Peace and Tranquility in the border areas. Peace and Tranquility will certainly assist in creating cordial atmosphere between the two countries to proceed towards solution of the border problem.

In line, the *third* round of India-China Joint Working Group on the boundary question met in Beijing on 13th May 1991. In the meeting the Indian side was led by the Foreign Secretary Muchkund Dubey and the Chinese side, by the Vice Foreign Minister Xu Duxin. The two sides were serious in talks and discussed better relationship and commitment of the two governments to seek a solution within the framework of an agreed approach. They were also determined that neither side would do anything to upset the tranquility along the border and both sides would address the issues in a spirit of accommodation and principle of mutual acceptability. They also discussed measures for the strengthening of peace and tranquility and mutual confidence in the border areas and exchanged their views on bilateral, regional and international issue.[67] An ultimate gain of this meeting was that two sides had a serious discussion about measures in terms of how to maintain peace and tranquility along the Actual Line of Control.

The *fourth* round of JWG on boundary question was held at New Delhi on 20th and 21st February 1992. Chinese side was led by Xu Duxin and Indian side by J.N. Dixit. During talks finally two sides agreed on the concept of maintaining peace and tranquility on the Line of Actual Control and a series of specific steps for it. In view of the confidence building measures they agreed to hold meetings more frequently, meet as and when necessary instead of within a rigid time frame. In course of the discussions leader of the Chinese delegation Xu Duxin said two important things. (i) The boundary question is complex and should not stand in the way of across the broad expansion of relations between the two countries and; (ii) The problem of boundary needs an approach of sincerity and patience. "Patience" means bridging the gaps, narrowing the differences on a long-term basis, on the boundary issue between the two countries will take time as it is considered a legacy of the past. This meeting had added significance because both delegations were composed of representatives from the Defense Ministry and an Army Officer of the rank of "Brigadier" to discuss the measures for the course of action in maintaining peace and tranquility on the Line of Actual Control. The fruits of this talks were that JWG moved from "concepts" to "specifics" and from "ideas" to "measures" with regard to stabilisation of the Line of Actual Control and building up on peace and tranquility there to settle the boundary problem. Throughout the discussions the atmosphere was candid, mutually accommodative, meaningful and positive.

In the same year (1992), the *fifth* round of JWG meeting on boundary question was held at Beijing on 28th and 29th October in which Indian delegation was led by Foreign Secretary J.N. Dixit and the Chinese side was headed by Xu Duxin, Vice Foreign Minister of the country. In the meeting the positive experience of implementing confidence building measures agreed at previous meeting was reviewed and further steps were considered by both. Points for further border trade was also discussed in detail.[68] This round of talk was especially to create a cordial atmosphere and expand an area of cooperations between the two countries. It too was conducted in a cordial and friendly atmosphere.

The *sixth* round meeting of Joint Working Group was held at New Delhi on 25th and 26th June 1993. The Chinese delegation was led by Tang Jia Xuan, Vice Foreign Minister and Indian delegation by J. N. Dixit, Foreign Secretary. In the meeting both sides expressed satisfaction at the manner in which the confidence building measures agreed upon at the previous meetings of JWG were being implemented. Different views were also expressed on further measures to ensure peace and tranquility in areas along the line of actual control between the two countries. Besides, attempts were made by both sides to arrive at a mutually acceptable settlement of India-China border question. As a part of steady and perceptible improvement in bilateral ties, an additional border trade point at Shipki La Pass has been introduced.[69] In this round of talks mainly additional measures were determined to ensure the peace and tranquility along with line of actual control.

The meeting of Joint Working Group appeared unending and the *seventh* round of talks on boundary issue were held in Beijing on 6th and 7th July 1994. However, before the talks India's Prime Minister P.V. Narasimha Rao paid a visit to China from 6-9th September 1993, in response to Li Peng's India visit between

11th and 16th December 1991. Earlier during Li Peng's visit the two premiers reiterated that a method to resolve the border issue "acceptable to both the sides" should be found through friendly consultations" at the earliest. Both leaders also agreed that the talks held by the JWG on border has increased "mutual understanding" and felt that the Group should intensify its work so as a method to resolve the border question is found at the earliest. They reaffirmed that until a final solution to the border problem is found, peace and tranquility along the border should be maintained.[70] In all fairness Li Peng's visit to India was a "milestone in the development of Sino-Indian relations," and was successful in achieving the goal of promoting understanding, cooperation and strengthening friendship between the two countries.[71] In line five bilateral agreements were also signed between the two countries during the visit.

Prime Minister P. V. Narasimha Rao's September 1993 visit to China was hailed as another landmark in bilateral relations. If Rajiv Gandhi was successful in cutting the ice, then Narasimha Rao's visit brought a thaw to Sino-Indian relations. In course of the visit Rao held two rounds of talks with his counterpart, met the Chinese President and the CCP General Secretary, Jiang Zemin, and other important political leaders. In the talks both sides reaffirmed their desire to solve the border issue through friendly consultation.[72] The visit witnessed a breakthrough on 7th September 1993 when at the conclusion of the talks both premiers signed four agreement, the most important among them was the Agreement on Maintenance of Peace and Tranquility along the Line of Actual Control in the Sino-Indian Border Areas. According to Article 9 of the Agreement the border issue should be resolved through peaceful and friendly negotiations; neither side should use force or threaten to use force against the other; the two sides should strictly respect and observe LAC before the border issue is settled and each side should keep its military forces in the areas along LAC to a minimum level; effective confidence building measures (CBMs) in the area along LAC should be worked out through consultations; any contingency that might arise along the LAC should be dealt through consultations between border personnel of the two countries.[73] The signing of other bilateral agreements and on maintaining peace and tranquility on the border, in particular, was pointer to the fact that both sides adopted a "realistic and flexible approach to the knotty border problem and were emerging into an era of mutual comprehension and understanding. Major Indian newspapers had hailed the agreement and reported, 'with the signing of the agreement maintaining peace and tranquility along the LAC indicated that Sino-Indian relations were entering a new phase of mutual trust and political understanding.'[74] It was the beginning of a new era in Sino-Indian relations. The Agreement could be regarded as a brainchild of the Joint Working Group's border talk.

In an important development on border issue during the visit both sides agreed to set up India-China Expert Group in implementation of the Agreement on Maintenance of Peace and Tranquility along the Line of Actual Control in the India-China border areas which was signed in Beijing on 7th September 1993. The first meeting of the India-China Expert Group was held at New Delhi from 2nd to 4th February 1994. It consisted of representatives from the Ministry of External Affairs, Defence and Home Affairs, the Army Headquarter and the Survey of India. In the meeting the Indian delegation was led by Shivashankar Menon, Joint Secretary (North-East) while Chinese delegation was headed by Fuxuezhang, Deputy Director Asian Department, and included the experts from various concerned departments.[75] In the meeting after discussion, both the sides agreed on many issues relating to its mandate, future tasks and methodology and noted with satisfaction that the situation along the India-China border area is peaceful.

The *second* and *third* meetings of Expert Group were held in Beijing and New Delhi respectively. The second meeting held on 21st and 22nd April 1994 and reviewed the progress made at its first meeting. In this meeting the two sides reached agreements on the work regulations of the Expert Group. The document which spells out the mandate for future talks and modalities of the Expert Group was signed by the leaders of the two delegations on 22nd April 1994.[76] The third meeting of the Expert Group was held from 2nd March to 4th March 1995 and Shivashankar Menon, Joint Secretary headed the delegation composed of delegates from the Ministry of External Affairs: Defence and Home Affairs, the Army Headquarters and the Survey of India. The Chinese delegation was led by Wang Chungi, Deputy Director General, Asian Department had included the members from Military and Foreign Affairs. The expert group reviewed the progress made at its first and second meetings. The achievement of the third meeting was:—

- The two sides recognised the importance of effective confidence building measures and discussed on further such measures.
- The two sides exchanged the views on the drafts prepared by India on prior notification on military exercises and prevention of air intrusions across the India-China LAC.
- The two sides also agreed that additional designated points for meetings between the border personnel of the two countries will be established at "Nathu La pass" in the Sikkim sector and a point to be, agreed in the middle sector of the India-China border areas. It is quite an important achievement of the third meeting of expert groups.[77]

In all the three meetings of the expert group both sides were determined about the nature of their tasks in terms of implementing the accord. They also agreed to prepare a framework for the implementation of the accord step by step.

In succession the *Seventh* round meeting of Joint Working Group, was held after the successful visit of Indian Prime Minister P.V. Narasimha Rao and took place on 6th to 7th July 1994. The Indian delegation was led by the Foreign Secretary while the Chinese delegation was headed by Tang Jiaxuan, Vice Foreign Minister. In the meeting the two sides continued discussions aimed at arriving at a fair, reasonable and mutually acceptable solution of the boundary issue. On the border Agreement signed during the visit of P. V. Narasimha Rao, both sides were pleased and noted that the situation along the India-China Line of Actual Control was peaceful and agreed to introduce additional points for meeting between the border personnel of the two countries. It was the additional important gain of this round of JWG meeting. The JWG meetings made the two sides understand gradually that (i) To deal exclusively with the border question, and (ii) Improving the bilateral ties for mutual benefits of both the countries.

In line the *eighth* round of JWG talks on border were held in New Delhi on 18th and 19th of August 1995. The leader of Indian delegation was Salman Haider while Chinese side was led by Tang Jiaxuan, Vice Foreign Minister. In this round of talks the Sumdorong Chu Crisis of 1986-87 was settled when both sides agreed to disengage the controversial posts in the area. Both sides agreed to retain one post so as to facilitate dialogue on disengagement of troops along the entire line. It was also agreed to set up a meeting point at Nathu La in Sikkim State of India and TAR border. Another development of the meeting was the recognition of "pockets of disputes" by both sides. These were Trig Heights and Demchok in Western Sector, Barahoti in Middle Sector, and Namka Chu Sumdorong Chu, Chantze, Asaphila and Longju in the Eastern Sector.[78] Reducing the number of troops from border post was considered by both sides as an important achievement of the eighth round of talks and at the end of meeting Salman Haider stated, 'This is a major and positive development where the two countries have gone beyond enunciating general principles on the implementation of the 1993 border peace and tranquility agreement.[79] Further, the *ninth* meeting of Joint Working Group was held in October 1996 at Beijing. In the meeting both sides agreed to increase reciprocal visits by military personnel with the rank of Major-General; to establish two additional meeting places along the eastern section of the Sino-Indian border for military personnel manning the disputed LAC.

Before the *tenth* meeting of JWG Chinese President Jiang Zamin paid an official visit to India from 28th November to 1st December 1996. During his four-day visit Jiang held cordial talks with President S. D. Sharma, Vice President K. R. Narayanan, Prime Minister H. D. Devegowda and External Affairs Minister I. K. Gujral. In their meeting both sides discussed bilateral issues and reached common understanding on many international issues. In course of the visit India and China signed four important agreements but the most valuable was the Agreement on Confidence Building Measures in the military field along the Line of Actual Control in India-China border areas. The agreement pronounced that the suggested measures aim at "a fair, reasonable and mutually acceptable settlement of the vexed boundary question. The very first Article of the Agreement stated, Neither side shall use its military capability against the other side." Even some Indian newspapers considered the agreement as "a virtual no war pact."[80] Speaking on the CBMs agreement India's Foreign Secretary Salman Haider said more reasonably, 'It is a step built on the foundation of the

Peace and Tranquility Agreement signed in 1993 and its full implementation advances the shared agenda of Sino-Indian cooperation.'[81] The Agreement also stipulated that both sides would exchange data on the military forces and armament to be reduced along the LAC, and give prior notice to the opposite side in the event of military exercises. In a nutshell, the 12-point agreement further elaborated the 1993 peace and tranquility agreement except the fact that 1996 agreement specified some of the CBMs on paper. The momentum of the exchange of high level visits by the two countries enhanced mutual understanding and confidence in general.

Jiang Zamin's visit was followed by the *tenth* meeting of Joint Working Group in New Delhi from 4th to 5th August 1997. Indian delegation was led by Foreign Secretary K. Raghunath while the Chinese side was headed by Tang Jiaxuan.[82] In the meeting the two sides exchanged their views on regional, multilateral and international issues of mutual interest and desired the constructive and cooperative relationship in the twenty first century. In addition, they reviewed the implementation of the Agreement on Confidence Building Measure along the line of actual control in the Sino-Indian border area. Overall the system of Joint Working Group proved quite effective in building confidence measure along the LAC and restoring lost trust between the Indian and Chinese people. As a result of the JWG talks the border areas were said to be comparatively peaceful.

The *eleventh* round of JWG meeting which was scheduled for May 1998, was delayed about a year in the wake of nuclear explosion by India in May 1998. The delay had two immediate reasons, first, soon after the BJP-led government came to power, some of its ministers made statements critical of China and a member of the cabinet even dubbed China as enemy No. I. It halted the wave of progress towards normalcy. Second, the justification for the Pokharan test was given as a security threat from China. It led China not to respond for holding the JWG meeting in May 1998. But finally the eleventh meeting to JWG took place in Beijing from 27th-28th April 1999. In the meeting JWG lost much time with India emphasising that it did not regard China as a security threat and China reciprocating these sentiments. Apart from a general review of the state of bilateral relations, including the situation in border areas, the meeting ended without any significant progress. Indeed the momentum of the earlier talks seemed to be lost. During the meeting, however, there was a subtle shift in Chinese official language: whereas its formula once used to be mutual understanding and mutual accommodation to resolve the border dispute, Beijing now advocates that the matter be "properly handled" with mutual respect. In the meeting India's Foreign Secretary K. Raghunath led the Indian delegation while Chinese side was headed by Yang Wenchang, the Vice Foreign Minister.

The *twelfth* and *thirteenth* round of JWG meeting held in New Delhi and Beijing respectively. The twelfth round of meeting took place 28th-29th April 2000 and Chinese Vice Foreign Minister Yang Wenchang led his country's delegation while his counterpart from Indian side was Lalit Mansingh, the Indian Foreign Secretary. In the meeting both sides reviewed the existing Confidence Building Measures (CBMs) and expressed satisfaction over the talks. They made agreement to adopt a "forward looking" approach and set up an expert group to solve the border dispute. Their discussions also included clarification of the LAC and CBMs between the two militaries.

In succession the *thirteenth* round of JWG meeting between India and China held in Beijing 31st July-1st August 2001. The Indian side was headed by its Foreign Secretary Chokila Iyer while Chinese side was led by its Vice Foreign Minister Wang Yi. In the meeting both sides agreed that the present momentum in bilateral relations should be maintained and enhanced through further high-level exchanges. They also reviewed the work being done by JEG on the clarification and confirmation of the LAC, and on the implementation of CBMs.[83] The leaders of the two delegations exchanged their views on the international situation and there was an agreement that the improvement and further development of India-China relations will make an important contribution to peace and stability in Asia and the world.

Likewise the *fourteenth* round of India-China Joint Working Group was held at New Delhi on 21st-22nd November 2002. Wang Yi led the Chinese delegation while Indian team was headed by its Foreign Secretary as part of the continuing engagement between the two countries to tackle the unresolved border problem.[84] In the meeting both sides described the occasion as "forward looking" but it was not clear if maps on the LAC were exchanged. According to the statement, 'Both side also viewed the functioning of the existing dialogue mechanism such as on counter-terrorism and security. The usefulness of these dialogues and need to sustain and broaden them was reaffirmed.'[85] Regional issues were also discussed and China said it did not see relations with India simply from a South Asian perspectives.

The *fifteenth* meeting of India-China Joint Working Group on the boundary question was held in Beijing from March 30-31, 2005. Indian delegation which included representatives from the Ministries of External Affairs, Home and Defence was led by Foreign Secretary Shyam Sharan. The Chinese delegation was led by Vice Foreign Minister Wu Dawei. The discussion marked a resumption of dialogue in the JWG process after a gap of two and a half years. It was held in three sessions and remain positive and forward looking. In the meeting both sides reviewed the ongoing process of LAC clarification and confidence building measures. They highlighted the importance of the implementation of the bilateral agreement of 1993 and 1996 for maintenance of peace and tranquility and for furthering confidence building measures in border areas so as to promote mutual trust and confidence which is essential for the objective of a settlement of the boundary question.[86] In addition, they also discussed the cooperation and coordination between the two sides on global and multilateral issues.

Earlier in third week of June 2003 Indian Prime Minister Atal Bihari Vajpayee paid an official visit to China. On arriving Beijing Vajpayee hoped that his talks with Chinese leaders would help in building better understanding and trust between our two countries. He also remarked further that India and China "have developed a wide convass of mutually beneficial cooperation" and have been developing and diversifying our relations even while simultaneously addressing our differences.[87] As regards the knotty boundary problem, both sides expounded their respective positions and reiterated their readiness to seek a fair, reasonable and mutually acceptable solutions through consultations on an equal footing. The two sides agreed that pending an ultimate solution, they should work together to maintain peace and tranquility in the border areas and restated their commitment to continue implementation of the agreements signed for this purpose.[88]

On border issue Atal Bihari Vajpayee's visit to China had proved a turning point in India-China relations. During the visit the two sides issued a joint declaration on Principles for Relations and Comprehensive Cooperation between India and China in the future. The declaration rolled out a road map for friendship and cooperation including on border dispute. In the talks the two sides agreed to appoint a Special Representative to explore from the political perspective of the overall bilateral relationship for the framework of a boundary settlement. India and China agreed to a three-phase settlement of the border dispute;

Phase I. The Agreement on the Guiding Principles to settle the border dispute.

Phase II. The Special Representatives of the two sides to construct a framework based on the guiding principles.

Phase III. Apply this framework on the ground in a single package deal involving give and take which will be worked on a political basis by the Special Representative.

The mechanism of India-China special representatives' border talks was established to work towards resolving border problems between the two countries. The importance of the talks with two key government officials – the National Security Advisor from India and State Councillor from China is seminal. In course of the visit India named its National Security Advisor Brajesh Mishra as its special representative to explore from the political perspective within the overall bilateral framework. China, too on its part, appointed Dai Bingguo, its senior-most Vice Minister in the Ministry of Foreign Affairs' as its special representative, signalling a strong desire on both sides to expedite resolution of the vexed boundary question.[89] During the visit talks and meetings were held in a "sincere and friendly atmosphere". They also agreed to continue maintenance of peace and tranquility on the Line of Actual Control (LAC).

2.3 Talks at the Level of Special Representatives (SR)

Prime Minister Atal Bihari Vajpayee's milestone visit to China had yielded "better than expected" results for the final settlement of the boundary dispute that has impaired the smooth development of Sino-Indian relations. The new step would go a long way to enhance mutual trust and understanding between China and India and lead to the final settlement of some of the outstanding issues.[90] Aiming to challenge the impass in the protracted boundary dispute between India and China and seek out a solution from the political perspective special representatives of the two countries had decided to hold the first round of border talks. Seeking to address the long-standing boundary dispute afresh the *first* round of talks held in New Delhi 23-24th October 2003 that focused mainly on evolving a framework for engagement between the two sides. They put their earlier failures aside, the two sides led by national security advisor Brajesh Mishra and Senior vice-minister of Chinese foreign ministry Dai Bingguo sought to engage each other to find a solution to the decade-old problem through peaceful negotiations. The two held day-long talks, first one-to-one and then assisted by officials. However, despite hesitations to move further on both sides considerable ground had gone into preparing for the first round, since the decision was made by the Prime Minister of India and China in June 2003.

The special representative of India and China conducted their *second* round of talks on vexed border issue in second week of January 2004 in Beijing as part of the political efforts for an early solution to the long-pending problem. India's National Security Advisor Brajesh Mishra and senior Vice Minister of the Chinese Foreign Ministry Dai Bingguo exchanged significant aspects of border problem in order to get an acceptable solution of the issue. Likewise in July 2004 the *third* round of special representative's talks on border problem was held in which Indian delegation was led by J. N. Dixit, India's new special representative. In May 2004, the change of guard took in India and as a result Dr Manmohan Singh replaced Atal Bihari Vajpayee as the new Prime Minister of the country. Soon thereafter India's special representative was also changed and in place of Brajesh Mishra, J. N. Dixit was made special representative to talk with Chinese representative. This time, like earlier, the Chinese side was led by Chinese executive vice Foreign Minister Dai Bingguo. The two sides exchanged views on wide range of subjects and agreed to hold next round of talks soon.

The *fourth* round of special representatives, talks on border issue between India and China held on 18-19th November 2004. On India's part National Security Adviser J.N. Dixit led the delegation while on Chinese side was its executive vice Foreign Minister Dai Bingguo. The two sides met in Beijing and concluded on a positive note with having "frank and detailed exchanges of views on the principles that could form the framework of a possible boundary agreement.[91] The in-camera discussions under the fourth round of talks were spread over three sessions and they discussed the very complex problem of border question. According to the press statement issued at the end of talks, it was said, 'We moved away from the introductory rounds of exchanges to fairly detailed discussions in two sections, firstly, principles and terms of reference on the basis of which the settlement of the boundary issue could be established. Secondly, the actual framework-an exchange of views on what we envisage how the boundary should be actually delineated on the ground. In both sessions, the discussions were candid. Both sides clearly spelt out each other's views and details regarding each principles and ingredient of what could be the framework.[92] Thus, certainly this round of talks had some meaningful movement forward and this momentum was likely to continue in further talks.

The first round of the special representative meeting established a three-step development strategy over the border dispute settlement: making the guiding principles and then setting up a framework agreement to implement the guiding principle and setting the borderline at last. During the fifth round of special representative talks in 2005 the two sides finally reached the agreement on the political parameters and guiding principles for the settlement of the boundary question. Reaffirming their commitment to Agreements signed in 1993 and 1996 the two sides signed a fresh agreement on 11th April 2005. Article 10 of the Agreement clearly states that the special representatives on the boundary question shall continue their consultations in an earnest manner with the objective of arriving at an agreed framework for a boundary settlement, which will provide the basis for the delineation and demarcation of the India-China boundary to be subsequently undertaken by civil and military officials and surveyors of the two sides. Both, the agreement and the end of first round of special representatives' talks had set the objectives for next or sixth round of talks to be held soon.

With a clear agenda in view the *sixth* round of talks between India and China on border issue was held 26-28th September 2005 in which the representatives of the two countries exchanged their views in a bid to find an agreed framework for a boundary settlement based on the mutually agreed political guiding principles India's National Security Advisor M.K. Narayanan and Chinese Vice-Foreign Minister Dai Bingguo held several rounds of formal and informal meetings. The sixth round of talks marked the beginning of the second phase of negotiations under the mechanism of special representatives. In this round the special representatives were mandated to work out an agreed framework for a boundary settlement on the basis of the agreement on political parameters and guiding principles for settlement of India-China boundary question.[93] In recent past the atmosphere surrounding the border issue has been greatly improved with the warming up of Sino-Indian relation and the leaders in both countries has admitted fairly good progress in bilateral ties and they also agreed to explore a fairly and reasonable framework guiding the solution to the border issue.

The decision to conduct the seventh round of India-China border talks at special representatives level was taken in January 2006 when Shyam Sharan, India's Foreign Secretary paid a visit to China and met Dai Bingguo, who was the Chinese special representative to the border negotiations. The Indian Foreign Secretary told the journalists, 'We are working together in the next round to try and evolve a framework for the border settlement. Both sides are committed to seek an early settlement on the basis of the political parameters and guiding principles for settlement of the India-China boundary question.'[94] As a follow up of the decision the two countries held their *seventh* round of border talks 11-13th March 2006 at New Delhi. In the meeting Indian National Security Adviser M.K. Narayanan and Chinese Vice Minister Dai Bingguo headed their respective delegation and a wide range of subjects were discussed. Earlier a statement issued after the sixth round of talks on the boundary question in September 2005 in Beijing had described those discussions as the beginning of the "second phase" of negotiations on the border dispute. During this phase, the special representatives are mandated to work out an agreed framework for a boundary settlement on the basis of the agreement on political parameters and guiding Principles for settlement of India-China boundary question, which was signed during the visit of Chinese Premier Wen Jiabao to India on April 11, 2005.[95] Following the progress made in the talks during the first phase, the two countries reached an agreement on a set of guiding principles that would assist the special representatives reach a settlement of the border issue.

In line the two-day *eighth* round border talks between special representatives of India and China were held 25-27th June 2006 in Beijing to find a political settlement to the vexed dispute. In this round India's Foreign Secretary M.K. Narayanan and his Chinese counterpart Dai Bingguo met officially and continued their in-camera session in an effort to resolve the boundary issue. Among other things, the earlier signed agreements on guiding principles commit both India and Chinese sides to arrive at a "package settlement" of the boundary question in a spirit of mutual respect and mutual understanding.[96] In the meeting the two sides exchanged their views on different aspects of the border issue settlement. Their talks were held in a cordial and friendly atmosphere.

Special representatives of India and China resumed the two-day border settlement talks into the *ninth* round in January 2007 but as earlier they refused to divulge details of deliberations. In the meeting India was represented by National Security Advisor M.K. Narayanan and China by Minister of Foreign Affairs Dai Bingguo. As an incentive to the talks, earlier Prime Minister Manmohan Singh met with Chinese Premier Wen Jiabao on the sidelines of the ASEAN meeting in Cebu (Philippines) and both agreed to pursue discussion with "great vigour and greater innovativeness". During Chinese President Hu Jinto visit in November 2006 both nations agreed to resolve the boundary settlement as a "strategic objective" as it would advance basic respective interests.[97] As agreed the special representatives shall complete at an early date the task of finalising an appropriate framework for a final, package settlement of the India-China boundary.[98] Pending the resolution of the boundary question, both sides shall maintain peace and tranquility in the border areas as a follow up of the agreements made in 1993, 1996 and 2005. The two special representatives exchanged their views on the framework of the boundary issue in a friendly and candid atmosphere.

In line, the *tenth* meeting of special representatives of India and China was held 20-22nd April 2007 to resolve the decades old border dispute. The talks were headed by India's National Security Adviser M.K. Narayanan and Dai Bingguo, Vice Foreign Minister of China at New Delhi where they discussed the framework for the boundary settlement on the basis of the Agreement on Political Parameters and Guiding Principles.[99] Thus, the meeting was aimed at pinning down a framework agreement for demarcating 2000 kilometer frontier as a prelude to a final package deal to resolve this contentious issue. As a key step that lead to the realisation of the proposal from both leaders to settle the border row politically rather than technically, this round of talks in India forms the tough leg of the road map and indicates the political will of both sides to expedite the negotiation process leading to a find settlement.[100] In the direction through several rounds of talks, China and India both have adopted a more realistic and self-restrained approach.

The *eleventh* round of talks between the special representative of India and China were held in Beijing 24-26th September 2007 and delegations were headed by India's National Security Advisor M.K. Narayanan and his Chinese counterpart Dai Bingguo. They held useful and positive discussions on the framework for the settlement of the India-China boundary question. In course of the discussions the special representative of India and China had decided to set up a working group to prepare a framework for the resolution of the boundary issue. The apparent progress on the boundary issue came ahead of the visit of Prime Minister Manmohan Singh as well as that by Congress President Sonia Gandhi.[101] The progress was disclosed by India's Foreign Minister Pranab Mukherjee after a 50-minute meeting with his Chinese counterpart Yang Jiechi. Mukherjee said, 'India-China is making progress in border negotiations and let us wait for the recommendations of the Working Group.[102] In fact, the boundary issue has hampered the development of bilateral ties, with frequent reports of incursions.

After a year long hiatus, India and China agreed to hold the *twelfth* round of border talks at special representative's level at Beijing 18-20th September 2008. M.K. Narayanan India's National Security Advisor and Dai Bingguo, Chinese State Counsellor headed their delegations. In this meeting the talks were held amid some tension in bilateral ties in the wake of attempts by China to block a consensus on India-specific waiver at the NSG meet in Vienna. On the first day of the talks Narayanan met the Chinese Vice President who said Narayanan that we both should maintain peace and tranquility in the area before the boundary issue is resolved. He hoped the framework for the resolution of the boundary issue would be fair and reasonable and added that the two sides should view the bilateral ties with strategic and long-term perspective and expand the common ground and properly handle the disputes so as to push forward the long-term and stable relations.[103] However, India and China failed to reach any specific agreements on the boundary issue in this round of negotiations but decided to pursue their goal for a fair and reasonable solution. In a brief statement the Chinese Foreign Ministry stated that the two sides concluded two days of in-camera talks. They exchanged in-depth views on a framework to solve the boundary issue and both sides agreed that both countries would carry out the guidelines of their leaders, maintain negotiations and seek a fair and reasonable solution accepted to both sides.[104] In the case of India-China relations on the one hand we found a booming bilateral trade, increasing people to people contact and a sustained exchange of high-level visits indicates a maturing of ties but on the other despite round after round of negotiations at varying levels over the last decades the two sides has not resulted in even being able to agree on the Line of Actual Control (LAC).[105] And still the border issue remains the most important in India-China ties.

After a gap of almost a year the *thirteenth* special representatives level talks of India and China held in August 2009, in the backdrop of recent attempts by China to block Asian Development Bank (ADB) aid for a project in Arunachal Pradesh. It was in this atmosphere that Chinese Vice Foreign Minister Dai Bingguo and India's National Security Advisor M.K. Narayanan met at New Delhi for the resolution of boundary question. In the meeting both sides expected to the demarcation of the boundary issue although a little earlier India's Minister for External Affairs S.M. Krishna had acknowledged in the Rajya Sabha that resolution of the boundary issue will take time and patience. He also said that the problem between the two countries is complex and the aim is to ensure peace and tranquility in the border areas.[106] From this two-day talks not much forward movement was expected as it was held in the backdrop of Beijing's fresh claims on Arunachal Pradesh. It is to mention here that for the last three years boundary discussions have been stuck on Tawang, a monastery town which China claims to be its own. China has maintained that Tawang, which is the birth place of the sixth Dalai Lama, should be given to the Tibetans in China. On the other hand, New Delhi has refused to accept the Chinese claims and has told Beijing repeatedly that Arunachal Pradesh is an integral part of India. The Indian side has also made it very clear that it will not accept any boundary settlement that involves exchange of territory of inhabited areas.[107] In the meeting the two sides also discussed regional issues along with matters of mutual interest.

The *fourteenth* round of India-China border talks between the special representatives was fixed on November 29-30, 2010, a month ahead of Chinese Premier Wen Jiabao's visit to New Delhi in which the two representatives had been instructed to address the issues with a "sense of urgency". In the meeting the Indian side was led by National Security Advisor Shivashankar Menon while State Councillor Dai Bingguo headed the Chinese delegation. In the wake of scheduled visit the special representatives had been given a wide mandate to discuss a range of issues beyond the border dispute.[108] The meeting was held at Beijing and after its conclusion India's Security Advisor Shivashankar Menon said that fourteenth round of boundary negotiations between India and China had made "steady progress" with both sides expressing willingness to arrive at a "fair, reasonable and mutually acceptable" solution. On border talks Menon said that negotiations were still in the second of three stages, focussing on arriving at a framework to settle the dispute in the western and eastern sections of the border. The first stage, which involved coming up with political parameters, concluded in 2005 with an agreement. The third and final stage will involve the actual process of delineating the border on maps and on the ground.[109] The Foreign Ministry statement of China said that it was committed to settling the issue through "friendly consultations". The statement had also added that both countries had made a joint pledge to seek a fair and reasonable solution acceptable to both sides.[110] However, Indian analysts viewed that the recent hardening of China's claims on Arunachal Pradesh, which it refers to as "Southern Tibet" is likely to rule out any narrowing of differences in near future.

On 16-17th January 2012 the special representatives of India and China concluded their *fifteenth* round of border talks in Beijing. The Chinese Foreign Ministry spokesperson Liu Weimin stated that besides the boundary negotiations, both countries will hold discussions on a wide range of bilateral, regional and global issues of mutual interest.[111] Even before the commencement of talks Chinese special representative and State Councilor Dai Bingguo issued a strong call for both countries to put aside their differences and seize "a golden period to grow China-India relations. In an exclusive article written in *The Hindu* stressed the fact that our Indian friends may have confidence in China's tremendous sentiments of friendship towards India.[112] In the meeting India's special representative and National Security Advisor Shivashankar Menon with his Chinese counterpart discussed a framework for the settlement of disputes in all three sectors– western, middle and eastern. This was in keeping with the 2005 agreement on political parameters and guiding principles which marked the ending of the first of three stages of negotiations. According to Article 3 of the agreement, the boundary settlement would be final covering all sectors of the India-China boundary.[113] The special representatives of the two sides agreed that they would prepare a joint agreed record for their governments on the progress made so far in the talks on the boundary question. According to a press release the Ministry of External Affairs, Government of India, an Agreement on the Establishment of a Working Mechanism on Consultation and Coordination on India-China border Affairs was signed in the presence of special representatives.[114]

Besides these, they also discussed other bilateral, regional and global issues. As agreed by the special representatives in the fifteenth round of talks, at the end of the year 2012, the Indian and Chinese special representatives, in a comprehensive report of all fifteen talks asserted that the two had made considerable progress on the border dispute. In the report called a "common understanding" they reviewed the long-running negotiations on a framework for settling the boundary dispute. This document was finally prepared during Shivashankar Menon's trip to Beijing in December 2012 where he said, 'There is work still to be done, both sides recognise that, and we have not allowed the boundary to prevent all round development of relations.[115] Likewise Menon's Chinese counterpart Dai Bingguo, who till fifteenth talks, continuously remained China's special representative, also called on both countries to "take a strategic and all round view, equally negotiate, respect and understand each other and make progress using the current mechanism" of special representatives on the border. He also added that he was convinced that the two countries had the capability and wisdom to resolve boundary question.[116] But despite cordial and friendly talks border areas remained a controversy of claims and counterclaims between the two countries. In the meantime, the Chinese law-makers had proposed the construction of a new high way linking southwestern Yunnan with Tibet, which would for the first time provide year-round access to a remote region which borders Arunachal Pradesh.[117] In Chinese view, it is a multipurpose project and apart from strategic aims, it would boost infrastructure in border regions and make them economically developed.

In the year 2013 on 28-29th June, the *sixteenth* round of special representatives meeting took place at Beijing in which India's National Security Advisor Shivashankar Menon and China's new special representative Yang Jiechi, an official known for his cautious demeanour and often unyielding approach, participated. At the time India and China were in the second round of a three-stage process, which involved agreeing to a framework to settle the boundary question in all sectors.[118] In the meeting the two countries followed thoroughly on the requirements of the leaders of the two countries and maintain the negotiation momentum, safeguard the peace and tranquility at the border areas, exchange views on bilateral relations as well as major international and regional issues and push for comprehensive and in-depth development of the bilateral relations.[119] In this round of talks India and China had discussed putting in place additional confidence building measures (CBMs) and strengthening mechanism for communication along the border. They also attempted to push forward the slow-moving negotiations to agree to a framework to settle the boundary dispute. In other words, this round of talks shifted away from the actual process of negotiation to finding ways to strengthen mechanism in place in order to ensure that incidents of incursions did not reoccur. According to a statement issued after the last day of talks, the two had discussed "ways and means of strengthening existing mechanism for consultation and coordination on border affairs and methodology to enhance the efficiency of communications between the two sides.[120] As to the then situation Indian special representative

Shivashankar Menon said that the current stage of agreeing the framework was "the most complex as it was" what will actually translate into the line.[121] However, the talks were held in a productive, constructive and forward looking atmosphere.

According to a press release by the Ministry of External Affairs, Government of India, the *seventeenth* round of talks between the special representatives of India and China were held 10-11th February 2014. India's National Security Advisor Shivashankar Menon and Yang Jiechi, State Councillor of China exchanged views on different subjects at New Delhi. The special representatives in the meeting made a positive evaluation of India-China relations in the aftermath of Chinese Premier Li Keqiang's visit to New Delhi and return visit to China by Indian Prime Minister Manmohan Singh in 2013. In course of the talks both sides stressed the need for continuing the momentum of high level exchanges, and enhancing people-to-people ties. They encouraged the holding of regular dialogues between the two Governments on all bilateral issues, including on counter-terrorism, disarmament and international security and maritime affairs on schedule.[122] These apart, the special representatives continued their discussions on a framework for a resolution of the boundary issue and maintenance of peace and tranquility in the India-China border areas.[123] Quoting the talks the Chinese special representative Yang Jiechi said, 'the parleys had yielded "initial results" enabling the two sides to properly handle their boundary - related differences and maintain peace and tranquility in the border areas. He also added further that the two sides have continued to take care of each other's concerns, properly manage our differences and helped create an environment favourable for the overall development of bilateral relations.[124] However, as disclosed by *Rediff News*, in this round of talks China raised the issue of code of conduct for troops on the India-China border. On China's part it was said that the proposed code of conduct aims at reducing/eliminating chances of conflict between the patrolling troops in the border area.[125] This proposal has made Indian side cautious and New Delhi is looking at the provisions of the code.

After the formation of BJP-led National Democratic Alliance (NDA) government in the country in May 2014 the Chinese President Xi Jinping paid a three-day (17-19th September, 2014) official visit to

India and signed with India a number of agreements in various spheres. His visit to India was aimed at creating greater cooperation between the two countries and in line he started his journey from Ahmedabad, the largest city in Indian Prime Minister Narendra Modi's home state of Gujarat. In course of the visit both leaders were eager to stress cooperation, with Modi, in particular, keen to secure Chinese funding to develop the country's dilapidated infrastructure. But on border issue the sweet taste of the visit turned into sour as in course of the tour incursions by the Chinese troops in Ladakh remained dominant in government and public as well. In the summit talks between the visiting President and Indian Prime Minister Narendra Modi the latter raised the issue seriously and in response Xi Jinping committed to resolve the border dispute with India at an early date.[126] He also added further that both sides are capable of effectively managing the situation through border-related mechanism so that they do not have a large impact on bilateral relations.[127] Indian Prime Minister also raised the issue while both were addressing a joint press conference. Modi reminded him that solving the boundary issue between the two is needed for growing economic cooperation. A clarification on the LAC is very important. It has been pending for years, it is time to start it again.[128] Thus, the agreements on a number of issues were signed during the visit but despite expectations in China of a breakthrough no progress was made on long running boundary row.[129] In the joint statement issued on 19th September 2014 both "the leaders stressed their country's commitment" to seek a fair, reasonable and mutually acceptable solution to the dispute in the light of April 2005 agreement between them.

On border issue the visit of Chinese President Xi Jinping to India in September 2014 was less than a landmark that failed to be a breakthrough or create an impression, different to the past. On the other, the visit highlighted the fact that still the border matters most for Indians as it is directly related to our security and sentiments. Since the last major flare up in 1986-87, India and China have created a confidence building measures regimes which has effectively maintained peace there. Although in recent past perhaps Narendra Modi was the first Indian leader to direct speak of the issue and that too, before China's supreme leader, yet the incursions and incidents on border indicate us in clear way that unsettled borders can never really be quiet borders.[130] And perhaps for this reason while talking with the Chinese President Narendra Modi reiterated that we should resolve the border at the earliest. He stressed the need to, at least work out a commonly accepted alignment of the 4,056-km long Line of Actual Control (LAC) that marks the border today.[131] Currently, there are some 14 places on the LAC where India and China's perception of where it lies differs, and this gives rise to the so-called "transgressions" or "incursions". Especially following the appointment of high level special representative in the wake of Atal Bihari Vajpayee's visit to Beijing in 2003, things moved fast and the two sides worked out a basic agreement on the Political Parameters and Guiding Principles for the settlement of India-China boundary question in 2005. In addition, the 17 rounds of discussions between the special representatives have done the required work, what is now needed is for the political leaders means Xi Jinping and Narendra Modi to finalise the settlement. In other words, as long as Beijing seeks to keep India unsettled in its own region; we cannot really develop ties which could be called friendly.

The visit of Chinese President in September 2014 was followed by the *eighteenth* round talks of special representatives on border issue between the two countries on 23rd March 2015. This round of talk took place in the backdrop of candid discussions between Prime Minister Modi and the Chinese President during latter's visit to New Delhi, but the matter was also raised earlier in February 2015 when Sushma Swaraj, India's Minister for External Affairs, visited China and spoke about the need for an "out of box" solution on the border issue in order to not leave it for future generations.[132] In the meeting India was represented by Ajit Doval, National Security Advisor while from Chinese side was Yang Jiechi, its State Councillor. Ahead of the meeting both sides were hopeful about the fruitful discussions since Prime Minister Modi and President Xi Jinping had emerged as strong leaders, the two nations had a unique chance to settling the issue. Before the scheduled talks Chinese Foreign Minister Wang Yi had said that China and India should "do more" to strengthen bilateral cooperation to clinch a final settlement of the vexed boundary problem. 'The dispute had been contained. At the moment, the boundary negotiation is in the process of building up small positive developments.'[133] It was the first round of negotiations after Prime Minister Narendra Modi came to power in May 2014 and as a result, the two sides were expected to focus on clarification of the Line of Actual Control.

In the 18th special representatives's level meeting held on 23rd March 2015, the representatives of India and China agreed to take "necessary steps" to maintain peace and tranquility in border areas. In an effort towards demarcating the contentious boundary, both sides also reinforced their commitment to the three-step process to seek a fair, reasonable and mutually acceptable resolution within the agreed guiding principles.[134] In the meeting while both sides broadly agreed to maintain peace and tranquility on the border, the representatives also noted the growing interaction between the border forces of the two countries and agreed to further expand such contacts. In addition, the two sides also exchanged views on regional and global matters of mutual interest and agreed to further consultations on counter-terrorism, maritime security, climate change, reform of United Nations and civil nuclear energy cooperation.[135] The statement from the Ministry of External Affairs noted, 'The special representatives continued the discussions to reach a mutually acceptable framework for resolution of the boundary question on the basis of the Agreement on the political parameters of guiding principles.[136] Their resolve to keep the border engagements tranquil had paved the chances of deepening their trade ties and other perspective relations in a brighter way.

In succession, Narendra Modi, the Prime Minister of India, paid a return visit to People's Republic of China between 14-16th May 2015. As a gesture of goodwill before the visit Hua Chunying, spokesperson of the Chinese Foreign Ministry said, Taking Prime Minister Modi's visit to China as an opportunity, we are going to further strengthen strategic mutual trust between two countries and deepen practical cooperation and cultural communication'. On her part she added, 'The boundaries question is an issue of common interest. So I believe that this question will be covered in their talks. We look forward to enhancing the communication with the Indian side to strive for "more progress" on the resolution of the boundary dispute with India during the visit'[137]. Earlier Prime Minister Modi also expressed confidence that his trip will lay the foundation for enhancing cooperation in a wide range of sectors and strengthen stability, progress and prosperity in Asia.[138] A significant groundwork for the visit had been done by

India's External Affairs Minister Sushma Swaraj and Foreign Secretary S. Jaishankar when they both visited China in course of a delegation tour in February 2015. Given the hard reality of a border dispute, the India-China relations stand in stark contrast to India's relations with other major and middle powers of the world.

At the start of his three-day trip Indian Prime Minister was hosted by President Xi Jinping in the city of Xian and the very next day on 15th May Modi met Li Keqiang, his Chinese counterpart. In the talks they both agreed to seek a "fair resolution" to border disputes arising from a boundary disagreement. The border dispute dates back to 1914 when Britain, which controlled India at the time, signed an agreement with Tibet which made the McMahon line the de facto boundary. Later at his speech at Tsinghua the Indian Prime Minister said; 'The solution we choose should do more than settle the boundary question. It should do so in a manner that transforms our relationship and not cause new disruptions.'[139] At the sametime Li Keqiang, the Chinese Premier also reiterated that the countries had 'enough political wisdom to manage and control differences'. 'Our common interests are far bigger than our differences.'[140] Earlier to this, the first day 90-minute meeting between Prime Minister Narendra Modi and Chinese President Xi Jinping was also focused on trade deficit with China and a decade-long border dispute. Amid signs of warming ties between two Asian giants the discussion at the Shaanxi state guest house was "substantive" and held in a "comfortable" atmosphere.[141] In the context Foreign Secretary S. Jaishankar also confirmed that the focus of the meeting was on increasing "mutual trust" and convergence between the two countries, who are attempting to come out of a relationship often fraught with mistrust and focus on boosting bilateral trade.

The Indian Prime Minister ended his state visit to China on 16th May 2015 and in course of the tour, 24 Agreements/Memorandum of Understandings totalling more than 22 billion US dollar was signed. The long list of deals range from railways to space including information technology and power among other areas. However, as earlier, the border issue remained the most intractable problem between the two countries. Still there are no indications that China is willing to move beyond the stability of the border. They are uncomfortable with the clause in the 2005 agreement which says 'there will be no transfer/exchange of territory with settled population, which put Tawang and Arunachal Pradesh beyond their negotiating agreement'. In addition, just before Modi's visit the Communist Party run *Global Times* accused Modi of "playing tricks" over the border issue, and demanded that to promote trust Modi refrain from visiting disputed areas in context of his tour to Arunachal Pradesh. It also emphasised that India should completely stop supporting the Dalai Lama and stop making the Tibet issue a stumbling block to the Sino-Indian relationship. It clearly conveyed China was no longer satisfied with the Indian position on the Dalai Lama and the Tibet issue.[142] Although the Joint Statement issued at the end of the visit touched on several points of issues between the two countries, overall it was cautious and no independent points were made– the recognition that mutual trust be generated, military ties be enhanced, peace and tranquility along the border be maintained, with hot lines to be established between the two militaries, relation not be made hostage to the border issue and, cooperation be present in counter-terrorism and a host of other things.[143] In a nutshell, from China's perspective the Sino-Indian relations and the border issue are linked to the issue of Dalai Lama's residence in India and the Tibet issue. India tried to appease China by signing on the dotted lines presen-ted by the Chinese on the status of Tibet in 2003, during Prime Minister Atal Bihari Vajpayee's visit to China, India got nothing in return.

But above all, Prime Minister Narendra Modi's visit to China has managed to break the ice and give a positive push to the perceptions about India-China relations on the street. The challenge remains whether he can build on this to address the long fostering border dispute and whether his government can engage China in the major bilateral and multilateral partnership which are developing.[144] Now there is hope that Modi and Xi Jinping, who had emerged as strong leaders, would take a new initiative on the border. It is possible that in their private talks they might have considered some steps and Modi's reference to early clarification of the Line of Actual Control (LAC) and Ajit Doval's focus on the boundary may be connected with that.

Apart from the recent visits the two phases of the special representative meetings were identified with the early five discussions from 2003 to 2005 as knowing each other's positions on the border dispute, while the meetings from sixth through ninth as more intensive in nature. After five meetings between the special representatives of both countries, in a joint statement in April 2005 the two countries, decided to solve the border dispute based on political parameters and guiding principles. The second phase from the sixth meeting in September 2005 explored the possibilities for initiating an agreed framework on the boundary dispute settlement. At the 15th special representative meeting in New Delhi in January 2012, the framework was exchanged. Interestingly, during the August 2009, 13th special representative meeting between M.K. Narayanan and Dai Bingguo, a Hong Kong-based newspaper *Ming Pao* reported that China was prepared to settle for 28 per cent of the disputed territory between the two countries.[145] In the context the current stage is seen as the most difficult that involves agreeing a framework to settle the dispute in western, middle and eastern sections of the disputed border. Over the years, the two sides have done a lot of work to achieve settlement of the issue, in particular, through the establishment of the mechanism of special representatives in 2003.

In a nutshell the overall status of India-China relations indicates both cooperation and competition but cooperation has no bounds while competition is limited. The current Modi dispensation in India sees infrastructure, construction and manufacturing as priorities for India's economic reform, and China can provide the equipment, technology and experience at a low cost. However, the border issue between the two is the biggest obstacle in relations between the two. Although in the past half century, the border area has been peaceful and India and China are still negotiating this issue. Both have signed a framework agreement and reached the several agreements to keep the border area peaceful. In the situation most analysts suggest that if India and China cannot solve the border issue in a short time, this issue should be put aside and instead both should focus on cooperation in other fields. At this juncture, the role of perceptions and images towards each other cannot be undermined which have created a wide artificial gap in their smooth and constructive relationships.

References

1. Sarvepalli Gopal, *Jawaharlal Nehru: A Biography 1956-64*, Vol. III (Delhi: Oxford University Press, 1984), pp. 303-304.

2. Verghese Koithara, *Society, State and Security – The Indian Experience* (New Delhi: Sage Publications, 1999), p. 68.
3. V. N. Khanna, *Foreign Policy of India* (New Delhi: Vikas Publishing House, 2004), p.113.
4. K. P. S. Menon, *Many World's Revisited – An Autobiography* (Bombay: Bharatiya Vidya Bhavan, 1981), pp.139-142.
5. *Ibid.* p. 270.
6. *Jawaharlal Nehru's Speeches 1949-1953*, Vol. II (New Delhi: Publication Division, 1954), p. 226.
7. Mira Sinha Bhattacharjea, '1962 Revisited', in G.P. Deshpanda and Alka Acharya (eds.), *50 Years of India-China-Crossing a Bridge of Dreams* (New Delhi: Tulika, 2001), pp. 430-432.
8. *Jawaharlal Nehru's Speeches 1949- 1953*, pp. 254-255.
9. Rajkumar Singh, *India's Foreign Policy: The First Study in Continuity and Change* (New Delhi: Samiksha Prakashan, 2001), p. 103.
10. For the text of the letter see *Indian Constitutional Documents: Munshi papers*, Vol. I (Bombay: 1967), p. 178.
11. Nancy Jetley, *India-China Relations-1947-1979: A Study of Parliament's Role in the Making of Foreign Policy* (New Delhi: Radiant, 1979), p.19.
12. Mira Sinha Bhattacharjea, '1962 revisited,' p. 435.
13. Memorandum of the Foreign Office of China, 3 November 1959 as quoted in Sarvepalli Gopal, *Jawaharlal Nehru: A Biography 1956-1964*, p. 83.
14. Mahendra Kumar, *Theoretical Aspects of International politics* (Agra: Educational, 1976), pp. 294-95.
15. *The Economist* (London), 4 April 1959.
16. M. Brecher, *India and World Politics* (London: 1968), p. 145.
17. *People's Daily* (Peking), 24 April 1959.
18. A.S. Whiting, *The Chinese Calculus of Deterrence* (Ann Arbor: 1975), pp.10-11.
19. B.M. Kaul, *The Untold Story* (Delhi: 1967), p. 368.
20. *Ibid.*, p. 387.
21. V.P. Dutt, *India's Foreign Policy* (New Delhi: Vikas, 1987), p. 279.
22. Vera Micheles Dean, *New Patterns of Democracy in India* (New Delhi: Motilal Banarasidas, 1961), pp.193-95.
23. Subramanian Swamy, 'Looking Beyond the Border Issue', *The Hindu*, 18 June 2008.
24. *Ibid.*
25. As quoted in Harish Kapur, *India's Foreign Policy 1947-92- Shadow and Substance* (New Delhi: Sage Publications, 1994), p. 132.

26. V.P. Dutt, *India's Foreign Policy*, p. 280.
27. *Asian Recorder*, October 1965 (New Delhi: 1965), p. 6715.
28. B.R. Deepak, *India-China Relations* (New Delhi: A.P.H. Publishing Corporation, 2001), pp.18-19.
29. *The Times*, 24 March 1977.
30. *India and Foreign Review*, 15 August 1977, p. 9.
31. *The Times of India* (editorial), 16 March 1978.
32. *The Sunday Standard* (New Delhi), 9 April 1978.
33. *The Hindustan Times* (New Delhi), 29 April 1978.
34. *The Times of India*, 21 January 1969.
35. *The Hindu*, 15 November 1971.
36. Girilal Jain, 'Foreign Policy Consensus-Some New Factors at work', *The Times of India*, 6 April 1977.
37. V.P. Dutt, *India's Foreign Policy*, p. 293.
38. *The Hindustan Times*, 10 December 1980.
39. *Beijing Review*, 13 July 1981.
40. *The Indian Express*, 14 February 1979.
41. Mahinda Werake, 'China and South Asia in the Eighties,' in Shelton U. Kodikara (ed.), *External Compulsions of South Asian Politics* (New Delhi: Sage Publications, 1993), p. 79.
42. *China's Foreign Policy* (Beijing: Foreign Language Press, 1983), p. 4.
43. *Beijing Review*, 21 March 1983.
44. Kuldip Nayar, 'Changes in China's Attitude', *The Island* (Colombo), 12 February 1987.
45. Sumit Ganguly, 'The Sino-Indian Border Talks 1981-89', *Asian Survey*, Vol. XXIX, No. 12, December 1989.
46. Naheed Khan, 'Wither Sino-Indian Relations – A Highlight Over Border Dispute', *Indian Journal of Politics*, Vol. XVII, No. 2, June 1983 (Department of Political Science, Aligarh Muslim University), p.74.
47. Satish Kumar (ed.), *Year Book on India's Foreign Policy 1985-86* (New Delhi: Sage Publications, 1988), pp.150-152.
48. Government of India, *Foreign Affairs Record*, Vol. XXVIII, No. 5 (New Delhi: Ministry of External Affairs, Publication Division, May 1982), pp.158-59.
49. B.R. Deepak, *India and China 1904-2004-A Century of Peace and Conflict* (New Delhi: Manak Publications, 2005), p. 312.
50. Gopal Ji Malviya, *Sino-Indian Relations Security Environment in Nineties* (Madras: The Director Publication Division, University of Madras, 1992), p. 90.

51. *Beijing Review*, 14 November 1983.
52. Sumit Ganguly, '*The Sino-Indian Border Talks 1981-89*'.
53. Satish Kumar (ed.), *Year Book on India's Foreign Policy 1985-86*, p. 153.
54. B.R. Deepak, *India and China 1904-2004- A Century of Peace and Conflict*, p. 317.
55. *Ibid*., p. 318.
56. Mira Sinha Bhattacharjea, 'India-China Talks: The Long Haul to Normalisation', *NCDS Bulletin* (University of Allahabad: Department of Defence and Strategic Studies, 1990), pp. 18-20.
57. Nikhil Chakravarty, 'The Chinese Shift', *The Indian Express* (Bombay), 27 July 1986.
58. *Beijing Review*, 10 August 1987.
59. *The Indian Express* (editorial), 19 November 1987.
60. B. R. Deepak, *India and China 1904-2004-A Century of Peace and Conflict*, p. 324.
61. *Ibid*., p. 325.
62. *Ibid*., pp. 325-26.
63. *The Indian Express* (Bombay), 21 December 1988.
64. *Ibid*., 23 January 1989.
65. *Deccan Herald*, 9 July 1989.
66. Ministry of External Affairs, Press Release (External Publicity Division, Government of India), 1 September 1990.
67. *Ibid., Press Statement of* 13 May 1991.
68. *Ibid., Press Release of* 30 October 1992.
69. *Ibid., Press Release of* 28 June 1993.
70. *Renmin Ribao*, 17 October 1991.
71. *Ibid*., 17 December 1991.
72. *Ibid*., 8 September 1993.
73. *The Hindustan Times*, 8 September 1993.
74. *The Time of India*, 8 September 1993.
75. *Ministry of External Affairs, Press Release* (External Publicity Division), 4 February 1994.
76. *Ibid., Press Release of* 23 April 1994.
77. *Ibid., Press Release of* 4 March 1995.
78. B. R. Deepak, *India and China 1904-2004-A Century of Peace and Conflict*, p. 350.
79. *Competition Success Review*, October 1995, p. 17.
80. *The Time of India*, 30 November 1996.

81. *The Hindu*, 30 November 1996.
82. Ministry of External Affairs, *Press Release* (External Publicity Division), 5 August 1996.
83. *The Hindu*, 2 August 2001.
84. *Ibid.*, 9 November 2002.
85. *Ibid.*, 23 November 2002.
86. Ministry of External Affairs, *Press Release* (External Publicity Division, Government of India), 31 March 2005.
87. *The Hindu*, 23 June 2003.
88. B. R. Deepak, *India and China 1904-2004- A Century of Peace and Conflict*, pp. 429-30.
89. *The Indian Express*, 25 June 2003.
90. *The Economic Times*, 30 June 2003.
91. *Ibid.*, 20 November 2004.
92. *Ibid.*
93. *Ibid.*, 29 September 2005.
94. *Rediff News*, 10 January 2006.
95. *The Hindu*, 9 March 2006.
96. *The Economic Times*, 26 June 2006.
97. Visit, whatisindia.com, 20 January 2007.
98. *The Hindu*, 18 January 2007.
99. *Oneindia News*, 23 April 2007.
100. Visit at www.chinadaily.com. cn, 24 April 2007.
101. *The Economic Times*, 25 October 2007.
102. *The Hindu*, 26 October 2007.
103. *Ibid.*, 19 September 2008.
104. *Ibid.*, 20 September 2008.
105. *Asia Times*, 19 September 2008.
106. *The Economic Times*, 5 August 2009.
107. *Ibid.*, 8 August 2009.
108. *The Hindu*, 29 November 2010.
109. *Ibid.*, 1 December 2010.
110. *Ibid.*
111. *Ibid.*, 15 January 2012.
112. *Ibid.*, 16 January 2012.
113. *Ibid.*, 16 February 2012.
114. *Press Release*, Ministry of External Affairs, Government of India (New Delhi), 17 January 2012.

115. *The Hindu*, 5 December 2012.
116. *Ibid.*
117. *Ibid.*, 14 March 2012.
118. *Ibid.*, 17 March 2013.
119. *Ibid.*, 25 June 2013.
120. *Ibid.*, 29 June 2013.
121. *Ibid.*
122. *Press Release*, Ministry of External Affairs, Government of India (New Delhi), 11 February 2014.
123. *Ibid.*
124. *Znews*, 12 February 2014.
125. *Rediff News*, 17 February 2014.
126. *The Hindustan Times*, 18 September 2014.
127. *Ibid.*
128. *South China Morning Post*, 21 September 2004.
129. *India Today*, Mail to day Bureau (New Delhi), 20 September 2014.
130. *The Economic Times*, 22 September 2014.
131. *Ibid.*
132. *Bharat Press*, 22 March 2015.
133. *Press Trust of India*, 22 March 2015.
134. *The Hindu*, 23 March 2015.
135. *Ibid.*
136. *Ibid.*, 25 March 2015.
137. *The Hindustan Times*, 18 September 2014.
138. india.com, 6 May 2015.
139. *Ibid.*
140. bbc.com, 15 May 2015.
141. *Ibid.*
142. hindustantimes.com, 15 May 2015.
143. visit www.southasiaanalysis.org/node/1778.
144. *Ibid.*
145. Manoranjan Mohanty, 'History Challenges Modi in China', *Economic and Political Weekly*, Vol.1, No. 22, 30 May 2015(Mumbai:2015), p.1.

Chapter III

Updated Border Perception and Peer Reviews

3.1 Perceptions Behind the Border Negotiations

Departure of the British from the sub-continent in 1947 deprived India of the necessary military strength that England had represented for so many years- a strength that was clearly indispensable for the implementation of viable defence system. In the post-Independence situation in India the new political leaders who were at the helm of affairs were unable to continue to follow a forward policy in the north. Poverty-stricken and problem-ridden India had, in their view, other priorities to judiciously use her unexploited resources. Furthermore, they had a different political goal, which was to contribute to the promotion of peace and welfare of mankind. In the meantime the regional security environment had also changed considerably from the time of the British. The new India had now to face an unfriendly and suspicious Pakistan. On her northern frontier soon after the termination of the Chinese civil war India had to reckon with the Chinese occupation of Tibet. It made border with China alive and unstable. The Indian political leaders had generally come to the conclusion that the border threat stemmed more from Pakistan than from China.

Thus, in Indian calculation Pakistan, not China, became the focal point of country's defence strategy. Though the possibility of attack on the sub-continent was only from the northwestern frontier region, they did not feel any need to extend their military strategy or expertise.

At the juncture, Nehru's conviction that China would not take any strong action against India played a decisive role. On the basis of different intelligence and diplomatic reports, he allowed himself to be convinced that China's growing adverse relations with the two superpowers and her serious domestic economic situation would restrain her from taking any military action. He, however, did not lack political understanding of the potential problems and, in a communication to K.M. Panikkar, the Indian Ambassador in China, noted that whenever China had a strong central government, it had intended to expand across its frontiers. This historical tendency had now been reinforced by a vigorously pulsating and dynamic new China, both radical and militantly nationalistic.

Indian Perceptions

The defeat and humiliation of India on the battlefield in 1962 generated a new mood in the country- a mood of re-evaluating country's concept of national security. For the first time India's foreign policy was no longer allowed to remain the *domain reserve* of the political leaders and accusing fingers were pointed at those who were guilty of having neglected India's defence. China, since the establishment of Communist rule on October 1, 1949, was viewed by India as a threat to its security. Despite his faith in peace, friendship and cooperation in dealing with the nations of the world Jawaharlal Nehru was alert to the danger from China and in 1952 he instructed the Director of Indian Intelligence to regard China as an intelligence target along with Pakistan.[1] India and China- the two giants of Asia were also assigned to play a role in the region and viewed in this context India always thought of China as a potential foreign policy partner who shared a concern to moderate the effects of superpower imperialism in world affairs.[2]

Despite apprehensions, Nehru could not believe that relations with China could or would deteriorate as they did in the late 1950s and the early 1960s. When it happened, his China policy failed to know the full extent of the change in Chinese motives and designs. Not after the outbreak of the war but even before in December 1958 it had become known in Delhi that the Chinese had established a number of posts in the Aksai Chin area of Ladakh, true to the intuitive approach to foreign affairs, Nehru said in the Indian Parliament, "The normal idea is that security is protected by armies. That is only partly true; it is equally true that security is protected by policies. A deliberate policy of friendship with other countries goes further in gaining security than almost anything else."[3] He called this attack a strange twist of history that had brought us face to face with something that we had not experienced in this way for over a hundred years or more. The Chinese aggression on our border during the last five years, bad as it was and indicative of an expansionist tendency, though it troubled us greatly, hardly led us to the conclusion that China would indulge in a massive invasion on India. Charging cynicism and duplicity on the Chinese side he drew the conclusion that Chinese interpretation of various lines changes with circumstances and that they accept the line which is more advantageous to them. Sometimes they accept part of a line and not the rest of it which is disadvantageous to them.

India, to Nehru's satisfaction, faced this challenge with 'new anger, new determination and new gratitude'- anger at Chinese perfidy, determination to accept no dishonourable settlement and gratitude to those countries which had rallied to her aid.[4] The reaction to Chinese behaviours was far from defeatist and led Nehru to speak of the war repeatedly as a blessing in disguise.[5] After independence, foreign policy became a responsibility of the national government under Jawaharlal Nehru. A variety of factors enabled him to play a unique role in this realm. His personal position was so dominant that, as one of his biographers remarks, he was "the philosopher, the architect, the engineer and the voice of his country's policy towards the outside world."[6] And lastly, his personal strength, acquired during the freedom movement, and greatly augmented after independence, established him as a world statesman par excellence, so that his opinion and authority could not be successfully challenged and undermined even by the events of 1962. But the conflict left a strong mark on it for a number of years in all the three spheres, domestic, regional and international. Nehru himself said that India had been living in an unreal world, and that "We are growing too soft and taking things granted," but he added "We are not going to give up basic principles because of our present difficulty."[7]

The conflict with China suddenly subjected foreign policy to what appeared at the time intolerable pressure. In the new situation there was not much scope for the stock in trade of Indian diplomacy-mediation, peace-keeping amelioration of tension with which she played in the past a dramatic role on the international scene. In preparing for a long phase of Chinese hostility, the domestic situation and the military requirements had to be placed in world context. India, experiencing a crisis of the spirit, had found herself, and this new mood should be utilised to achieve both industrial advance and military readiness.[8] Defence and developments were parts of the same process; and planning, socialism and non-alignment were all ways of preparing the nation to face renewed Chinese aggression. Real strength, as Nehru said on January 18, 1963, came not from the purchase of arms but from the building of an industrial base which could be converted, when the need arose, into a war machine, the development of power and transport, increased productivity in agriculture, improvement in public health and spread of technical education. Thus, in domestic dealings the war crisis reinforced the importance of the kind of socialism suited to India.[9] On the other exercise in favour of the search for a way to honourable negotiations with China remained in active consideration.

Nehru's successors- Lal Bahadur Shastri, Indira Gandhi and others who succeeded to the throne had not only reaffirmed their resolve to cling to old lines of policy, but had moved in measure albeit still tentatively towards negotiations with China. On assuming office Shastri had made it clear that if the intention of China was really to arrive at a settlement and if Peking would not put forward at the negotiating table claims to large areas of territory with threats to take them by force, then there could be negotiations between the two countries. He clearly viewed Chinese motives behind the attack and said in Parliament on 20 September 1965, "The basic objective of China is to claim for itself a position of dominance in Asia, which no self-respecting nation in Asia is prepared to recognise.[10] The annual report of the Ministry of External Affairs for the year 1964-65 also spelt out India's perception of Chinese motivations. It said, "India was the key to the 'vast intermediate zone' of Asia, Africa and Latin America, China would like to see India reduced to the status of a secondary power in Asia and to destroy the policy of non-alignment which has earned for India so much respect and prestige in the Asian-African world."[11] After Shastri, Indira Gandhi became the Prime Minister of India who, in a statement, on February 16, 1966, reiterated that India was prepared to talk with China "should proper conditions arise."

However, apart from keeping the door opened for talks with China, post-Nehruvian strategy was also faced with a dangerous situation and India finally resulted in the adoption of a dual method of upgrading the armed forces, and of seeking a military alliance with the Soviet Union. It gave a new direction and a broader definition to the concept of national security. Gradually successors of the throne gave the concept of national security a wider dimension and created a triple defence strategy–a strategy of upgrading India's armed forces, a strategy of seeking a military alliance and, finally, a strategy of greater institutionalisation of the Indian system for the identification of national security objectives.[12] In her quest for national security, India has indeed come a long way since her independence. She has, through the years, acquired a military clout that no one in the region can challenge – probably not even China in the conventional sector.

Perceptions of China

In contrast of India, the People's Republic of China had a long history of a tacit but clear strategic military doctrine. Since the third century B.C. till 1911, the 'barbarians' from across the land frontiers remained the main threat to the Chinese empire. Whenever they threatened any part of the regime, armies were raised to repel them or to extend the empire in the process of subduing them.[13] For a brief period in pre-revolution phase China became weak and unstable because of warlordism and internal warfare between Nationalist and Communist forces. It was followed by the establishment of a strong central government in China which adopted a doctrine, combined with Soviet strategic thinking and the Communist party's experience in fighting Japan and the Guomindang armies for several decades. By 1949, the geopolitical situation had changed and the Soviet Union had become China's ally, while the United States of America which had been China's ally all along, had now become an enemy. Thus, the Chinese strategic military doctrine, in early fifties, identified US imperialism as the grand strategy to encircle China prior to invading it. Even India's forward policy in the border area was interpreted as part of US imperialist encirclement of China.

In formulating Chinese attitude towards India and the world at large Mao Zedong played a significant and decisive role. Mao's theoretical analyses of formidable power, especially those written in his early years, and his old leadership of the peasants in China have earned for him a unique place in world history. But basically he was an outstanding Chinese figure, rooted in indigenous tradition. A hard-headed nationalist, he was determined to regain for his country not only equality among the nations but a prime position in Asia. He combined throughout his life the roles of both a revolutionary and a nationalist and at the start, each strengthened the other. Under his leadership and inspiration China became an ambitious nation and a skilled practitioner of *realpolitik.*[14] By the time India and China had awakened modern communication, broke down the physical barriers and brought them face to face in a period when they were going through an acute phase of nationalist stirrings and hyper-sensitive responses to foreign countries, because of their experience with imperialism and rather late emergence as nation-states, abrasive responses that rubbed off against each other too.

In the years following China's attack on India people felt a need to reassess the motives behind the aggression. It was a failure of diplomacy which is, in fact, meant management of international relations by means of negotiations; the method by which these relations are adjusted and managed by ambassadors and envoys; the business or art of the diplomat. Possible motives are important to be mentioned here not only because they are related to China's general policy in foreign affairs but because they will reveal the extent to which those motives have determined the nature of Sino-Indian relations. Motives behind the attack were closely related to the Chinese anxiety to keep the Sino-Indian border issue alive. It also explained the causes of the series of Chinese intrusions into the Indian territories during the 1960s. Even hardening of the Chinese attitude towards India in late fifties and early sixties was based on country's calculation of gain and loss. It is said to be a mixture of Chinese imperialism militant nationalism, and revolutionary zeal of militant communism.[15]

Desire for attainment of great power status, as considered by many, was the prime motive behind the Chinese attack. For several years in the beginning India introduced Communist China to the world, especially to Asia. After some years they knew that China is able to make more rapid and greater progress than India, former's dependence on the latter for status became intolerable. As a first step China insisted on India accepting a subordinate status, renouncing non-alignment and generally moulding her foreign and domestic policies to suit China's view of herself and of the world. Viewed in this perspective if the creation and non-recognition of India's northern frontier was the expression of independence in world politics, the aggression of 1962 was intended to show that China had not only the desire but also the capacity to be a great power.[16] However, a scholar, Neville Maxwell, considering the effects of India's forward policy and its unilateral declaration of ceasefire argued that military action by China was decided on to bring India to the negotiating table and to show her that any attempt to achieve a settlement on her own terms, by moving into Chinese-held territory, was futile.[17] On the other the Chinese showed their reasonableness in having border settlements with Nepal, Pakistan and Burma.

While dealing with the People's Republic of China we can hardly overlook the strategic aspect of the issue. In fact, one other purpose of the Chinese military action was to hold on to the Aksaichin and the strategic highway which is so vital for controlling the difficult provinces of Tibet and Sinkiang. As the war was an expression of the politico-military strategy of China, Nehru, keeping it in view, said in November 1962, "I don't see any real compromise. What they have in mind is different from our thinking. There is no bridge between us." But later on he also added 'India was not going to be one of the small fish which this huge crocodile in the pond of Asia was seeking to devour,[18] In the face of China's attitude that either one is for them or against' a self-respecting nation like India could hope for no lasting friendship with her.[19]

Ideological differences between China and the Soviet Union had also motivated the former to launch a massive attack on India. The Sino-Soviet rivalry at the time was centred in Asia and China regarded India as an ideological obstacle and sought a dominating position in Asia. In addition to this the Soviet influence of Asia has been much more than the Chinese influence. Obviously, Chinese aggression was launched in the hope that the attack on India would compel the communist parties of Asian countries to come to the Chinese fold. It, however, realised a deeper objective, that was to find out what attitude would the Soviet Union take towards China after the aggression and it became clear that the Soviet Union could not be relied upon even in a conflict with a non-communist country. In international arena the behaviours of China was criticised widely and was based on the fact that it had forgotten the futility of war as a traditional means of the achievement of great power status. The Chinese behaviours in post-aggression period also testified that the attempt made on the part of China had been to build up her power and not bother about the settlement of the border question.

Perceptions Experienced and Analysed

In post-1962 period relations between India and China were put on rails with the establishment of ambassadorial level contact in April 1976. It could not be done earlier because Peking was engaged in a full-scale campaign against India whose chief purpose was to carry the conviction that India was no longer non-aligned but was firmly in the imperialist camp. In the meantime China shifted its position on Kashmir, moved closer to Pakistan and gradually became a major source of military and economic aid to Islamabad. Particularly in case of Nepal and Sri Lanka, China adopted the policy of creating or encouraging dissensions between them and India. The border question was, in addition, made complicated with Pakistan giving China a direct access to the disputed territory of Kashmir. It was reported at the close of the sixties that Pakistan was building a road from Mor- Khun in Northern Kashmir to Khunjareb Pass on the Kashmir-Sinkiang territory. The entire alignment of the road ran in Indian territory under Pakistani occupation. The road was strategic one and would help extend the Chinese road network in the Tibet-Sinkiang area into Northern Kashmir. The Government of India viewed that 'it will give easier access to Chinese troops from areas under the illegal occupation of China in North-east Kashmir and from Tibet into the Gilgit area in Pakistan-occupied Kashmir which lies to the North of ceasefire line.[20]

China's strategic relations with Pakistan and construction of Karakoram highway on a disputed land with the help of the former had marred the prospect of border talks between the two. But in spite of these negative developments India, on her part, did not shift its policy towards China either on Tibet or on Taiwan. It also backed fully China's efforts for representation in the United Nations. By the time Indira Gandhi took the reign of administration in January 1980 a lot of change had been made in China's internal and external policies. Considering the proper perspective, she opted for a policy of establishing contact with the Chinese. As a major breakthrough she met Huo Guofeng, her Chinese counterpart, on the occasion of Tito's funeral in May 1980 and an agreement was announced when Huang Hua, the Foreign Minister of China, visited New Delhi in June 1981. With no major gain on the border side it could be counted as slow serpantine movement of adjustment and accommodation. They agreed that the officials of the two countries should take up the problems and seek settlement through periodic and ongoing discussions. Huang Hua mentioned that the three principles: historical background, existing realities and national sentiments of the two countries should constitute the framework for addressing the border problem. Among the positive developments, the most important was Indian Prime Minister's visit to Beijing in December 1988.

For India the central issue was border problem but with the visit of Rajiv Gandhi in December 1988 India changed the track and decided to push relations with Beijing ahead without waiting for a border settlement. Indian view received further impetus in May 1992 when R.Venkataraman, the President of India, visited China and emphasised the creation of conditions of tranquility on the border. During the visit they acknowledged in their statements that the border problem was a serious road block and needed redress through serious negotiations. Side by side several meetings of Joint Working Group (JWG) were concluded to strengthen the process of peace and tranquility on the border and both sides agreed to facilitate greater mutual confidence in their relations.[21]

The two countries moved in direction of getting peace and tranquility on the border and as a mark of success they agreed to keep the border dispute apart and develop friendly relations when P.V. Narasimha Rao, the Indian Prime Minister paid a visit to Beijing in 1993. Until the border dispute is resolved, Rao and Li peng agreed to maintain peace on Line of Actual Control (LAC). They also greed to undertake specific confidence building measures like informing each other on their military exercises, but unfortunately no consensus was arrived at the reduction of troops on the border. It seems that the original impetus given and policy orientations initiated by Deng Xiaoping, Rajiv Gandhi, Li Peng and Narasimha Rao has lost momentum.

As a result of the understanding reached between the two during Narasimha Rao's visit to Beijing "to skirt border dispute" and develop friendship Jiang Zemin, President of China and Head of the Chinese Communist Party paid an official visit to India in November 1996 and among others, signed an Agreement on Confidence Building Measures. The signed agreement provided that the two countries would reduce their military strength along the Line of Actual Control and that no military activities would be undertaken by either country that affected the other country. The preamble of the agreement laid stress on the relevance of Panchsheel and stated that it was aimed at a fair, reasonable and mutually acceptable settlement of the complicated border issue. However, Atal Bihari Vajpayee, who was the leader of opposition at the time, called for cautious approach towards China. He wondered why President Jiang Zemin was maintaining a mysterious silence on the border issue.[22]

Differences between India and China on many other issues have been narrowed down but by no means eliminated. Some of the operational confidence building measures have been put in place since 1993, but the CBM's agreed upon in this time and later in 1996 can be fully implemented only after the problems affecting the Line of Actual Control are settled. The fact of the matter is that the Chinese seemed reluctant to take even the interim step necessary to move towards a solution of the boundary question, namely, to delineate the Line of Actual Control in the seven segments where there is a difference of opinion between China and India.[23] China has no intention to resolve the boundary question. It remains opposed to India's nuclear weaponisation and missile programme. On the other Chinese defence cooperation, particularly with Pakistan, remains a major security concerns of India to which there has been no satisfactory Chinese response.

Even today, China remains concerned about India's policies on Tibet. This concern is heightened by the incremental support that the

Dalai Lama is getting from the international community. The China visit of Atal Bihari Vajpayee, the Indian Prime Minister, in July 2003 was a classic exempler of Indian diplomacy in practice. Despite elusive statements and concessions from the Indian side, the Chinese spoke in measured terms on Sino-Indian relations and gave no ground. In the period since the negotiations began, China has emerged as a global economic and political force and strengthened its leverage vis-à-vis India, both directly and through its mass transfers of weapons of mass destruction to Pakistan.[24]

As viewed by the Indian establishment China desires a normal relationship with India, they seem insistent about having this on their own terms. Another Indian view is that Chinese relations with Pakistan and Myanmar could be an exercise for creating a Chinese cordon sanitaire around India. In an atmosphere of mistrust, net result would not be easy to come by. Prolonged and hard-nosed discussions would follow. But as they are neighbours, big countries, vast landmasses, ancient civilisations, modern, independent, nationalist countries they have to live together and learn to make adjustments and accommodations.

3.2 Updated Perceptions of Border Dispute

Theoretical Dimensions

The rise of India and China are undoubtedly a major feature of contemporary global politics. In post-colonial era, we find that more than sixty years after the establishment of formal diplomatic relations between the Republic of India and the People's Republic of China, tangible relations between these two Asian giants are not as predictable, solid, and stable as many in both countries might consider desirable.[25] The relationship between the two rising Asian powers will not only exert a profound and far-reaching influence over Asian security, but is also seen as a decisive factor of reshaping international order. Currently, the major issues of India-China relations include, the nuclear issue, the boundary problem, the Tibet issue, regional competition and cooperation, and their relations in the global context. These are the reasons for the current gap between the friendship repeatedly declared as an objective by both governments and its lack of actualisation. As a result, the Sino-Indian relations have been constrained by the asymmetry between their threat perceptions: India tends to be deeply apprehensive of threats from China, while China appears comparatively unconcerned about threats from India. This position has made it difficult for China and India to forge shared knowledge and to set a common agenda around which their expectations could converge.[26] In the circumstances India will be on a perennial quest for changes in Sino-Indian relations, such as a final resolution of the border issue and securing more credible nuclear deterrent against China. On the contrary, China will be in favour of the status quo, and feel no urgent need to sort out the disputes.

In general, perceptions and misperceptions of threat become a variable in the strategic policies of states. The end of Cold War and emergence of new powers have tested and stretched the theoretical framework. In the new context, too, international relations theorists have long analysed threat perception as the estimated intent and capabilities of the adversary state. Based on such analysis, not always wise or right states adopt countermeasures to cope with the perceived threat. These have often taken the form of balancing, through internal strength, either military or economic or both, or external partnership with allies. Some other states try 'band wagoning' by joining another power while some others seek a constructive engagement through Confidence Building Measures (CBMs) to reduce the threat.[27] In the case of India-China relations misconception have developed over the years and they continued to remain in the forefront due to unresolved issues like the border dispute. Such misconceptions may have grown from "images" formed towards the end of the colonial era, from self-images and convictions of righteousness, from ideology, from wishful thinking, or from errors in communication and mutual understanding in the years immediately preceding the 1962 conflict.

In relations between India and China, all things apart, perceptions and images about each other have remained a dominant factor in determining the nature of their relationship. Neither conflict nor cooperation nor indifference between the two is an inevitable consequence of their geographical location or historical past. Rather, the tone and content of their bilateral relationship at any given time is a product of policies pursued by the two governments within the context of specific international and national environments that could and did change. Thus, in case of India and China foreign or national security policies are shaped by many determining and variable factors, including objective resources, internal and external pressures, and the priorities and quality of national leadership. Perceptions and images-generally preconceived in leadership and public alike-are bound to play important role :

- in affirming (or not) the desirability and feasibility of a policy direction;
- in interpreting history and delineating the lessons to be learned from it;
- in reinforcing attitudes, and also making it difficult to change attitudes, by diluting attention paid to contradictory signals;
- in simplifying complex or inexplicable phenomena by reducing them to something comprehensible within an existing mental framework; and
- in consolidating a policy-making elite.[28]

These theoretical perceptions and images towards each other apart, both India and China, the two of the most populous countries in the world, have been moving up the ladder, militarily, economically, and politically, but each has its own priorities, strategies, successes, and failures. In today's world countries themselves are the masters of their own fate and are well on their way to take their rightful place as leading economic powers in the international comity of nations. China is undoubtedly ahead of India in the development success story. The remarkable rise of China in the last three decades has had mixed global reactions. While many countries have welcomed this rise, some other nations, especially some of China's neighbours and even the US have viewed it with concern. In the context both India and China as third world countries, share a mirror image perception of each other of encirclement. One prominent example of this perception is Pakistan's all-weather friendship with China.[29] Many in India believe that a nuclear Pakistan is the creation of China to a large extent; and for China, the existence of a strong and confident Pakistan, able and willing to challenge India confers important strategic advantage by forcing India to spread its armed strengths in two fronts.

Status of India and China in Comparison

The increasing gap in military and strategic strength between India and China is of concern to India. In comparison to China, India is far less in a viable nuclear and conventional deterrence. At its present level of strategic strength India does not have the option of following a hostile and confrontational attitude towards China. Contrast to the relative reasonable understanding of China's economic growth, India's perception of China's military build-up, by and large is negative. China's combination of rising nationalism, its key ideological role in regime stability, and the realpolitik strategic culture has made China's military power build-up a potent factor for uncertainty, insecurity, and instability in Asia. In the circumstances the combination of Peoples Liberation Army's (PLA's) size, growing strategic and conventional capabilities, organisational restructuring and adoption of a new strategy of preparing for high tech limited warfare are factors that its Asian neighbours have to take seriously. From the beginning the sense of China's threat perception has been occupying the Indian strategic horizon with PLA's entry in Tibet in the year 1950, through the Sino-Indian border war in 1962, Chinese nuclear test in 1964, and the strategic ties with Pakistan since 1965, right up to India's nuclear test in 1998.[30] Indian negative perceptions of China's military build up were obvious, especially during the event of India's nuclear test. Since then, perceptions have become more positive as a result of the recent changes in Chinese Asian diplomacy, improved Sino-Indian relations and its greater sensitivity to some of Asian concerns.

Analysts of India view seriously China's long-term and deepening military relations, nuclear and missile cooperation in particular, with Pakistan, the principal rival of India. They took notice of China's adjustment of its South Asian Policy in recent years, characteristic of which is its dealing with India and Pakistan separately. In line China's apparent neutral position in the Kargil conflict, and China's continuing endeavour to improve its internal export control regulation and actively participate in international non-proliferation regime made them apprehensive of China's words and deeds. India is also anxious on China's deepening and close defence relations with India's immediate neighbours as an Indian analyst quote, 'While India hopes to surround Pakistan its immediate adversary and to contain China's long-term security threat, China and Pakistan are pursuing similar aims of strategically squeezing Delhi.[31] In the context the reality of China's supplying nuclear and missile technology to Pakistan, military ties with Bangladesh and Myanmar, and the building of the deep-water Gwadar Port in Baluchistan gave us clear indication. China's military ties in the region around India remain a matter of concern, including the fact that the bulk of its arms exports are to the region. In the sphere India's regional strategic concern extends from the Persian Gulf in the west to Straits of Malacca in the east and from the Central Asian Republics in the north to near the equator in the south. In a nutshell, both India and China are likely to see peaceful ties, but in the medium to longer run, a rising China as the most powerful state in Indian's neighbourhood will affect India's national interests politically, militarily and economically.

In comparison to military and strategic viewpoints, in economic sphere there is much to learn from China. Cooperation with China is the need of the hour to achieve India's objective of broad-based development. In the journey towards prosperity in the twenty first century China should be looked upon as India's partner and both countries should work together to make transition from a unipolar to a multipolar as smooth as possible. India must understand China better and cooperate with it in international forums, and China on its part should accept the importance of India in tackling international issues of common interests.[32] China knows it well that it would take decades to seriously compete with the US for global hegemony, it has focussed its strategic energies on Asia. Its foreign policy is aimed at enhancing its economic and military prowess to achieve regional hegemony in Asia. China's recent emphasis on projecting its rise as peaceful is aimed at allying the concerns of its neighbours lest they try to counterbalance its growing influence.[33] China's readiness to negotiate with other regional states and to be an economically responsible power is also a signal to other states that there are greater benefits in allying with China rather than opposing its rise in any manner. In addition, while declaring that it will be focusing on internal socioeconomic development for the next few decades, China has actively pursued policies to prevent the rise of other regional powers, or at least to limit their development relative to itself. Especially in case of India, this manifests itself in its cultivation of Pakistan as a close ally. From supplying nuclear and missile technology to building its military infrastructure, China has done one all it can to help Pakistan be an effective counterweight to India.[34]

On the other the general understanding of India in China is dominated by its backwardness, poverty, underdeveloped infrastructure and scarce supply of daily commodities. Further the basic principles of the democratic system, independence of foreign policy, India's diplomatic relations with the international community and especially with the major powers like United States, domestic affairs and comprehensive developments are noted among the general Chinese public positively.[35] As to the perception of each other's strengths and weaknesses, the Chinese public as well as the academia believe that compared to China India has deeper integration with outside world. China does not enjoy the stature as India at the international level due to many historical and political reasons. At the diplomatic level, India is perceived as a tough player and negotiator. However, India lags behind China in the pace of economic development. In particular, China has been heavily influenced by the portrays displayed by the chief correspondents of the People's Daily in India. They projected India in a pessimistic light and see no future for the country in the global arena; the general belief in the country is that China has left India far behind in terms of economic and social development and it will take India decades to catch up with it.[36] As a result when they talk about India, they are concerned about how its system has been mired by various social problems such as caste, dowry, female infanticide, untouchability, social injustice, poverty, and the feudal justice system. In their view, caste and religion are so deep-rooted in the Indian social system that instead of pushing for reforms, each political party has turned these into vote banks.

Regional and Global Compulsions

This apart, in global context China views India as a rising power when measured in terms of wealth. India, for example, is described as rising in relative terms when compared to the United States and many other countries. At the sametime, Chinese experts do not necessarily view India as rising in respect to China. In 1990, the Chinese and Indian economies were roughly the same size. Today China's economy is more than three times as large as India's, and the gap between the two continues to widen. Further China does not see India as an ally in the geopolitical sense-the two are not security partners. But China does view India as a rising power that can help China limit the potential influence of the United States in various arenas, especially in international institutions. Regarding the military dimension of the border dispute Chinese military writings continue to express concern about the potential for an armed conflict with India. Nevertheless, Beijing approaches such as a conflict from a position of considerable strength. With few exceptions, China already controls the disputed territory that it values most, principally the territory in the western sector known as Aksai Chin. In other word China is more or less satisfied with the status quo in terms of actual control of disputed territory. In addition, because of the geography of the region India faces real challenges in projecting military power over disputed areas, especially those held by China. China occupies the high ground and its forces can move easily across the Tibetan plateau. By contrast, India must seek to transport its forces uphill into high altitude areas and cannot easily shift troops laterally along its border with China.[37] However, from the recent past China began to view India's rise as a largely positive development that promotes China's own interests and objectives more that it threatens or challenges them.

Likewise in the Indian Ocean, China views any limits on its ability to access this body of water as a potential threat, especially in the event of an armed conflict in East Asia. Beijing also acknowledges the capabilities of India's navy and its ambitions in the Indian Ocean. For now, however, China is not seeking to match these capabilities. Instead as one Chinese analyst says; India seeks access to the Indian Ocean "indirectly" by strengthening its commercial and political relationships with other littoral states, especially Pakistan and Burma.[38] In the context, it is important to understand the broader parameters in which these perceptions have formed; India and China exist in a structural situation where China is much stronger and wealthier than India. As a result China can threaten India more than India can threaten China. Consequently, Beijing may underestimate concerns in New Delhi about growing Chinese power. For the same reason, New Delhi may exaggerate the threat posed by China, as China sees the United States and not India as the principal strategic competitor.

Thus, recently the Chinese experts have demonstrated a growing sensitivity to the increasingly negative views of China within India and have encouraged their government to take action to reverse this trend. These experts have floated a variety of proposals to improve what they describe as "strategic trust" including increased support for what each country views as its core interests, dialogues on areas where interest may conflict, and genuine progress moving to resolve the border dispute. At this juncture China's strategy is to find all the areas where it can cooperate with India and to do so. That is, Beijing pursues comprehensive economic, political and international engagement with New Delhi to buffer the overall relationship from specific challenges and sources of friction, such as, India's bid to join the UN Security Council as a permanent member. Such comprehensive engagement seeks to create a situation in which both countries have a vested interest in sustaining generally cooperative ties by increasing the costs of reverting to a more confrontational relationship. However, despite this positive and encouraging sign many points of friction between them exist that can darken the prospect of good/healthy relationship between India and the People's Republic of China.

To conclude the relationship between India and China is complicated by layers of rivalry, mistrust, and occasional cooperation. It is a subtle, unseen, but ongoing and deeply felt collision, the affects of which have left a convoluted lineage. Tensions between the two in any point of time have come to influence everything from their military and security decision-making to their economic and diplomatic maneuvering with implications for wary neighbours and far away allies alike. Developments on the disputed Himalayan borders are central to Indian's internal debate about the credibility of its strategic deterrent and whether to test nuclear weapon again. Being the weaker power, India is far more concerned about the overall military balance tilting to its disadvantage. India sees everywhere because of Beijing's "hexiao gongda" policy in South Asia; "uniting with the small" Pakistan, Bangladesh, Nepal, Burma and Sri Lanka to counter the big India. When combined with Chinese nuclear and missile transfer to Pakistan and a dramatic increase in the Peoples 'Liberation Army's (PLAs) incurions and transgressions across the Line of Actual Control (LAC), even very recently in September 2014 when Chinese President was on India's three-days official visit, the official Indian perception of China has undergone a dramatic shift. Now, China is being widely seen as posing a major security threat in the short to medium term rather than over the long term.

In response to China's "hexiao gongda" policy in South Asia India has strengthened its strategic links with Afghanistan, Tajikistan, Mongolia, Vietnam and Burma– countries on Beijing's periphery. Further the Indian military is strengthening its forces in preparation to fight a limited conflict along the disputed border, and is working to balance Chinese power projection in the Indian Ocean. That balance includes a strategic tilt towards the United States that has also had a damaging effect on Sino-Indian relations. Although the leaders from both countries often repeat the ritualised denials of conflict and emphasise burgeoning trade ties, such platitudes cannot obliterate the trust deficit. Although a small section of China's strategic thinkers seem to hold positive view of India for China's future, a majority of them keep a wary eye on India's great power dreams, its military spending and weapons acquisitions, and the development in India's naval and nuclear doctrines. As the pivotal power in South Asia, India perceives itself much as China has traditionally perceived itself in relation to East Asia. Both desire a peaceful security environment to focus on economic development and avoid overt rivalry or conflict. Neither power is comfortable with the rise of the other. Both seek to envelop neighbours within their national economies. Both are nuclear and space powers with growing ambitions. Both yearn for a multipolar world that will provide them the space for growth and freedom of action. And both remain suspicious of each other's long-term agenda and intentions. Each perceives the other as pursuing hegemony and entertaining imperial ambitions. Faced with exponential growth in China's power and influence, India feels the need to take counterbalancing measures and launch strategic initiative to emerge as a great power, but these are perceived as challenging and threatening in China.

In the circumstances, India needs "a more coherent" China strategy. Putting the border issue, the economy, and military engagement into separate compartments does not work beyond a point. We need better calibration at the highest levels for more meaningful engagement. From an Indian strategic perspective, its core security interests lie in the sub-continent territorial integrity, economic development, peaceful and a secure periphery and those can never be sacrificed or mortgaged for greater cooperation with China at the global or institutional level. At best, improving cooperation between the two in various spheres as well as cooperationg more on global issues of common interest, will in the long-run help to reduce perception gaps and create the right conditions for settling the disputes.

3.3 India's Look East Policy : A Relook Required

The new government formed in India on 26th May 2014 under the charismatic leadership of Narendra Modi and bolstered by its own majority in the Lok Sabha will, undoubtedly be, in a position to take bold steps in the domain of foreign policy along with India's Look East Policy (LEP) which was a response to a unipolar world, marked by the end of the Cold War and the demise of USSR. The aim of all governments from the days of Jawaharlal Nehru have been to make India a major world power and the Look East Policy, officially announced in 1992, was a part of India's re-assessment of its role in the wider region, and looking at Southeast Asia as a neighbour which mattered politically and economically. India's foreign policy evolved as a "dual" pattern, encompassing a global as well as a regional role. The two roles were run on a very different basis, as relations with India's neighbours were conducted on a much more realistic policy course as opposed to the moralistic international policy.

A Historical Sketch

India has a long-standing history of engagement with East and Southeast Asia. Its vision of Eastern neighbour was shaped by the strength of India's geographical proximity, similarity of historical experiences, cultural identity, economic interests and common strategic concerns in relation to the countries in the vast stretch of geo-strategically important Indian Ocean and its economic and strategic significance.[39] In addition, India has a long history of trade and cultural exchanges with East Asia. Trade links with East Asia stretch back to millennia to the Silk Road and Calicut emerging as a major trading port in South Asia. Meanwhile cultural and religious bonds date back to Emperor Ashoka's spread of Buddhism beyond the subcontinent in the third century B.C. The exchange of pilgrims, explorers and traders continued until the onset of British rule over India in the eighteenth century, after which India ceased to be an independent actor on the international stage.[40] Further in the nineteenth and twentieth centuries large scale Indian emigration to Southeast Asia took place as a result of colonialism through the indenture or Kangani system which took away Indians to work in rubber, tea and coffee plantation and also by free emigration of traders, clerks, bureaucrats and professionals. Thousands of Indians were mobilised to fight in the Indian National Army (INA) in Malaya and to contribute to the cause of Indian independence. After Independence, Indians continued to migrate to Thailand, Malaysia, Singapore, Brunei and Indonesia in search of employment, with the pace picking up from the 1970s onwards.[41] The Indian community constitutes 7.3 per cent of Malaysia's population, five per cent of Myanmar's population and 9.71 per cent of Singapore's population.

Politically too, Jawaharlal Nehru said prophetically while addressing the First Asian Relations Conference in April 1947, 'We are of Asia and the peoples of Asia are nearer and closer to us than others...In the past her culture flowed to all these countries and they came to her in many ways. Those contacts are being renewed and the future is bound to see a closer union between India and Southeast Asia.'[42] Forming a common cause with Asian leaders such as Indonesian President Sukarno and Chinese Premier Zhou Enlai on decolonisation, Western imperialism, Socialism, national Sovereignty, equality and a developing world solidarity, Nehru helped to forge the "Bandung Spirit" of 1955. However, this phase of India's engagement with East Asia perished with India's border war with China in 1962, preoccupation with Pakistan and inability to meet its development needs which caused India to turn inward. It marred the prospect of India's dream of resurgent East Asian Solidarity towards peace, progress and prosperity.

Ever since the Sino-Indian War of 1962, China and India have been strategic competitors in South and East Asia. China has cultivated close commercial and military relations with India's neighbours and rival Pakistan and competed for influence in Nepal and Bangladesh. After Deng Xiaoping's rise to power in China in 1979, China began reducing threats of expansionism and in turn cultivated extensive trade and economic relations with Asian nations. China became the closest partner and supporter of the military junta of Burma, which had been ostracised from the international community following the violent suppression of pro-democracy activities in 1988. In world politics too India refused to be part of any defense pact or to take sides against either the Western powers or the Communist bloc. India's relations with the superpowers during the Cold War were difficult as its non-aligned status was never really accepted by the US who saw India as being in the Soviet camp. India's desire for economic self-sufficiency also went against the grain of the concept of free market economy, which was being pushed by the Western powers. On the other hand relations with the Soviet Union were cordial with substantial trade and barter trade underlying the relationship. In a nutshell, India never subscribed to the communist world's ideology, trying to combine a socialist economy with a democratic system at home.

Looking at Look East Policy

In that kind of situation India developed and enacted its Look East Policy which represents its efforts to cultivate extensive economic and strategic relations with the nations of Southeast Asia in order to bolster its standing as a regional power and a counterweight to the strategic influence of the People's Republic of China. Initiated in 1991, it marked a strategic shift in India's perspective of the world. In fact, the qualitative and structural changes brought about by the end of the cold war led to the new orientations in the foreign policies of India and countries of Southeast Asia. The new policy was started with the aim to enhance economic relations with the ASEAN countries and has reached towards the strategic, political and institutional linkage.[43] As a result India moved towards Southeast Asia to build a multi-dimensional ties with these countries. In response, the Southeast Asian countries by leaving all inhibitions of the past came closer to India to develop warm and friendly relations with it. Perhaps, contrary to China, the rise of a democratic pluralist secular India has been viewed by ASEAN and East Asia with more welcoming optimism. China is still trying very hard to enhance its "Soft Power" image in its relationship towards the ASEAN countries, but due to its authoritarian nature and a bitter war-torn past, its rise makes them suspicious.

Pursuing Look East Policy by India in early 1990s with a lot of vigour and glare witnessed a good gesture from opposite side and in

1992 India became sectoral dialogue partner with ASEAN and full dialogue partner in 1995. In July 1996, Inder Kumar Gujral, the then Minister of External Affairs attended an ASEAN conference in Indonesia for the first time and expressing the new Indian government's approval of the policy said, 'We see the full dialogue partnership with ASEAN as a manifestation of our Look East destiny...India would work with ASEAN as a full dialogue partner to give real meaning and content to the prophecy and promise of the 'Asian country' that is about to draw upon us.[44] With gradual development India-ASEAN relations got a wider dimension toward the end of 1990s and the beginning of 2000. In 1998, the then Indian Prime Minister Atal Bihari Vajpayee intended to accelerate India's Look East Policy. In the first inning of National Democratic Alliance (NDA) the concept of "external neighbourhood" was popularised by Indian leaders such as I.K. Gujral and Jaswant Sinha. After almost a decade of initiation, the policy assumed a more pronounced strategic flavour and expanded to the countries other than ASEAN member like Australia, Japan and South Korea. Jaswant Sinha heralded the second phase of the Look East Policy in 2003, by saying, 'The first phase of India's Look East Policy was ASEAN centred and focused primarily on trade and investment linkages. The new phase of this policy is characterised by an expanded definition of 'East' extensively from Australia to East Asia with ASEAN at its aim. It also marks a shift from trade to wider economic and security issues including joint efforts to promote the sea lanes and coordinate counter-terrorism activities. On the economic side, phase II of Look East Policy is also characterised by arrangement for FTA and establishing institutional economic linkage between the countries of the region and India.[45] Beyond the concept of immediate neighbourhood, there are two other concepts- the countries of East and Northeast Asia are perceived as 'far eastern neighbours' while the ASEAN countries as 'near eastern neighbours.' Expansion of neighbourhood area has served most importantly India's economic and security related interests especially in post-9/11 periods.

However, the beginning of the Look East Policy was economic-centred. The 1991 economic reforms saw the birth of a new role for international economic and trade relations. India suddenly had to engage with the post cold war world and reassess its foreign policy priorities. The opening up of the economy to international players also meant that foreign relations had an economic dimension and trade became a foreign policy tool. Leaving Swadeshi, economic self-sufficiency behind and engaging in international trade was India's new way forward. Especially under the first NDA government India's foreign policy formulation has been conducted on the basis of trade and power priorities as a mechanism to hegemony. At a larger level, this move fits in with globalisation and the increasing power of business in government policy formulation, not only in Asia but in the world at large. In the economic realm, the Look East Policy provided a tremendous encouragement to economic ties between India and the ASEAN member states resulting in the constitution of a number of institutional mechanism to promote economic exchanges. After interactions Malaysia and Singapore emerged as the 10th and 11th in terms of approved investment received by India in 2002. Thailand was in the 18th and Indonesia and Philippines were in 33rd and 35th position respectively. In recent times, India's export to Malaysia and Thailand have improved significantly from US$ 773.69 million in 2001-02 to US$ 3956.98 million in 2010-11 and US$ 633.13 million in 2001-02 to US$ 2792.80 million in 2010-11 respectively.[46] Overall, Singapore has continued to remain the largest market in ASEAN for India's merchandise exports, followed by Indonesia, Malaysia and Thailand. Cumulative FDI from Singapore to India has increased from US$ 1.3 billion in 2005-06 to US$ 17.15 billion in March 2012. Similarly, FDI from India to Singapore has increased from US$ 3.1 billion to US$ 23.41 billion between 2004-05 to 2011-12.[47] In the circumstances it is hoped that India's economic integration with the East Asian region will grow gradually. Recently, it has assumed a greater economic dimension. Given India's economic reforms and the attendant efforts to integrate with the regional and global economy, it is but natural that Indian diplomacy, particularly in its relation with ASEAN countries will focus more on economic issues like trade, investment, goods and services.

New Thoughts on Look East Policy

India's recent attempt to build a closer relations with East Asian countries within the framework of its Look East Policy has been a success in economic sphere and to some extent in defence fields at multilateral and bilateral levels. Even at political level, beginning with its sectoral dialogue partnership with ASEAN, India graduated first to full dialogue partnership with attendant membership of the ASEAN Regional Forum (ARF), then to mechanism of ASEAN-India Summit, at par with ASEAN plus China, Japan and South Korea and finally to the membership of the East Asian Summit. These interactions have resulted in considerably greater integration with the rest of Asia than is commonly realised.[48] In sphere of defence India is engaged with Southeast Asia at both multilateral and bilateral levels. At multilateral level, India is an active participant in the regional security mechanism, the ASEAN Regional Forum and since 1995 the Indian Navy has been hosting a biennial naval gathering called MILAN at Port Blair. According to some analysts there were several objectives of these naval exercises with Southeast Asian countries. Besides intended to balance China's influence, it was obviously underscoring India's emergence as a major player in the Asia-Pacific region. It was also likely to stem the flow of arms across the Bay of Bengal insurgents in the Northeast and it also demonstrated the Navy's ability to operate far from home. At bilateral level too, India has established and strengthened defence-related relations on various aspects with countries of the region and primarily with Singapore, Japan, Malaysia, Indonesia, Vietnam, Myanmar, Thailand, Philippines, South Korea etc.

Despite this, on the other, things changed rapidly in the early 1990s as India adopted the strategy of globalisation and liberalisation, the policy-makers of South block started exploring all possible avenues of India's dream of becoming a regional big power.[49] From earlier and till date China has seized the leadership of the Eastern region practically and even today India is not in a position to deter Beijing in any of its sinister design against New Delhi. In the context India's Look East Policy has been more reactive to what China has been doing in the region than a proactive one attempting to make a distinct Indian mark and "getting others to want what you want." Undoubtedly, the region now looks towards India because of its potential as an economic powerhouse and partly to balance China's overwhelming economic and strategic influence, in comparison to economy. India's role in the security and strategic aspects of Southeast and East Asia is still quite marginal. Observers of India's Look East policy have found the conspicuous absence of a strategic vision of a future Asia-Pacific, that can inform its policies and actions in the coming years and its will to establish its rightful place in the Asian balance of power. If India has to emerge as a major power in the Asia-Pacific it has to have not only a vision of its own economic future but also a vision of its future strategic role in the region. India's hesitation in taking a more open and assertive role is informed not only by its limits of military and economic power, but also by its intent to avoid a direct confrontation with China which considers Southeast Asia as its sphere of influence.

In promoting India's strategic objectives, as many analysts believe, its soft power image in the region would be more helpful than its hard military power and P.V. Narasimha Rao, the then Prime Minister of the country, also laid emphasis on India's historical and cultural relations with the region in a lecture delivered in 1994 at Singapore. He said these relations very old and strong and there was nothing new in India's looking towards reinforcing cooperative linkages with its Eastern neighbours. India's soft power image is very high in the countries of Southeast Asia due to their shared heritage and civilisation and they are now called its 'civilisational neighbours.' Besides, a democratic tradition of more than six decades, Mahatma Gandhi with his concept of non-violence and peaceful conflict mediation as national hero and India's long engagement in multilateral institutions are indicators that seem to qualify as one of the leading soft powers of the twenty-first century.[50] Internationally, the way the Indian Navy helped in Operation Sahayaata and Operation Sadbhavana in post-Tsunami and post-Lebanon crisis in 2004-05 and 2006 respectively earned the goodwill of the people of East Asia and PIOs of Lebanon. This altruistic humanitarian assistance giver image is vital for India to promote its soft-power with a robust demonstration of its hard or military power.

Another area India can make an impact in, is in the field of higher education. During his visit to Indonesia in April 2005, commemorating the Bandung Conference, Prime Minister Manmohan Singh declared that India intended to stay engaged by sharing experiences gained from our own development process-with nations in Asia. He said on the occasion, 'Human resource development holds the key to employment and wealth creation, particularly in this age of globalisation. This has been our strategy and we have laid particular emphasis on training and skills development as we globalise.[51] In the region Indonesia has been one of the prominent beneficiaries of Indian technical cooperation programmes meant for fellow developing countries. Everywhere in Asia, there is greater demand among the younger generation to learn English, the language of globalisation. Myanmar and the two least developed countries of the region Indochina, Cambodia and Laos, can benefit from India's abundant English language teachers, who could help those countries at much less expense than the British or Australians.

In line, India has a lead in information technology and Indian IITs and IIMs have a very high reputation in those countries. Many Southeast Asians have expressed their interest not only to come and study in these institutions but also open their campuses in their countries particularly in Indonesia.[52] The success of Indian companies like Infosys Technology and Wipro Technologies in the Information Technology sector, success of other multinational companies like the Tata Group and Reliance Group; and the worldwide recognition of the academic excellence in training and research have contributed to the new image of India as a country with English educated, enterprising people.

However, to develop and strengthen India's multi-dimensional relations with the countries of Southeast Asia, much more is left to be done. India's soft power can be increased by augmenting funding for cultural activities, promotion of tourism as a means of people to people contact, presentation of Islamic cultural heritage and monuments before the Muslims of Indonesia and Malaysia. At the juncture India needs to give its Look East Policy a more vigorous soft power thrust by initiating an innovative political and cultural charm offensive to give added substance to shed a different, positive light on India's foreign policy.

References

1. B. N. Mullik, *The Chinese Betrayal* (New Delhi: Allied Publishers, 1971), p. 84.
2. Jawaharlal Nehru, *Indian Foreign Policy: Selected Speeches, September 1946 – April 1961* (New Delhi: Government of India, 1961), p. 395.
3. *Ibid.*, p. 79.
4. Sarvepalli Gopal, *Jawaharlal Nehru: A Biography 1956-1964*, p. 239.
5. *The Hindu*, 27 April 1963.
6. Michael Brecher, *Nehru: A Political Biography* (London: 1959), p. 564.

7. *Jawaharlal Nehru's Speeches 1957-1963*, Vol. IV (New Delhi: Publication Division, 1964), p. 230.
8. *Lok Sabha Debates*, Vol. 13, 27 February 1963 cols. pp. 1307-42.
9. *The Hindu*, 20 January 1963.
10. *Asian Recorder, October 1965* (New Delhi: 1965), p. 6715.
11. *Annual Report 1964-65* (New Delhi: Ministry of External Affairs, 1965) p. 28.
12. Harish Kapur, *India's Foreign Policy 1947-1992-Shadow and Substance*, pp. 27-34.
13. Giri Deshingkar, 'Strategic Doctrines', in G. P. Deshpanda and Alka Acharya (eds.), *50 Years of India-China-Crossing a Bridge of Dreams*, pp. 333-34.
14. Sarvepalli Gopal, *Jawaharlal Nehru: A Biography 1956-1964*, pp. 238-39.
15. Mahendra Kumar, *Theoretical Aspects of International Politics*, pp. 301-2.
16. *Ibid.*, p. 303.
17. Maxwell, N., *India's China War* (London: 1970), p. 348.
18. *The Hindu*, 4 January 1963.
19. *The National Herald* (Lucknow), 18 and 31 January 1963.
20. *Foreign Affairs Record*, July 1969 (New Delhi: Government of India, 1969), p. 142.
21. *The Indian Express*, 2 February 1992.
22. *The Times of India*, 3 December 1996.
23. J. N. Dixit, Beijing on Our Mind; *The Hindustan Times*, 3 August 2000.
24. Brahma Chellaney; 'Forever Shanghaied', *Ibid.*, 29 July 2004.
25. Surjit Mansingh, 'Perceptions of India and China Relations at the End of Colonial Era,' in Madhavi Thampi (ed.), *India and China in the Colonial World* (New Delhi: Social Science Press, 2005), p. 224.
26. *The Hindu*, 24 March 2014.
27. *Ibid.*
28. Surjit Mansingh, 'Perceptions of India and China Relations at the End of Colonial Era,' pp. 225-27.
29. Nabeel A. Mancheri and S. Gopal, 'Perceive China's Rise?,' *Foreign Policy Journal*, 22 September 2014.
30. Zhang Guihong, 'India's Perceptions of and Responses to the Rise of China: An assessment,' visit www.asianscholarship.org.
31. *Ibid.*
32. Nabeel A. Mancheri and S. Gopal, 'Perceive China's Rise?.'
33. Evan S. Medeiros, 'China Debates Its Peaceful Rise Strategy?.' at http//yaleglobal yale edu/display article 4118.

34. Harsh V. Pant, 'Indian Forign Policy and China,' *Strategic Analysis*, Vol. 30, Issue 4, October 2006.
35. Jia Haitao, 'Chinese Perceptions of India and Its Rise,' China Studies Centre, IIM, Madras, 5 March 2013.
36. B.R. Deepak, 'A Bleak View of India from China,' *India Today*, June 16, 2011.
37. Erin Fried, 'China's Responses to a Rising India,' *The National Bureau of Asian Research*, 4 October 2011.
38. *Ibid.*
39. Sourabh Jyoti Sharma, 'Soft Power' and India's Look East Policy-Present Role and Future prospects', *South Asia Politics*, Vol. II, No. 7, November 2012 (New Delhi: 2012), p. 46.
40. Chietigj Bajpayee, 'India Rediscovers East Asia,' *Asia Times*, 31 October 2007.
41. Jayita Mukhopadhyay, 'Indian Diaspora in South East Asia: Predicaments and Prospects,' *The Indian Journal of Political Science*, Vol. LXXI, No. 3, July-September 2010 (Meerut: 2010), p. 997.
42. Chietigj Bajpayee, 'India Rediscovers East Asia'.
43. Jyoti, 'India's Look East Policy : In Its Second Phase,' *Global Journal of Pharmaceutical Sciences and Education*, Vol. 2, No.1 (2013), p.1.
44. *The Times of India*, 25 July 1996.
45. From the text of Jaswant Sinha's Speech at Harward University, Cambridge, 29 September 2003.
46. Jyoti, 'India's Look East Policy : In its Second Phase'.
47. Ahmed, E., 'India-Singapore Ties Underpinned by Strategic Interests,' at www.newstrackinpia.com.
48. Subhash Shukla, 'The Evolution of India's Look East Policy,' *Dynamics of Public Administration*, Vol. 29, No.1 (2012), pp. 1-20.
49. Jayita Mukhopadhyay, 'Indian Diaspora in South East Asia : Predicaments and Prospects,' pp. 996-97.
50. Sourabh Jyoti Sharma, 'Soft Power and India's Look East Policy-Present Role and Future Prospects,' pp. 47-49.
51. Baladas Ghosal, 'Some New Thoughts on India's Look East Policy,' Institute of Peace and Conflict Studies, No. 54, October 2007 (New Delhi: 2007), p. 3.
52. *Ibid.*

Chapter IV

Understanding Kashmir : Problem and Perception

The region Jammu and Kashmir, an area of 86,000 square mile located in northwest India and northeast Pakistan, has been violently disputed by these two South Asian neighbours since 1947. With partition of the Indian sub-continent, the region was split as well with two-thirds going to India and a third going to Pakistan. Since then India continued to resist conducting a plebiscite by the population of the region while Pakistan, times without number, renewed its call for a referendum by Kashmiris. On being defeated in Kashmir related declared wars and emergence of Bangladesh in December 1971 Pakistan began to wage a proxy war through the Pakistan-based extremist groups along Indo- Pak borders and inside Indian territory which later became a single major hurdle in normalisation of Indo-Pak relations. Several round of talks and attempts made by governmental and non-governmental agencies failed to providc an acceptable solution of the problem of Jammu and Kashmir followed by a war-like situation prevailing between the two countries for decades. Even today India continues to assert its sovereignty or rights over the entire region of Kashmir but Pakistan maintains that it is a disputed territory.

4.1 Complexities of the Problem

India and Pakistan have been in a state of war over Kashmir ever since 1947. India is fighting for Kashmir as proof of its adherence to the secular way of life. Kashmir should be with India as it proves that a Muslim majority area can be part of a predominantly Hindu secular state. This is the great value of Kashmir being a part of India, the country with the second largest Muslim population in the world. Pakistan wants Kashmir because it is a Muslim majority area and thinks that it belongs to it by right. Islam, whether as a separatist force that had not aligned itself with the mainstream anti-colonial movement or as a movement that sought to create a national state for its people, has always been at the root of the conflict between India and Pakistan. The matter is more evident in Kashmir because Kashmir, unlike the rest of undivided India did not follow the logic of partition based on religion. The first Indo-Pak war of 1947-48 ended in a ceasefire with Kashmir being divided between the two countries. Pakistan has always looked at this situation as an unfinished task that would be complete only after Kashmir becomes an integral part of Pakistan. But the Government of India has, no doubt, a good legal reason of the view : The Ruler of Jammu and Kashmir had unconditionally acceded to the Indian Union; the accession was accepted by a freely-elected Constituent Assembly of the State of Jammu and Kashmir in 1951; and was reaffirmed in the State's Constitution in 1956. Thus, the whole of Jammu and Kashmir becomes an integral part of the Indian Union. Kashmir is vital to us from many points of view. Kashmir is also vital to Pakistan and so there is an inherent conflict in the situation.

Solution of the Kashmir problem is important not because it is a Muslim majority area but because it has the key to normalisation of relations between India and Pakistan. At New Delhi and Islamabad the presence of a deeply ingrained conflict mentality, not to say a culture of mistrust, seemed to have made any initiative towards cooperation and accommodation unacceptable to domestic public opinion in both the countries. There was hardly a country which did not carry its ghost about with it and, for India, it was the ghost of Pakistan. Behind that ghost lay the history not only of the recent past but also of the many years preceding freedom. Relations with Pakistan appeared to be a continuation of the old communal conflicts, and there could be no real solution till that basic conflict in the minds of the people in Pakistan and India was resolved. Jawaharlal Nehru, the then Prime Minister of India, in his letter to Chief Ministers, on 1st November 1957, did not claim that India was free from this communal temper, but it did not dominate everything else as in Pakistan. No Government in that country had any policy except of fear and hatred of India and, till that ceased, the future was dark.[1] He, however, accepted his failure to win the goodwill of the Government of Pakistan.

As the sub-continent was partitioned on the basis of religion and in the background of communal riots, it became the single determinants that govern Pakistani action. For India this jingoism did not last long. In those days when Kashmir became part of India emotions were high, and quite legitimately so. India was still a very young nation-state and threats from neighbouring Pakistan loomed large in the post-partition national psyche. The nation-state is popular endorsement of territory. This implies that in all authentic nation-states territory is sacralised. Territorial acquisition are not just a matter of geography, there is a profound sense of cultural attachment to them. It is quite useless to look for rational reasons behind this sentiment.[2] However, Jingoism differs from patriotism and the latter goes a step further. Patriotism is also concerned with people who live on the soil, and puts people on a par with the soil, Jingoists are never happy with it. Jingoism is dismissive of people and of cultural diversities. It is solely besotted by considerations of territory. A patriot is also devoted to the soil but realises that the best way of firming up national boundaries is by paying attention to the people who live within it.[3] In both instances territory is critically important.

It was this cultural attachment of the people of India that looked to Kashmir as its integral part. The territorial bond that unites and vivifies the Indian nation-state is not just a sub-continental characteristic. In the relative placid environment of Canada too there is an equal feeling regarding territory. It was seen when a section of English Canadians started considering the possibility of letting Quebec go it met with an interesting response. Unfortunately we have become to use thinking of every problem or most of the problems in terms of communalism of Hindu versus Muslim or Hindu and Sikh versus Muslim and so on. That has been unfortunate legacy of ours, and the extent to which it took us cannot be forgotten by us nor the tragedies that it has led to. Even at this juncture, the case of Kashmir stands apart, because Kashmir is not a case of communal conflict. It may be a case of political conflict or a case of any other conflict, but it is essentially not a case of communal conflict.[4] We have cast eyes on

Kashmir not for any gain but because of old bounds, because of old sentiments and new sentiments also. Kashmir is very close to our minds and hearts and if by some decree or adverse fortune Kashmir ceases to be a part of India, it would be a wrench and a pain and torment for us.[5]

In this connection it is worth assessing that whether Kashmir is a symptom or a disease. The two would have found some other reason to stay distant because they have not yet overcome the religious differences, which led to the partition of the sub-continent. After the constitution of Pakistan on the basis of the two-nation theory, the rulers or political parties have been at pains to run down secularism in India. It is a secular state, as is clearly and unambiguously stated in its constitution, in contrast to the theocratic states of Pakistan, Bangladesh and Sri Lanka and unlike all its unitary neighbours India has inherited a quasi-federal state structure. Pakistan has been insisting on describing India as a Hindu country. On being influenced from the approach there have been serious suggestions from Pakistan to divide the state on the basis of Hindu and Muslim, the formula used at the time of partition. Such proposal have never been taken into consideration as it would harm the Indian polity as well as the Muslim population in the country. The two countries, if arrayed as Muslim Pakistan and Hindu India can hardly find a solution to the problem of Jammu and Kashmir, which demands a secular approach, transcending religion.[6] The ground has to be prepared from where the nettle of communalism must be uprooted.

Accession and Thereafter

Accession of the state of Jammu and Kashmir to the Union of India was followed by an invasion on the part of Pakistan and a fighting had taken place on a large front along almost the entire border of the Kashmir State and Pakistan. In the post-accession phase the state of Jammu and Kashmir became an integral part of Indian Dominion territory which had thrust upon the latter a constitutional duty to defend the state with the active support of Kashmiri army and the public as well. There arose an urgency about these matters, for the first step that must be taken was to put a stop to the fighting and this could only be done if the invaders returned across the border in Pakistan. Since Pakistan was unwilling to cooperate with India in this matter, the alternatives left with India was to send its Armed Forces across Pakistan territory to deal effectively with the invaders, or to request the United Nations to ask Pakistan to do so. Any resort to the first course would have involved armed conflict with Pakistan.

New Delhi, in an effort to avoid a full-fledged war with Islamabad and to try every available method to find a peaceful solution, made a reference to the Security Council on January 1, 1948. Our making a reference on this issue to the Security Council of the United Nations was an act of faith, because we believe in the progressive realisation of world order and a world government.[7] In regard to Kashmir, Nehru was pained because it had got entangled in external politics, in the relations between India and Pakistan. He added that it got entangled was not odd, but the manner of its entanglement was odd. The problem became all the more complicated because of the involvement of the Great powers, particularly the USA. Since it was taken up in the Security Council in January 1948, India had hoped that the United Nations would uphold India's genuine cause. But it did not happen as the attitudes of the United States and the United Kingdom were very much favourable to Pakistan rather than to India. The extremely partisan attitude of the United States on the issue of Kashmir was absolutely anti-Indian and suicidal to her interest and also for maintaining peace in the subcontinent.[8] This is another heavy burden which we have to bear. Our experience of international politics and the way things are done in these higher regions of the United Nations, has been disappointing in the extreme.

In the light of the then prevailing international context, if not militarily, but diplomatically, we have reached almost a crisis over the Kashmir issue. This development on Kashmir owed quite a variety of factors, connected with everything except the merits of the Kashmir issue. The Americans who voted for the partition of Palestine and thereby alienated the sympathies of the Arabs seemed anxious to win back Arab support which was essential for them in view of the oil situation and the possibility of war in the Middle East. The Arab League in February 1948, threatened withdrawal of oil concessions if the United States continued to support the partition of Palestine. Both, the USA and the UK also seemed to be a fear in mind that if Pakistan becomes weak internally the situation might be exploited by Soviet Russia. But above all, the achievement of independence and a desire to maintain our own foreign relations, free of attachment to blocs, had brought us sharply against the ugly forces of power politics.[9] India held the pro-Pakistan position of the USA and this belief grew in when we saw that there was not only substantial change in the Security Council's attitude to Pakistan. The United States neither took any stern action against Pakistan nor criticised the presence of its troops in Kashmir since October 26, 1947. Though it had no doubt regarding the legal validity of Kashmir's accession to India, it accepted the position that the accession should be chalked out in the light of a plebiscite to resolve the issue finally.[10]

First of all, this 'reference of the people' was mentioned in a letter written to the Maharaja of Kashmir by the then Governor-General at the time of accession and later the pledge was accepted by the Indian leaders. Though it did not form a part of the agreement made between the Maharaja and the Government of India, in the phase of cold war and mainly due to power politics of Great Powers, the issue of Plebiscite overshadowed the accession of Kashmir to the Union of India. As per the spirit of the accession the Indian government tried to fashion its actions and honour the pledge it gave to the people of Jammu and Kashmir. Its responsibility was two-fold: To protect them from invasion, rape, loot, arson and everything that accompanied that attack. The second was given unilaterally to the state's people to decide finally what their future was to be. But the last one was more important. There seemed to be a good deal of misunderstanding about Kashmir's accession in people and in some newspapers, mostly abroad that something had happened in last three weeks that had made this accession complete.[11] In the circumstances India made a declaration that it would abide by the will of the people of Kashmir as declared in a plebiscite or referendum. However, it could not held because the Plebiscite was conditional upon Pakistan pulling out all its troops, regular or irregular from the state.

It is a general feeling of the people in India that excessive idealism, its lack of experience in diplomacy at the time of independence, and an overly accommodative trait of Hindu culture, led India to make one mistake after another in handling the Kashmir question. Our policy on Kashmir has never been full-proof from strategic and tactical points of view while negotiating Pakistan on Kashmir issue. The overall objective was neither clear nor consistent. India adhered strictly to the certain ideals which had shaped its thinking and action during our freedom struggle. It even did not care to ponder over its opposite number Pakistan which had a different gospel. They were not for unity but disunity, not for construction but for destruction, not for peace but for discord, if not war. But many who thought that practising a good neighbourly policy is a purely one-sided affair with the responsibility for it to be borne entirely by this country have now become sadder and wiser and realise that such a policy needs the willingness and cooperation of the two parties to be developed satisfactorily and cannot be implemented on unilateral basis, though unilateral steps may help on appropriate occasions. In most mature countries, this would need no special emphasis and would be taken for granted. Unfortunately, this basic flaw pervades not only in our security policy but also in our economic planning and in various other aspects of our national life.

Pakistan's Game Plan in Kashmir

Pakistan's foreign policy has always revolved round the idea of annexing Kashmir. If anything, Islamabad's intentions have acquired greater urgency since the Bangladesh war for it to do to India what it believes India did in 1971. This is why Pakistanis do not hesitate to tell their Indian interlocutors that they feel insecured and incomplete without Jammu and Kashmir. Several US congressional studies, think-tank reports, task-force-on-terrorism findings and CIA revelations have named Pakistan for aiding and abetting the proxy war. Yet, not a day passes without Pakistan passing strictures on India's management of Jammu and Kashmir. The proxy war waged by Pakistan has also falsified the latter's claim that it is interested in the plight of Kashmiri Muslims. Its true interests are geostrategic and economic. Although it is more than the truth that the proxy war is unwinable by either side, Pakistan's aim is to make the cost for India holding Jammu and Kashmir high, diplomatically, politically and militarily.

Traditionally, terrorism is a highly organised enterprise that fits into a clear political strategy. It has been filling the news for most of our lives, and will doubtless go on demanding the attention of our children and grand-children as well. Even in the past terrorism was almost a part of the strategy of an armed national liberation movement, and in the colonial context it usually worked in the end. The reason why it worked so well in anti-colonial struggles was that it did not have to defeat the imperial power's superior military forces in order to win. They were a long way from the home, and there was a limit to how many lives and how much money the imperial government would spend to hang into its possessions. But the early, easy successes of terror tactics in the anti-imperial context left everybody with a great inflated notion of what the technique could achieve against an established national government with local roots.[12] Governments and armies that cannot "go home" – because they are already at home – simply do not give in to terrorism. After several years and more than 80,000 deaths, the Islamic fundamentalists, terrorist war against Algeria's crypto-military regime is no closer to success. They are capable of doing much harm but they are not politically serious people.

While India has traditionally been on the defensive, Pakistan made Jammu and Kashmir the core issue and the root cause of India-Pakistan dispute. Pakistanis and the world are fed on a routine diet of propaganda on television, radio and print media about Indian Army atrocities and human rights violations in Jammu and Kashmir.[13] Pakistan's initial strategy in Kashmir has settled down to three-pronged mutually supportive thrust line;

- Work for negotiations with India in an agenda which would discuss the Kashmir issue on the basis of not only the Simla Agreement but also the UN Resolutions, thus bringing the issue of plebiscite/self-determination into bilateral/multilateral talks. So far Pakistan's own obligations under the UN Resolutions (the basic reason why the resolution could not be implemented) are not even alluded to;
- Strategy of overt support and covert action for a low - intensity proxy war fought by non-regular forces constructed on the ideology of religion based subnational separatism;
- Prepare for, and if necessary escalate to a regular war preferably in a manner that creates perceptions of India being the initiator of such war.[14]

The above strategy was aimed to seek the Pakistan's objectives of destabilising India and its developmental plans, undermine its secular policy and feudal structure, push the Indian states towards increasing dependence on force and damage India's standing in the international community particularly at a time when it is receiving added recognition and respect. Pakistan would actually be pursuing a low-cost high-benefit strategy where the real price would be paid by the Kashmiri and other Indians. The proxy war could be sustained by Pakistan for a long time as long as some Kashmiris are willing to keep the conflict alive. Pakistan would try to avoid war as long as it sees the basic objectives being met by the other elements of its strategy without paying a direct price which is bound to be heavy.[15] We can hardly hope to win the low-intensity proxy war being waged against us if we do not have the undoubted capacity to win a possible regular war, whether it is of short or long duration. Winning the proxy war was itself requires a cool assessment of the evolving situation and elements of the Pakistani strategy so as to evolve appropriate responses, political as well as military.

It is said that the situation in the valley could not have taken such a serious turn since 1989 had the government handled militancy more effectively in its earlier stages. The policy-makers of India were knowing Pakistan's plan. The details of the Pakistani plan were given in "Operation Topaz", published in one of the issues of the *India Defence Review* in 1988. Later on the plan was put into operation in stages. At each stage it tested government's will and preparedness to fight it. First, a number of explosions, without causing much damage, took place in Srinagar. This was followed by attacks on police stations and selected killings to terrorise the people. The three main objectives before the militants were : (i) to demoralise the state police by targeting those officers who dared to take action against them; (ii) to drive out the Kashmiri Pandits from the valley; and (iii) to create a communal divide between Hindus and Muslims.[16] The key to the Kashmir problem lies in controlling its internal situation.

India has been for years at the receiving end of cross-border terrorism in Kashmir and surrounding areas. Scores of innocent civilians are mercilessly gunned down at all to frequent intervals, and bomb explosions kill and maim hapless victims in buses and trains as well as in the market place. At this stage our own strategy will have to rest on five concurrent elements.

- Keep the avenues for peaceful solution of the conflict with Pakistan open;
- Political and administrative measures to restore normality in Kashmir with the use of force where incapable;
- Sustained politico-diplomatic efforts to mobilise international support in countering Pakistan's proxy war for sub-national separatism;
- Active use of force against infiltration and terrorist activities which are an important component of the proxy war;
- Adequate preparedness to deter imposition of a direct war.

4.2 Cross-Border Terrorism and Indian Response

Differing Perceptions

In past the border areas had served as a heaven for terrorists, who after obtaining training and arms in Pakistan, crossed over into India and fanned out all over the country. There has been a steady one-way traffic of illegal immigrants from Pakistan to the border areas. The importance of the problem lies in the fact that not only human traffic but arms and narcotics find easy access into India. Reports from various parts of the country confirm that they smuggle arms and narcotics in large quantities. Unfortunately, there are many godfathers, agents, touts, etc. on the Indian side who not only provide shelter and food to the illegal migrants but all help needed to remain unnoticed. The defence forces with the help of local people and the police must break up these gangs, round up the agents and touts and send the godfathers to prison. What is needed is not a fence along the border but a highly efficient intelligence machinery capable enough to identify the illegal migrants and stop the trans-border commerce in humans, drugs and arms.[17] In August 1986, the Indian Parliament adopted a resolution in pursuance of Article 249 of the constitution whereby the Centre assumed special powers to create a security belt to deal directly and swiftly against large scale infiltration, illegal traffic in arms, drugs and secessionist and terrorist activities on international borders. Not only the entire border of Pakistan from Kashmir to Kutch but our borders with Bangladesh and China also need to be protected. It is time India told its people the real and full story about Pakistan's role in the unrecognised war in Jammu and Kashmir which the latter has been waging since its first invasion in October 1947.

Terrorism, it is said, has become endemic to modern society. It continues to be generated by recurrent social crises, arising from the increasing marginalisation of some sections of society caused by the indescriminate spread of capitalism and the free market economy, through the much vaunted process of globalisation. At its root the terrorist movement is born out of frustration and despair. Despair caused by social marginalisation, economic decline and political defeat. Someone once said that "young hope betrayed, transforms itself into bombs". Perceived injustice if allowed to continue unresolved, would transform into despair and then violence. According to Leon Trotsky the two emotions central to terrorism, are despair and vengeance.[18] The causes of these issues and the form they take, whether it be terrorism or otherwise, must be studied and understood in a scientific and objective manner.

With the start of cross-border terrorism by Pakistan the Kashmir dispute assumed alarming proportions. Pakistan's historical record of its commitment to honour its agreements and treaty obligations, which it freely entered into, not only with India, but also with other countries has been extremely poor. The 1947 Standstill Agreement with Jammu and Kashmir, the 1948 UN Resolution, 1949 Karachi Agreement, 1954 SEATO and CENTO agreements, 1966 Tashkent Declaration, 1972 Simla Agreement, 1988 Geneva Accords with Afghanistan, 1999 Lahore Declaration, and so on stand out. When the Kashmir agitation picked up steam the Berlin Wall was being pulled down, the mighty Red Army had been forced out of Afghanistan by rag-tag bands of Islamic guerillas a year earlier and geographical boundaries were being redrawn across Eastern Europe and Central Asia.[19] Thus, it was no surprise then that the votaries of *azadi* thought that India too would close shop in Kashmir. But this did not happen.

However, Pakistan's waging a covert war through trans-national terrorism has a strong religious base. It was during the regime of General Zia-ul-Haq that Islamabad began to use terror as a weapon to fight war. The strategy had found a sound footing from a book '*Quranic Concept of War*' written by Brigadier S. K. Malik (Lahore, 1979).

In it, the Holy Quran was interpreted as requiring the believers to use terror as weapon of war. Unfortunately, the military dictator at that time, strongly recommended the book and its conclusions by stating that it brings out the "Quranic philosophy on the application of military force, within the context of the totality that is "JEHAD". The volume concluded that "*jehad*", the Quranic concept of total strategy, demands the preparation and application of total manpower and military instrument is one of its elements. It went on to say further that "The Holy Quran lays the highest emphasis on the preparation of war. The test of utmost preparation lies in our capability to instil terror into the hearts of the enemies". The merging of the concept of *jehad*, war and terrorism has also been pursued by Pakistan in the trans-national terrorism it imposes in Jammu and Kashmir. Incidentally, a combination of *jehad* terrorism war has also been pursued by Pakistan in Afghanistan for nearly three decades.

There can be no doubt that India is the victim of sustained low-level aggression by secessionist forces encouraged and abetted by Pakistan. The present thinking on terrorism can be divided into two schools of thought. One school of thought places the terrorist beyond the pale of civilised society and considers him anathema to civilisation and stigmatises him as a plain murderer who needs to be eliminated. But the second school of thought encourages an in-depth study of, and a systematic approach to understand and eradicate, the reasons that bring about such upheavals. The rational political, social and economic aspirations of peoples which when frustrated continuously give rise to full blown terrorism of the modern day, must be sifted out of the process of terroristic actions and looked at separately. Those political aspirations must be addressed honestly and seriously. The solutions that are employed must be made effective–legally and constitutionally, politically, economically and socially. The overall gained impression from the cross-border terrorism is that it relates to the second school of thought. Peace is more than the simple absence of war. It entails active engagement in the battle for identifying and rectifying the root causes of conflict.

The problem of cross-border terrorism took an alarming shape during 1988-89 for which solid ground had been prepared by the parties concerned. First, on the part of New Delhi it was a time to face realities on the ground and examine carefully the causes for the sense of alienation that the Kashmiris feel. The government is well advised to go into the history of the Kashmir issue in order to understand and appreciate how and when things went wrong and how the impass of this particular type came about. It is an open fact that the Government of India has, from the beginning, been ignoring the political, social, economical as well as cultural needs of the people of Jammu and Kashmir. The successive governments of the National Conference well alternated by the direct rule of New Delhi proved a disaster in real sense of the term. Farooq Abdullah's behaviour during his curtailed first term in 1983-84, has been described as that of "a little boy with a toy", and during the second as "a virtual abdication of governance."[20] He acquired the *sobriquet* "disco chief minister" because he was frequently sighted in discotheques in India cities, and he spent much of the rest of his time playing golf or vocationing abroad. His colleagues in government earned a reputation for corrupt practices. In a nutshell, the Kashmiris feel that Delhi's behaviour has been atrocious in that it has chosen to ignore them completely.

The wars of 1965 and 1971 had succeeded in freezing the problem of Kashmir, however, the post-war agreements with Pakistan failed to keep the promises inherent in those documents. The Simla Agreement of 1972 in particular provided that the two would respect the ceasefire line of December 17, 1971, and that neither side would seek to alter it unilaterally irrespective of mutual differences and legal interpretations. They also agreed to refrain from a threat or a use of force as the agreement itself was based on the principles of bilateral diplomacy and durable peace. Notwithstanding the benevolent spirit of Simla Pakistan continued to raise the issue of Kashmir at various international fora. A little latter of the signing of the agreement, Zulfikar Ali Bhutto, the then Prime Minister of Pakistan, had clearly stated that there would be no compromise on the principle of self-determination in Kashmir. General Zia-ul-Haq followed the same militant line on the matter and succeeded in keeping the issue alive at both, bilateral and international levels. However, the issue had become critical and closely related to it was Pakistan's perception regarding its role in the State of Jammu and Kashmir.

Domestic as well as international are the two important determinants that govern Pakistani action in the State. The period that was responsible for initiation and growth of cross-border terrorism largely witnessed the power rivalry between the democratically elected ruling elite and the military. Prime Minister Benazir Bhutto inherited a mixed economy. Tied to these were two experiments of democratic rule, one of which was carried out by her father; and populist Islamisation process that was used by all as a tool for legitimacy. Her task was not just to undo autocracy but build an economy and industry that had for long been propped up by external aid. Her success at keeping the army at bay had also been uncertain. Therefore, militant posture for her became a need of the hour and in such a situation Kashmir remained the most readymade tool.[21] In addition, it was just a chance that both India and Pakistan were embroiled in grim problems outside Kashmir–India in Punjab and Assam and Pakistan in the volatile steamy city of Karachi where armoured personnel carriers were now common sight in the streets. There were host of problems for Pakistan in other states as well apart from the continuing and running battle between the federal and Punjab government.[22] The then government of Pakistan was beholden to the army and to the President to remain in office.

At that time India too was ruled by a minority and weak government headed by V. P. Singh, supported by Bharatiya Janata Party and Hindu fundamentalism. The situation in India convinced Pakistan that this was the time to liberate Kashmir. Among the military stalwarts, General Chisti, Arif and Gul were of the view that when the government in India is weak it is vulnerable to military and political pressures in the valley along with direct and indirect international wish to settle the issue of Kashmir. Hence, they calculated that the situation would either lead to the decapitation of India by the loss of Kashmir and parts of Punjab as a result of developments on the ground or to an Indo-Pak deal by a softened and chastened India, and a tough and principled Pakistan. Finally they concluded that in either way, militarily or diplomatically, India would lose in Pakistani thinking and 1971 would be revenged and with Pakistani getting its parity with India.[23]

So far as the international determinants of the Pakistani action in Kashmir was concerned, it was tied to Islamabad's perception about

India's position regarding the state of Jammu and Kashmir. In the first place, Pakistan must have reason to believe that India would be reluctant to mobilise itself into a war over the issue. Reason for such a reluctance would lie both in civilian and military thinking in India. Democratic systems are rarely tuned to instantaneous response in the face of crisis because it is linked to the decision-making process of the political system. In India, while the military would be consulted, the decision about the war would be basically political. Islamabad's second perception was related to the situation in Kashmir itself. As the Government of India had implemented democracy in Jammu and Kashmir half-heartedly and on the other Pakistan perceived the accession on Kashmir to India as one attained by force, the Kashmiri population would welcome intervention by Pakistan to liberate it from India.

But finally was the consideration of international support that Pakistan hoped, particularly from the US and China. Pakistan has reason to believe that both United States and China along with others would extend international sympathy. Given the religious dimension of the issue Pakistan also counted on the continued support of the West Asian countries. At that time the Soviet Union, India's only ally was in a state of internal influx and Gorbachev himself had been supporting freedom movements in Eastern Europe. The Soviet system was also trying to cope with demands for change from its own ethnic minorities and nationalities. In Pakistan's perception India would find it difficult to get international support over its position in Kashmir. However, Pakistan's initial efforts to project Kashmir on the world stage failed because the major powers had other preoccupations and were loath to add a hoary contentious issue to their agenda.[24] The Simla Agreement came in handy for the world to put away the issue of Kashmir as the world knows that there can not be a radical solution short of war.

Deepening of Pak Policy

Pakistan has been using terrorism as an instrument of State policy, waging a low-intensity covertly planned conflict against India for over the last 25 years. This policy is predicated on the Pakistani calculation that as long as the levels of intrusive terrorist violence remains short of a threshold, Pakistan could inflict damage upon India without attracting any punitive action against itself. There is also the Pakistani assessment that important powers would be willing to tolerate the situation in Jammu and Kashmir as long as this terrorist violence does not expand into a general conflict between India and Pakistan. As a result the latter's collusion with *jehadi* groups operating in Kashmir has weakened Islamabad's ability to influence any future political dispensation in the Valley. Pakistan's chosen Kashmir policy has also exacerbated domestic problems in multiple ways that do not require retelling. This debilitating condition can only be changed if the Pakistani leaders come to accept the proposition that a principled position on the Kashmir dispute can not be successfully advanced through unprincipled means.[25] The real thrust of Pakistani terrorism in Jammu and Kashmir is not to give a chance to the people of the state to vote for their future but to channel the overflow of arms and mercenaries from the war-ravaged areas of Afghanistan. The involvement of foreign mercenaries and international religious extremist organisations has become a challenge for the Indian agencies. Unfortunately, these covert mercenaries are supported not only by Pakistan but by some other Islamic countries as well. Extraneous vested interests have developed in terms of Pan-Islamic agendas, narco-terrorism, arms sales and so on, which negatively affects the prospects of a reasonable dialogue focused on specific issues related to Kashmir.

Sporadic cross-border incidents along the Indo-Pak border were so surprise for New Delhi because it did not pose a threat to the either side. However, it got an alarming rate at the close of the Eighties and especially with the Soviet's withdrawal from Afghanistan. The Pakistani military's Inter-Services Intelligence (ISI) had, during the 1980s military regime of General Zia acquired resources and autonomy as well in co-ordination with the Central Intelligence Agency (CIA), who sponsored war against the Soviet take-over of Afghanistan. In the post-withdrawal phase the ISI was in a position to focus on the new war in Kashmir. It began to recruit Kashmiri youths for training and arming in Pak-controlled camps. It got, for the first time since 1947, a large number of Kashmiris' prepared to join the terrorist organisations managed and maintained by the ISI.[26] It was revealed in the recent book, *The Lost Rebellion*, written by Manoj Joshi, that once General Zia and Pakistan's ISI concocted the scheme of recruiting local disaffected Kashmiris, and arming and training them to become insurgents. Till 1987, Pakistan received only a trickle of recruits, but that turned into a flood after Rajiv Gandhi forced the National Conference into a shot-gun marriage with the Congress in 1987 and Farooq Abdullah allegedly rigged elections in the Valley to ensure his return to power. What followed then was a genuine insurgency?

The whole story began in late 1986 when Farooq Abdullah concluded a rapprochement with the Congress regime at the centre. Under its terms, he was reinstalled as chief minister pending fresh Assembly elections in March 1987, which he undertook to contest in alliance with the Congress Party. This alliance was deadly opposed by the Muslim United Front (MUF) coalition. It was mainly represented by a new generation of young men who born in the 1960s. The organisation was formed as an independent, pro-people entity to fight NC's opportunistic alliance with the detested Congress at the polls. The process and its outcome irrevocably tainted Farooq Abdullah and his supporters in the eyes of their former voters as just another clique, serving as tools of the Indian state in return for the spoils of political office.[27] This was the moment when the valley and some of its contiguous areas lost all residual confidence in India's political system. With this, the Kashmir conflict witnessed a changed mood of the younger generation in the Valley.

Apart from this internal factor, there were international elements too that gave a helping hand to Pakistan and the ISI in spreading their network in the state of Jammu and Kashmir. International events, particularly that took place in late 1989 and early 1990, played an important role. The first Palestinian intifada against Israeli occupation was a significant reference point, as was the collapse of repressive one-Party regimes in central and eastern Europe after mass demonstrations in the autumn of 1989. It was noted by a Srinagar scholar, "We felt that if the Berlin wall could be dismantled, so could be the Line of Control."[28] The young Kashmiri guerillas, for their part, were inspired by the 1989 Soviet withdrawal from Afghanistan in the face of Afghan Mujahideen resistance and success of Tamil Tiger guerillas in Sri Lanka against the vastly superior Indian force. It also became clear soon that these foreign expeditions were fundamentally misguided and increasingly costly in terms of resources and combat casualities.

From here onwards, the ISI has successfully financed, cultivated and armed a powerful section of the Kashmiri people. By 1990, there were over 30 militant groups in Kashmir and 29 of these had been receiving assistance and shelter in Pakistan. A US task force on terrorism and unconventional warfare, set up by a House Republican Research Committee, covered, in its report, various aspects of Islamic terrorism, its origin and spread to Afghanistan, Sudan and Iraq. The report held ISI responsible along with Pakistan for abetting and sponsoring terrorism in Kashmir as part of its over all effort to promote Islamic international terrorism. It noted that in 1986 Pakistan expanded its operations to sponsor and promote separation, primarily in Kashmir, as a strategic long-term programme.[29] Among the most crucial activities of ISI were to propagate religious fundamentalism in small but lethal doses and train and indoctrinate selected leaders from Kashmir to create militant cadres. The report said that several youth from Kashmir valley and Poonch district in Jammu region were given extensive training in the use of automatic weapons, sabotage and attacks on security forces.[30] The US State Department and the various reports published by several agencies confirmed that the extent of the growing state support for terrorism and insurgence in Kashmir is clearly reflected in the evolution of the organisations operating there.

The relation between the two had undergone a sea change when they exploded nuclear devices in May-June 1998. After the explosion, Tariq Altaf, a Pakistani Foreign Office spokesman, reiterated Nawaz Sharif's assertion saying that Pakistan was ready to have a non-aggression pact with India but 'after just settlement of Kashmir dispute'. He urged India to take up the Kashmir issue on "priority basis" as it was root cause of tension between the two neighbours. Despite the fact that Vajpayee had cautioned Pakistan not to internationalise the Kashmir issue, the militants–mostly from Afghanistan and Pakistan find it easier to shoot and kill the people in the mountainous parts of Jammu and Kashmir region. Further Pakistan's ISI wanted to involve the Jammu region in violence to show the international community that the entire Jammu and Kashmir was disturbed – to strengthen its points of plebiscite in the state.[31] In a nutshell, the militants were doing what they had been assigned to do while Pakistan was claiming that it was not involved in any manner in the armed militancy in Jammu and Kashmir.

The net result of cross-border terrorism was the full-fledged war between the two at Kargil sector. It broke out in May-June 1999 which ended in a humiliating defeat of Pakistan at India's hand. Formerly Islamabad had fully expected the big powers to intervene because of the potential nuclear peril, thereby effectively internationalising the Kashmir dispute. When nothing of the short occurred, and the entire exercise became dangerously counter-productive, Islamabad decided to pull back the intruders from Kargil.[32] But the end of Kargil war did not mean the end of continuing hostility to India. The so-called withdrawal of Pakistani forces from Kargil the border had not regained normalcy and guns continue to boom. Added to this was the calculated revival by Pakistan of cross-border-terrorism, and resort to provocative anti-Indian action along various points across the LoC.

As an after-effect of Kargil the Government of Nawaz Sharif was overthrown in a military coup on 12 October 1999. General Pervez Musharraf, Chief of Army Staff, took over the Administration and again a new chapter of military rule was opened in Pakistan. The new ruler, in a televised announcement on 17 October 1999, as a gesture of goodwill towards India, declared unilateral military de-escalation along the border. His address also included an offer to resume "result-oriented" talks with India on "all issues" but said, "Pakistan would continue its support to the Kashmiri people for their right to self-determination" and added that India must honour all UN resolutions on Kashmir. At a later stage in July 2000 when Bharat Bhushan, a correspondent of *The Hindustan Times*, asked General Musharraf about different aspects of terrorism, the latter had replied that as far as the hardware and the weapons of terror were concerned, "We certainly want to curb the uncontrolled display and holding of weapons and we are taking action in this direction. But this is easier said than done. To disarm and de-weaponised a region completely is next to impossible."[33] On the ideological front he presented his own definition of *jehad* and distinguished it from terrorism. He refused to equate these two perhaps in reference to Kashmir and said, "jehad means struggle in the path of

God, opposing victimisation against Muslims wherever it exists. But the world at large did not share Musharraf's perception of *jehad.*

In this context, on times without number Islamabad has been told by countries of the world and its leaders as well to stop cross-border terrorism and reminded the assurance that the former had given to world organisations. Recently in the year 2002, the two most powerful associations of nations–the Group of Eight and the European Union through their adopted statements agreed that "Pakistan must put a permanent stop to terrorist activity organising from territory under its control. It called on Pakistan to take further concrete action in accordance with the assurances it has already given and with its international obligations, including UN Security Council Resolution 1373 (2001), to stop infiltration across the Line of Control and to prevent terrorist groups from operating from territory under its control, also through closing of training camps."[34] What seems to be clear, and all agree, is that the General has not done enough to curb militants. As military head and President Musharraf would have no problem in ordering terror camps in PoK to be closed. Of the powerful nations, Washington and London even doubted the power the General has over the *jehadi* groups. They believe that Musharraf's influence is limited, that large numbers of ISI officers operate independent of him. They refer to the December 13, 2001, attacks on Indian Parliament and the Karachi suicide attack on French nationals as evidence that Musharraf is not the puppet master of all *jehadis.*

But despite many stresses and strains on the Pakistan military over the last few years, the present day regime's chain of command remains intact. The logistical and communication linkages between the ISI and the Pakistani army units on the one hand and terrorist cadres on the other continue. The pattern and number of infiltrations from Pakistan into India across the LoC have been more or less at the same level. The terrorist training and launching camps which were closed briefly after January 12, 2002, in which Musharraf promised a crackdown on terror, have been reopened and relocated in other parts of Pakistan and PoK, the northern areas, the Punjab and the North-West Frontier Province. There are an estimated 70 to 75 such camps which continue to be active. India also has information that the Harkat-ul-Mujahideen and Lashkar-e-Taiba cadres are now located in PoK. There are at least

12 launching camps being used for funnelling terrorists across the LoC into India in Jammu and Kashmir. The estimate of the Indian security forces is that there are about 3,000 to 3,500 militants under training in Pakistan.

India and the US both are uncertain about the future course of action that Musharraf would like to take. But they need to keep the working closely on the goals they share in relation to Pakistan. Not only for the present but also in recent past India's threat of war and US diplomacy have worked well in conjunction, with each reinforcing the other's message to Pakistan. Recent revelations of Pakistan's help to Iran, North Korea and Libya in their nuclear weapons programmes have further fuelled American distrust and the latter had expressed its unhappiness. Equally on the other the Western world, including the Chinese should also pause and reflect on the consequences of supplying sophisticated arms and technology to Pakistan. Transferring the M-11 missiles to Islamabad, even in unassembled form, is to give into the hands of potential forces of destruction, the wherewithal to strike at civil society in the name of *jehad.*

One possible way to minimise Indo-US pressure on Islamabad to end the cross-border terrorism is to start a dialogue between the two and thereby improve relations. Difficulties are more with Pakistan than with India. Today there is a rare consensus on this in Pakistani civil society, born of very diverse reasons. The religious parties favour this on the ground that it would increase Pakistan's capacity to resist pressure by the US to get more deeply involved in the 'war against terror', Pakistan's liberals, both in politics and business, want it in order to further consolidate the economy. With its much smaller economy, it cannot indefinitely continue to try and match India. While nuclear weapons now provide it security against any alleged Indian hegemonism, nuclear sabre-rattling of the Kargil war period will not work. Equally, it is no longer possible for Islamabad to back proxy forces, even in the name of religion. This is more so because such forces are now turning against their Pakistani army mentors.[35] The demands for public funds for education, public health and so are no less compelling.

Kashmir is the speed-breaker on the road connecting India and Pakistan. Kashmiri Muslims are unhappy with our presence, but they are also doubtful about having close relations with Pakistan. With its best chance ever to end the scourge of cross-border terrorism, India needs to closely monitor the ground situation, continue to breathe down Pakistan's neck, and speak up whenever the circumstances demand. India's insistence on deeds, not just words reflects not only the emergent maturity in its foreign policy but also signals that war as an Indian policy option remains primed for exercise if Musharraf refuse to understand the matter in proper perspective.

Continuation as a 'Core Issue'

Once, in Pakistan's view the problem of Jammu and Kashmir was accepted as a "dispute", it began to consider the same as 'core issue'. In yester years, whenever, Indian over-cautiousness had taken the form of hedging after agreeing to discuss the problem of Jammu and Kashmir along with other issues which need to be resolved between the two countries, Pakistan had joined the offer of talks to the condition that the core issue of Jammu and Kashmir be settled first of all. On the dispute they failed to present any concrete suggestion officially except the context of outdated UN resolution. Over the years Pakistan has fashioned the terms of reference for discussion on Kashmir in the following concepts: Self-determination, the Muslim identity of the people of Kashmir, violation of human rights, the denial of representative government in Jammu and Kashmir[36] etc. There is no doubt that we had to contradict these Pakistani arguments to establish the validity of our views on the status of Kashmir.

First of all, Pakistan needs to get rid of the imprisoned mindset that far from being "Core" the issue of Jammu and Kashmir is one of many, and certainly not central to peace talks. There is socio-economic and socio-cultural growth to consider. However, over the years, India has also developed a duality of approach in case of Kashmir. Right from the period 1977 till 1996, on the one hand we have said that the Kashmir issue should be discussed and resolved "bilaterally with Pakistan", on the other, we connived from discussing the substance of the issue on the basis of the argument that the status of Kashmir as an integral part of India, cannot subject to any negotiations. Instead of adopting this contradictory logic we could have boldly agreed to discuss the Kashmir issue with Pakistan, emphasising that the substance of the dispute is Pakistan questioning the legality and constitutionally valid status of Jammu and Kashmir as an integral part of India . Our refusing to discuss the Kashmir issue specially and in substance has affected the credibility of our stance in the international community of which Pakistan has taken full advantage.

With the change of guards in New Delhi and Islamabad the talks between the two revived during 1996-97. It was for the first time since 1972 that New Delhi agreed to have talks with Pakistan on Kashmir. Earlier India pledged its support to the Simla Agreement but did not discuss the future of Kashmir. We made ourselves believe that there was no need to have talks with Pakistan. But Islamabad continued to treat the issue as a dispute between India and Pakistan and always emphasised on the third party mediation/intervention and wished its solution as per the UN resolution. No Indian government can accept the secession of Jammu and Kashmir and no Pakistani government can accept the LoC. At Simla in 1972, the LoC was sought to be imposed in the wake of a military defeat. It failed as such attempts do eventually. It is worse than pointless for a leader to embark on a peace process unless he is clear and realistic about the product he seeks, the concessions that are on offer and the ones he is himself prepared to make.[37] Both must be ready for a compromise and then only move forward.

Three round of Secretary–level talks were held between the two countries, the first followed, when the two Prime Ministers met at Male on 12 May 1997. In the talks, right from the beginning, Pakistan insisted that unless the "core issue of Kashmir" was solved, bilateral relations would never improve. It also implied that the Indian approach of normalising relations in other spheres would only serve to provide a cosmetic touch and would not materially alter the relations. While India continued to insist that it was ready to discuss Kashmir, normalisation of relations in other spheres, especially commercial, economic and people to people would help accelerate the process of normalisation.[38] The new dispensation was, no doubt, hopeful of solving the issue of Kashmir, was cautioned, 'The Gujral doctrine should not become a mantra. It is a commendable policy and has worked well in Sri Lanka, Bangladesh and Nepal. But in the case of Pakistan it must be applied to the extent that we get the right response from the other side. The doctrine's success will depend on matching deed for deed'.

The second round of Foreign Secretary–level talk was held in Islamabad in June 1997. As a proof of good gesture, New Delhi in haste, to achieve forward movement, agreed to constitute six working groups to discuss as many as problems it had identified. Islamabad's allegation was that there was no separate group constituted on Kashmir. The Government of Nawaz Sharif would have been satisfied if only a separate group was constituted to resume talks on Kashmir as disclosed by the Pakistani premier in conversation with Kuldip Nayar, a visiting Indian journalist, 'I do not mind how long time it take provided we begin to discuss Kashmir.'[39] However, discussing Kashmir as a separate subject in a separate working group does not automatically imply that India would compromise in any manner on the status of Kashmir. Pakistan always discussed Kashmir as the first item on the agenda, but moved on to discuss other subjects in a practical manner. The eight point charter of priorities chalked out by the Foreign Secretaries during the talks also included confidence-building measures.

In the third round of talks that started in New Delhi, in the middle of September 1997, they did not succeed in breaking their earlier position. The Foreign-Secretary-level talks ended with no forward movement on outstanding bilateral issues, particularly a mechanism for discussing Kashmir due to the apparent lack of desire on Pakistan's part to show any progress. The deadlock on Kashmir issue continued as a Pakistani foreign office spokesman quoted, "Pakistan considers Kashmir as the "Core Issue" which must be addressed urgently and effectively and a resolution on this contentious issue found in accordance with the UN resolutions. In the circumstances, the talks failed and even the opportunity provided by the President of the US in New York, where the Prime Ministers of India and Pakistan were meeting with the former, could not procure any concrete result as Islamabad missed no time to clear that the talks with India would continue only after the 'core issue' of Jammu and Kashmir was given "due place" and discussed and negotiated in a "substantive and specific manner."

The political relation between the two was charged in March 1998 when a Bharatiya Janata Party-led coalition took over in New Delhi under the premiership of Atal Bihari Vajpayee. It culminated soon by explosion of nuclear devices by India on 11 and 13 May 1998, followed by Pakistan on 28 and 30 May. The nuclear tests done by them have introduced a new sense of urgency in Indo-Pak relations and unfortunately refocussed attention on Kashmir as a focal point of the dispute between the two countries. It meant the linkages between Kashmir and the possibility of the use of nuclear weapons took a more serious dimension. The nuclear game in South Asia now requires mature handling by both countries if they are to demolish that the argument of non-nuclear weapons state that the developing countries are too irresponsible to handle such weapons of mass destruction. At least, the explosion has made Kashmir an international issue. Since Kashmir was where the conflict was occurring, the world demanded that India and Pakistan either denuclearise themselves or settle the Kashmir dispute.

As indicated by the world opinion, they are bound to change the *status quo* or to accept it. It provided Pakistan an opportunity to internationalise its dispute with India, especially Kashmir. While expressing for a dialogue with India, Islamabad has also indicated its wish for an international guarantor in respect of any bilateral accord that might be reached. Nawaz Sharif, while addressing a joint session of the two houses of Parliament on 6th June 1998, added that today world attention has been diverted to Kashmir. They are realising now that without its solution peace cannot return to South Asia and at the same time criticised the leading powers for their failure to implement the UN resolution on Kashmir for the right of self-determination of the Kashmiri people. In the same vein, Atal Bihari Vajpayee, the new Prime Minister of India, while taking part in a debate on nuclear issue in the Rajya Sabha on 8th June 1998, reiterated New Delhi's desire for earliest resumption of official talks with Pakistan on all outstanding issues including Kashmir but ruled out any third party mediation in the dialogue process.

Two important events of the recent past were Atal Bihari Vajpayee's visit to Lahore in February 1999, followed by a return tour paid by General Pervez Musharraf to New Delhi in July 2001. On both the occasions though no forward movement seemed to be taken, exchange of views took place. The Lahore Declaration signed by the two

Prime Ministers, issued on 21st February, resolved to intensify efforts to settle all outstanding issues, including Jammu and Kashmir. However, the Declaration contained Pakistan's inability to reflect any softening of the position on Jammu and Kashmir. At Agra, Musharraf insisted on the centrality of Kashmir to the peace process but also indicated at the famous breakfast on July 16, 2001 that the plebiscite idea was abandoned. Conceptually, the conflict in Kashmir has four important dimension impacting on Indo-Pak relations and the future of South Asia as a whole. First, the role of state actors, second centrifugal forces who at the present are out of power structure, third the question of security and insecurity engulfing the people of Jammu and Kashmir and fourth the broad question of religion and ethnicity.[40] If these four dimensions are analysed the process of conflict resolution in Kashmir could be understood in a better manner and normalcy in Kashmir then would be projected as a peace in real sense otherwise it is then a myth.

4.3 Event of 9/11 and Kashmir Problem

In the recent past India has been considered increasingly as an emerging power and a key stabilising player in the South Asian subcontinent. In the situation the international community is no longer keen to discuss Kashmir or force a solution; it knows India will not be pushed. The stress is now on India and Pakistan finding their own answers, and not much attention is being given to the wishes of the Kashmiris themselves.[41] However, the event of 9/11 proved a turning point not only in the history of America but in the concepts of Kashmir issue too. The dynamics of Kashmir conflict have undergone a drastic change since 9/11 due to dramatic changes brought by US War on Terrorism in the region. The US focus on fighting terrorism, extremism and Islamic fundamentalism, most of the times all linked together has put tremendous pressure on Pakistan's Kashmir policy. The event of September 2001 had helped create a favourable environment for India in three ways. First, India could succeed in framing Pakistan as a part of the problem of terrorism, as there was an organic link between Pakistan's support for radical Islamic groups in Kashmir and Afghanistan. This has highlighted the role of Pakistani intelligence agencies in supporting the Taliban and other radical Islamic militants operating in Kashmir and Afghanistan. Second, India has been able to get the US support in fighting terrorism and both countries have been applying joint pressure on Pakistan to abandon support for such radical Islamic groups operating from Afghanistan and Pakistani-controlled territories. Third, the distinction between terrorists and freedom fighters has been blurred in the post-9/11 phase. In the name of freedom fighters, these radical groups are involved in terrorist activities.[42] With the blurring of distinction between freedom struggle and terrorism, international community has become more intolerant to terrorism.

In broader sense India argued the resistance in India-held-Kashmir is primarily a issue of terrorism and that Pakistan is sponsoring and supporting "Cross-border-terrorism" in Indian Kashmir. Even before 9/11 and US war on terrorism, India had consistently accused Pakistan of waging "proxy war", "low-intensity conflict" and "cross-border-terrorism" in India- held Kashmir.[43] The event of 9/11 provided India a golden opportunity to push forward its own agenda of counter-terrorism in Kashmir. Consequently, India tried to combine the issues of War on Terrorism and Kashmir so as to draw maximum benefit from the changed international opinion in favour of fighting terrorism, lock stock and barrel. In line India strongly contested in Pakistan's inclusion in the US war on terrorism and repeatedly urged on the US to include Kashmir in its war on terror. New Delhi also questioned Pakistan's credentials in becoming partner in US counter-terrorism strategy while being a "source", "hub" or "epicenter" of terrorism and offered unconditionally to the US, all material and operational support for its military campaign against terrorism in Afghanistan.

In past decades Pakistan has always looked at Kashmir struggle as a freedom struggle and supported the right of self-determination for the Kashmiris and pledged moral, political and diplomatic support to the Kashmir cause. Ever since 1990 uprising in India-held-Kashmir, Pakistan stepped up its support for the Kashmiris that allegedly included material support to the fighters in Kashmir.[44] In the context Pakistan was deeply concerned about the potential fallout of 9/11 on its Kashmir cause that unleashed US global war on terror and included Pakistan, its regional ally, in this fight. After 9/11 Pakistan cleverly drew a distinction between freedom struggle and terrorism and made concerted effort that War on Terrorism (WoT) should not affect the Kashmiris fight for the right of self-determination. Pakistan distinguished between the "acts of legitimate resistance and freedom struggles and acts of terrorism". Pakistan's concern flowed from its principled stance and support to the freedom struggle in Kashmir, which increasingly came under pressure from India and world opinion after 9/11. At the United Nations General Assembly (UNGA) Musharraf observed: 'the just struggle of a people for self-determination and liberation from colonial or foreign occupation cannot be outlawed in the name of terrorism.'[45] In the same year (2002) Musharraf in his speech at the South Asian Association for Regional Co-operation (SAARC) Summit, stated, 'We regard terrorism as a grave threat to civil society. We abhor violence, we are determined to eliminate terrorism and therefore, fully implement the SAARC Convention for Combating Terrorism.'[46]

Thus, Pakistan has adopted dual policy in relation to terrorism in Kashmir. Within the broader international setting Pakistan has repeatedly condemned terrorism in all forms and manifestations, but strongly believes that terrorism or terrorist activities cannot be eradicated unless the causes of terrorism are removed. There are at least five elements in Pakistan's definition of terrorism. First, Pakistan considers terrorism a threat to humanity and human civilisation and in principle condemns all acts of terrorism anywhere in the world. Second, Pakistan maintains that the root causes of terrorism should be addressed as a part of the international campaign against terrorism. Third, the fight against terrorism should include "State terrorism" implying case of Kashmir. Fourth, a distinction should be drawn between freedom struggles and terrorism. Fifth, a distinction should be made between the Islamic religion and terrorism.

But in post-9/11 period Musharraf, although slowly, came to the ground realities in Kashmir. Earlier the Pakistani military establishment had a wrong perception that as long as Pakistan co-operated with the United States against Taliban and Al Queda, Washington would turn a blind eye to its policy in Kashmir. This proved to be a miscalculation as there was a growing recognition within Pakistan that proxy war and the use of terror, violence and religious extremism in Jammu and Kashmir are not globally accepted, but are counterproductive, in almost everyway. Gradually even Musharraf had realised that Pakistan's support for insurgency only helped undermine the political credibility of militants.[47] Under growing Indian/US international pressure,

Musharraf defined parameters for Kashmir struggle, while keeping the commitment to Kashmir cause intact. In his 12th January 2002 speech, Musharraf pledged, 'No organisatation will be allowed to indulge in terrorism in the name of Kashmir.... Anyone found involved in any terrorist act would be dealt with sternly. Strict action will be taken against any Pakistani individual, group or organisation found involved in terrorism within or outside the country.[48] He banned Lashkar and Jaish that India alleged were involved in such activity but at the same time, reiterated Islamabad's commitment to Kashmir struggle, 'Kashmir runs in our blood.... We will continue to extend our moral, political and diplomatic support to Kashmiris. We will never budge an inch from our principled stand on Kashmir.[49] However, the external pressure to roll back the Jihadi culture and cross-border terrorism had, no doubt, demoralised the groups operating in India. Equally significant, the world community has made it clear to Islamabad that regardless of the moral legitimacy of Pakistani claims on Kashmir, its policy of waging a low-intensity war using Islamic fundamentalist proxies in Jammu and Kashmir is unacceptable. What makes the situation worse for Musharraf was Pakistan's domestic elites stand divided on his Kashmir policy. The Islamic parties want him continue the Jihadi in Kashmir while mainstream opposition parties and liberal intellectuals were in favour of dismantling the Jihadi infrastructure and had made a strong case for terminating the insurgency in Indian Kashmir. These liberal intellectuals and mainstream politicians were of the opinion that so long as the military-intelligence establishment continues to allow such militant groups to operate from within the Pakistan-occupied territories to continue their operations in Indian Kashmir, Pakistan will be unable to achieve domestic and external peace.[50] For decades, Pakistan tried simultaneously to be both Islamic and modern. Modernism demands secularism even where a state religion exists. Now, after September 2001, Pakistan could no longer ride both the horses.

In last decades the Indian discourse on Kashmir has too changed drastically. The country's mainstream discourse traditionally considered the issue as one driven and created purely by Pakistani interference. Everyone seemed oblivious to the fact that Pakistan had been given the space for this interference due to India's traditional mishandling of Kashmir. This mainstream thinking was infused in the media discourse.

Bollywood films and popular writing portrayed Kashmir as a terrorism-infested region that needs to be cleansed of Pakistani agents.[51] It tended to draw a picture of Kashmiris as supporters of terrorism and Pakistan. This thinking is undergoing a positive transformation. At present there is a growing awareness about the nuances of the Kashmir problem, and about the follies that the Indian state has committed there.[52] Statecraft has failed Kashmir in spite of plethora of talks and proposals primarily because of their poor outreach, lack of sincere political will and absence of a mass-centred approach.[53]

Thus, for varied reasons after 9/11 the US was in a position to influence both India and Pakistan to mutually resolve all contentious issues. Even before 2001 India hoped that President Bill Clinton would address the problems that the Indian Government faced in Kashmir, sympathetically, especially after his efforts in Israel and Northern Ireland. But there was no commitment from the US administration become embroiled in what the issue was widely regarded as a matter for the UN. The attack on America by Al-Queda and tracing of that organisation's headquarters to Afghanistan changed the security environment in South Asia that followed the announcement of George William Bush that America was to launch a war on terror.[54] At the juncture India quickly equated the event to the terrorist attacks of Islamic groups in Kashmir as a similar problem. The American-led coalition operations in Afghanistan in 2001, the severe international pressure on Musharraf to wind up the Jehadi culture and the presence of US Special Forces in Pakistan sent shock waves through its military-intelligence establishment. The changed circumstance in a new way, encourage anybody to think that the US can be an effective mediator in bringing both India and Pakistan to the negotiating table. Among the reasons, the first is that America is close to both New Delhi and Islamabad, it has entered into a historic nuclear deal with India and has chosen Pakistan as its ally in its global war against terrorism. Secondly, as the world sole superpower that US has proved that it can haughtily influence the course of events. Thirdly, Musharraf must be expecting a sympathetic response from the US by cooperating it in every possible way to combat Islamic terrorism.[55] In addition, the US too needed India-Pakistan cooperation to fight its war on terrorism, which was mainly directed against Al-Queda and its operatives/ remnants in the region. In the situation although it refused to include

Kashmir in its war on terror mission, but it persisted exerted pressure on Pakistan to address India's concern on terrorism. Thus, the US factor, as a mediator, encouraged both India and Pakistan to stick to the peace process and start a fresh dialogue despite a series of terrorist violence in different parts of India.

Indo-Pak Relations in Post- 9/11

In fact, in a tense Indo-Pak relations, a thaw between the two countries began in April 2003 that resulted in a ceasefire on the LoC on 26th November 2003. Further on 6th January 2004, at the end of the South Asian Association for Regional Cooperation (SAARC) summit in Islamabad, the two sides signed a joint statement that revived composite dialogue. The joint statement formed the basis of current composite dialogue that hinged on drawing a delicate balance between India's concern on terrorism and Pakistan's apprehension regarding the marginalisation of the Kashmir issue. The statement, issued on the occasion said, 'The resumption of the composite dialogue will lead to peaceful settlement of all bilateral issues, including Jammu and Kashmir. In it, Islamabad agreed that it 'would not permit any territory under Pakistan's control to be used to support terrorism in any manner.'[56] In the summit the two countries also agreed to resume talks after a gap of almost two years and it ended the diplomatic impasse since the Agra Summit of July 2001. Agra Summit failed as Pakistan insisted on a solve-Kashmir-first policy and India refused to let Pakistan get away with that line.[57] India also refrained its stand for the need to discuss all (eight) issues instead on just focusing on Kashmir, which has been Pakistan's core demand.

India and Pakistan conducted three round of talks between February 2004 and September 2006. From the first round of talks held in March 2004 Kashmir and terrorism have dominated the composite dialogue. The experience of peace process indicates that India and Pakistan sharply differ regarding progress on Kashmir and terrorism. Pakistan feels that there has not been concrete progress on the resolution of Kashmir while it has done everything to address India's concern about cross-border terrorism. Conversely, India feels that Pakistan has not given up the Jehadi option on Kashmir and questions its sincerity and commitment to curb cross-border terrorism. The joint statements issued at the end of each round of talks on the peace and security in Kashmir and the foreign secretaries review talks, show that both sides want to register the importance they attach to their respective concern on Kashmir and terrorism. For instance in September 2004, the joint statement at the end of the foreign secretaries review meeting underscored, 'carrying the process forward in an atmosphere free from terrorism and violence' and continue with the serious and sustained dialogue to find a peaceful negotiated final settlement of the Kashmir dispute.[58] Likewise in October 2005, the joint statement issued at end of second round talks reiterated that possible option for a peaceful, negotiated settlement of the issue of Jammu and Kashmir should be explored in a sincere, purposeful and forward-looking manner.[59] It also reaffirmed determination not to allow terrorism to impede the peace process. Earlier in an additional effort in November 2004, Dr Manmohan Singh during his first visit to Srinagar, called on young people to join him in the adventure of building a new India and a new Kashmir.[60] His expression was a step further in solving the issue peacefully. In 2006, five working groups were set up by the Prime Minister to facilitate the peace progress at ground level. These were: On Ensuring Good Governance headed by N.C. Saxena, on Confidence Building Measures across segments of society in the State headed by Mohamed Hamid Ansari, on Strengthening Relations across Line of Control headed by a former foreign secretary M. Rasgotra, on Economic Development of Jammu and Kashmir headed by D.C. Rangarajan and on Centre-State Relations headed by Justice S.A. Saghir.[61]

In an important development on the issue Dr Manmohan Singh and Pakistani President General Pervez Musharraf met in September 2006 that followed a joint statement issued on 16th of the month. In the meeting the leaders decided to continue the joint search for mutually acceptable options for a peaceful negotiated settlement of all disputes between India and Pakistan including the issue of Jammu and Kashmir in a sincere and purposeful manner. It emphasised the need to build on convergences and narrow down divergences. The leaders strongly condemned all acts of terrorism and agreed that terrorism is a scourage that needs to be effectively dealt with. They decided to put in place 'an India-Pakistan anti-terrorism institutional mechanism to identify and implement counter-terrorism initiatives and investigations.' The leaders on both sides have showed considerable political will and commitment to sustain the composite dialogue on Kashmir and terrorism.

The leadership on both sides had, during the dialogue process, showed considerable political will and commitment to sustain the composite dialogue on Kashmir and terrorism. But their statements from time to time have voiced sharp difference in their respective stances over improving situation in Kashmir and the resolution of the dispute. Indian leadership has continued to highlight the issue of cross-LoC infiltration and terrorism and connected it directly with the reduction of troops from the valley and improvement of human rights situation there. In contrast Pakistani leadership continued to make efforts to keep Kashmir at the centre of the dialogue and emphasised on the Kashmir specific Confidence Building Measures (CBMs) that may provide relief to the Kashmiris on the ground. In this context it is also a fact that the militants trained and armed by the Pakistani army and the ISI are not entirely creatures of Pakistani state. These militant groups are semi-autonomous in nature and often pursue their agenda independently on the priorities and policy shifts in Islamabad. Some militant groups such as the Lashker-e-Taiba have vowed to continue the fight in Jammu and Kashmir regardless of any changes in Pakistan's agenda.[62] It was despite the fact that after the event of 9/11 the US has categorically told Pakistan to help destroy the Taliban and its Islamic associates, or risk being treated as a terrorist state itself.

Unfortunately for a brief period in 2006-2007 New Delhi suspended composite dialogue after Mumbai train blasts on 11th July 2006 which was restored only when Pakistan agreed to the formation of an anti- terrorism institutional mechanism to address India's concern on terrorism. A joint anti-terror panel was set up in this regard which had its first meeting in March 2007. However, sharp differences between the two had arisen in the very first meeting as Pakistan maintained that incidents inside the Indian State of Jammu and Kashmir would not come in the purview of the anti-terror panel while India insisted that it should cover all terror incidents whether they are in India or Kashmir. In their last round of foreign secretaries talks held on 13-14th March 2007, the two sides agreed to ensure implementation of already agreed Kashmir-related CBMs.

Thus, the net result of the last three rounds of talks showed that the normalisation process has moved forward, while conflict resolution process has not showed much concrete progress. So far there have been some Kashmir-specific CBMs such as a ceasefire on the LoC, resumption of Srinagar-Muzaffarabad bus service in April 2005, the opening of five cross-LoC points in the wake of earthquake of October 8, 2005, starting of Poonch-Rawalkot bus service and an agreement on the truck service on Srinagar-Muzaffarabad route. In addition, All Parties Hurriyat Conference (APHC) leaders were allowed to pay few visits to Azad Jammu and Kashmir (AJK) and Pakistan, and India and Pakistani journalists visited the two Kashmirs. There was agreement on monthly flag meetings along the LoC between the local area commanders. The benefit of the Kashmir-specific CBMs have, however, been limited due to the difficulties in way of their operationalisation. But in the whole process US has played an important role in initiating and sustaining India-Pakistan composite dialogue. It had extended support to bilateral efforts to resolve Kashmir dispute. US is interested in ensuring strategic stability and durable peace in the region. The US war on terrorism would continue to engage US in the region that in return would imply that US would stay actively engaged in India-Pakistan peace process.

No Forward Movement

In the history of Kashmir dispute, the year 2008 is important for various reasons. It witnessed the successful assembly election in the State of Jammu and Kashmir, change of guard in Pakistan but above all – the worst terror attack on 26th November 2008 in which Mumbai, the financial capital of India, was the target. The 26/11 attack on Mumbai was in several respects very different from those in the past. It was a bold, brave frontal, ferocious attack in which terrorists were well prepared. Once again the attack demonstrated how incapable India is as a nation to prepare itself to fight against terrorism. It not only shocked the nation, but also gave us an impression that we cannot boast of preparedness, but the reality is all together different.[63] Naturally the terror attack in Mumbai at different places in the city had furthered India-Pakistan relations in all spheres near collapse and created a war-like situation between the two countries.[64] At the time the main concern of US policy-makers was somehow not to let this grave provocation cause an escalation of India-Pakistan tension that would give Pakistan a ruse for not concentrating on its task on the western front.[65] Even in the years 2010 and 2011 several terror attacks were made in different parts of the country, at New Delhi and Mumbai in particular. Thus, the large scale terror activities on the part of Pakistani extremist groups had marred the peace prospect of the problem of Jammu and Kashmir.

Even after closing the composite dialogue and earlier, perhaps under international pressure Pakistan took several steps to further the new ideas. It extended support to the moderate faction of the All Parties Hurriyat Conference, and distanced itself from the hardline faction led by Ali Shah Geelani. The "back-channel" diplomacy was used in arriving at a compromise on the issue of travelling documents, regarding the Srinagar-Muzaffarabad bus service. Back-channel negotiations also began discussing the four-point formula – which many observed was secretive, but made significant progress in developing areas of aspirational convergence. The LoC was thrown open for travel and trade and intra Kashmir dialogue got underway – albeit in a non- structured and sporadic manner. As a new government came into power in 2008, the back-channel dialogue came to a halt. Zardari's government has gradually reverted to Pakistan's traditional stance- but continues to support cross-LoC interactions, which is very much in line with the vision of Pakistan People's Party (PPP) for "soft LoC." In August 2008, President Zardari advocated a policy of "soft borders" so that the people of the two parts of Kashmir can meet, travel and do business – but without compromising Pakistan's traditional position on Kashmir.[66] Zardari's administration has pulled back its sponsorship of Jihad in Kashmir, and has stated that it wants a solution through a tripartite dialogue that involves Kashmiris and fulfils the aspirations of the Kashmiri people. The President Musharraf earlier and his successor in Pakistan have given assurance to India and the international community that terrorist would not be allowed to use the territories under their control. However, the Pakistan establishment is not true to its words and continues to encourage the Jehadi elements.[67] Pakistan has become the chief proponent of Islamic Jehadi terrorism and unashamedly adopts it as an instrument of state policy to achieve strategic gains.

Among the proposals put forward by Musharraf and other Pakistani leader to resolve the Kashmir issue was the Chenab Formula road map. Based on the "Dixon Plan" the Chenab Formula assigned Ladakh to India, Gilgit Baltistan (G-B) to Pakistan, proposed a plebiscite in the Kashmir Valley and split Jammu into two – halves.[68] On 5th December 2006, Pakistani President Pervez Musharraf told an Indian TV channel that Pakistan would give up its claim on Kashmir if India accepted some of his peace proposals, including a phased withdrawal of troops, self-governance for locals, no changes in the borders of Kashmir and a joint supervision mechanism involving India, Pakistan and Kashmir.[69] Musharraf stated that he was ready to give up the United Nations' resolution regarding Kashmir.

In sum, despite forward movements in change of government from Musharraf to Asif Ali Zardari to Nawaz Sharif, Pakistan continues to wage half-hearted "war of position" replete with private doubts, symbolic posturing and petty opportunism. Its support has not helped unify or energies the insurgency in Kashmir into a winning movement. The resulting stalemate appears stable and unlikely to be upset in the absence of a conventional India-Pakistan war. Since war is not an option, Pakistan's policy is reduced to bleeding India. To date, the Government of Pakistan and Azad Kashmir have spent millions of dollars to mobilise international support behind the question of Kashmir. Islamabad's jet setting, patronage soaked lobbying for a UN recommended plebiscite has elicited no significant international support during the last seven years of Kashmir insurgency. Cumulatively, Pakistan's score has been pathetic zero, despite the hectic international itinerary of former Prime Minister Benazir Bhutto and the ever travelling delegations headed by the Punjabi Politician Nasrullah Khan. Also recently the Security Council even dropped Kashmir from its agenda, and it was only retroactive Pakistani lobbying that was able to obtain a temporary reprieve. The most that the Pakistan has been able to achieve are favourable resolution from the Organisation of Islamic countries.

In the year 2008 the State of Jammu and Kashmir witnessed a seven-phased assembly election starting on 17th November and finishing on 24th December 2008. Inspite of calls by separatists for a boycott, an unusually high turnout of almost 50 per cent was recorded.

The National Conference Party, which was founded by Sheikh Abdullah and is regarded as pro-India, emerged with a majority of seats. On 30th December, the Congress Party and the National Conference agreed to form a coalition government, with Omar Abdullah as Chief Minister.[70] On 5th January 2009, Abdullah was sworn in as the eleventh Chief Minister of Jammu and Kashmir. In this assembly election the people of Kashmir embraced ballot over 'bullet' or boycott and elected a young dynamic leader to power. This election was hailed as the beginning of 'real change' in Valley. The people expected that their young leader would be the voice of the Kashmiri and represent Kashmir in New Delhi.[71] Abdullah's promise of peace and prosperity and the vow of 'zero tolerance' to human right violations tempted the people to vote for NC-Congress coalition. Although in the years following the assembly election the state remained tense and in several activities the role of security personnel was in question, in general it registered a peaceful image and definitely it was a good news for the well-wishers of Jammu and Kashmir.

In the meantime the history of insurgency that was continuing for the last two decades also appeared slow in recent years. Despite concerns at the continued operations of Jihadi groups, violence in the State remains in decline. In 2007, there were 170 civilian deaths; last year 83 were killed. The security forces and the Jammu and Kashmir police lost 79 personnel last year down from 122 in 2007.[72] According to the Government of India Home Ministry, 2008 was the year with lowest civilian casualties in 20 years, with 89 deaths, compared to a high of 1,413 in 1996. In 2008, 85 security personnel died compared to 613 in 2001, while 102 militants were killed. The human rights situation improved with only one custodial death, and no custodial disappearances. Many analysts say Pakistan's preoccupation with Jihadists within its own territory explains the relative calm.[73] Further too, the relative calm period moved on. In the year 2007, 472 terrorists were killed; while just 239 were shot dead in 2009. Improvised explosive device use fell from 56 in 2007 to 23 in 2009; grenade attacks from 107 to 56. The decline in violence, has oddly, made it difficult for the two keys actors in the peace process – the Jihadist and Kashmiri secessionist politician to reach for New Delhi's olive branch. Above all, the assembly election held in 2008 had made it clear to the Hurriyat that its constituency in Jammu and Kashmir is contradicting. 'Elections are ultimately projected as a sort of referendum by India, and that is why we have called for a complete boycott of such a process' disclosed Mirwaiz, a separatist leader and in a statement issued on the eve of assembly election called it a last chance to the so-called mainstream politicians to join the separatist movement.[74] As a result the Kashmir secessionist politicians have come to realise that their political position rests on weak foundations.

Changing Perceptions on Kashmir: Global and National

Not only the internal situation of the State of Jammu and Kashmir but the US approach on the issue underwent a significant change over the decades as direct and indirect mediator between the concerned parties of the dispute. In the context there are two key points that are vital in understanding the US approach to the Kashmir dispute. First, the US does recognise that it is an international issue, and the final closure will require the endorsement of the United Nations Security Council (UNSC) leading to the removal of the UN Military Observer Group in India and Pakistan (UNMOGIP) from both sides of the Ceasefire line. This fact has not changed and I do not know why anyone would scour world media daily to catch snippets on Kashmir in order to reassure their psyche that Kashmir issue is still an international issue, when in fact that status has neither changed nor has been disputed by the major powers. The second point, though, is even more important. The US position on resolving the Kashmir issue has changed over the years. This change is neither dramatic nor topsy-turvey; it is merely a slow evolution that was inevitable given the knowledge and depth of comprehension within the US national security apparatus that existed about the dispute in 1947-48 as compared to today, as well as by growing stature of the bilateral relationship between the US and India.[75] Garnishing that deep chasm between the past and the present, official views of the US towards the Kashmir issue major changes have taken place within Pakistan before and after the 9/11 attacks, which end up reinforcing the core reasons that led to change in the US policy.

As such Barak Obama, on becoming the new President of the US repeated, what has been a long standing bipartisan view of both Democrats and Republican governments that the Kashmir issue should be resolved bilaterally by India and Pakistan. Today all major powers echo the statement made by President Obama that the Kashmir dispute can only be resolved by the two countries themselves.[76] Although the US President Obama expressed his intention to try to work with India and Pakistan on Kashmir but in view of several criticisms appeared in media later he became reluctant on the issue. In an editorial in the *Washington Times* Selig S. Harrison, Director of the Asia Programme at the Centre for International Policy and a senior scholar of the Woodrow Wilson International Centre for Scholars called it Obama's first foreign policy mistake.[77] Another newspaper *The Australian* called Obama's idea to appoint a presidential negotiator 'a very stupid and dangerous move indeed.'[78] Likewise, Reihan Salam, in an editorial in *Forbes,* noted, 'The smartest thing President Obama could do on Kashmir is probably nothing. We have to hope that India and Pakistan can work out their differences on Kashmir on their own.[79] Even according to *Financial Times*, 'India has warned Obama that he risks 'barking up the wrong tree' if he seeks to broker a settlement between India and Pakistan over Kashmir.'[80] Undisputedly, the problem of Jammu and Kashmir has been recognised by the big powers of the world as bilateral one between India and Pakistan to solve on their own.

In a recent attempt during the period of United Progressive Alliance (UPA) government, a new term 'quiet diplomacy' was discovered and propagated as a possible solution to the Kashmir problem. Speaking to journalists on the sidelines of an All India newspaper editor's conference India's home minister P. Chidambaram disclosed, 'We are working on quiet diplomacy and added that such efforts are essential to take the process forward.'[81] Earlier in April 2006 too India and Pakistan agreed on quiet diplomacy to further the solution of Kashmir issue. Under it, major initiatives will be taken up at the top level, rather than being discussed in the media. According to *The Dawn* (Karachi), 'Back-channel diplomacy will be used to debate proposals like self-government demilitarisation and independence. In the process some intellectuals and former bureaucrats and general of the two countries will meet and discuss various solutions. They would later brief their government about the outcome of their meetings and various proposals for resolving the dispute.'[82] However, even at the beginning the initiative was criticised by pro-freedom leader and Harriyat Conference chairman

Sayed Ali Geelani who said that the offer is aimed at forcing a compromise solution on the people of Jammu and Kashmir against their aspirations, sacrifices and over six-decades long struggle. 'Quiet diplomacy is secret diplomacy where people will decide things and force a solution on Kashmir.'[83] He urged the people to be cautious and remain firm on their resolve and added that if we compromised at this juncture we will always have to move backwards. In the context the separatists bullet that killed the moderate Hurriyat leader, Fazl Haque Qureshi had also, to a great extent, wounded the prospect of quiet diplomacy for settling the Kashmir problem.

In addition to the efforts made by individual countries and the people of Jammu and Kashmir itself, the region South Asia is well aware and anxious to solve the dispute amicably. Most countries of the region believe that the communal fanatics will not give up unless they are reduced to non-entities in a secular configuration of South Asia's unity in diversity, as in the European Union. In Europe, too, a similar scenario interstate feuds had resulted in the devastating Second World War. Consequently, the 1950s had the vision to sign the Treaty of Rome, establishing the European Economic Community (EEC). They affirmed in its preamble that signatory states were determined to lay the foundations of an ever closer union among the peoples of Europe. They specifically affirmed its political and economic integration creating a customs union, colloquially known as the 'Common Market.'[84] The establishment of South Asian Association for Regional Cooperation (SAARC) in 1985 also contained several characters and ideas of EEC. With its formation it was hoped that the organisation would encourage India and Pakistan to cooperate like Germany and France to overcome their enmity after decades of devastating wars. The Heads of State /Government of the region including India, Male, Sri Lanka and others felt the need of common currency like the euro that would boost South Asian's economic and political stability. Through the efforts and effectiveness of SAARC the South Asians expected to fabricate a secular umbrella to isolate the communal forces of the region as in Europe where the Basque in Spain, the Italian Catalan, and the Irish IRA terrorists have been reduced to non-entities.[85] The first step in this direction would be the introduction of a common currency that, like the euro, would accelerate trade and commerce and, more importantly, unleash the centripetal force to help consolidate economic, political and cultural cooperation among South Asian countries.

At large the concept of peace suggests not only the absence of conflict, violence and hostility but it also signifies an ambience of prosperity, be that economic, social or cultural. Without delving and getting stuck into the ruins of history, Kashmir, in the most recent times has been showing some semblance of peace. But, the million dollar question is, is this really an era of peace or just another short-lived phase of calm before it could once again turn into the storm of conflict that we got to witness on several occasions in past? In Kashmir, the psycho-social fallout of the lingering conflict situation has not been diagnosed appropriately, nor have they been tested with keen interest. In the context India's key failure has been to eradicate its culture of exclusion, which privileges religious identity over citizenship. Each bomb represents an idea and each idea, in turn, is rooted in a larger political and cultural context. Policing can arrest perpetrators, not the historical processes which create them. Even though ideological sources and material resources of the Indian Jihad are global, the specific conditions in which it grew are local.[86] India in the decade since 9/11, has failed to engage with, and address, those conditions. India's key failure has been its inability to hold honest national conversation about communal violence, and the ways in which it is embeded in our cultures: a key cause of the persistence of the Jihadist movement.

The general elections to the 16th Lok Sabha held in April - May 2014 proved a watershed in the political history of independent India. For the first time a non-Congress political party, the Bharatiya Janata Party, was able to get an absolute majority on its own in Parliament. The present victory is unprecedented as it has given the opportunity to BJP to form government without dependence on allies. Narendra Damodardas Modi was first named a year ago by BJP as its chief election campaigner and later as the Prime Ministerial nominee who took the oath of office on the evening of 26th May 2014. In comparison to his earlier pro-Hindu image, during the election campaign and on becoming Prime Minister of the country, Modi was said to have totally changed himself into a moderate. His approach towards politics and political ideology reminded his vision of a secular India as he declared in a Chintan Baithak at Jaipur in 2004, 'I do not treat citizens as minority or majority. I treat them as equal citizens of a modern state with equal rights and equal opportunities.'[87] Now he is the Prime Minister of the country and the world powers, one by one, turned towards him and all are set to re-engage with an India, which is, energised, rooted, and self-confident.

With the coming of new government in India in May 2014 people at large expressed mixed reaction to the Problem of Jammu and Kashmir. Congratulating Narendra Modi for his Party's landslide victory in Lok Sabha polls, Peoples Democratic Party patriarch Mufti Mohammad Sayeed hoped that the new BJP government would take tangible steps in finding a lasting solution to the Kashmir problem.[88] In a statement issued in Srinagar the PDP leader expected that the Modi government would pursue an agenda which would be politically - inclusive and developmentally - intensive.[89] Earlier the BJP has all along been calling for greater integration of Jammu and Kashmir with rest of India. Party's manifesto issued on the eve of 16th Lok Sabha election also mentioned the abrogation of Article 370 after discussion, return of Kashmiri Pandits and working on their resettlement, equal and rapid development of all the three regions of the State - Jammu, Kashmir and Ladakh, good governance, better infrastructure, educational opportunities for peolple of Valley as its target in coming years. In August 2014, Narendra Modi paid a visit to Jammu and Kashmir, although he refrained from touching any political issue facing the State and said that his government intended to win hearts of people through development.[90] However, it should be remembered here that Kashmir is not an economic issue but a political problem requiring a political solution as both separatist and mainstream politicians have been saying all along. Elsewhere, his development plank may have instant takers but in a place like Kashmir, he would not be able to strike a chord with people by ignoring their political alienation. At the juncture, it is too early to say anything concrete about the future approach and engagement of the new government on Kashmir.

References

1. Sarvepalli Gopal, *Jawaharlal Nehru- A Biography, 1956-1964*, Vol III (Delhi: Oxford University Press,1984), p. 84.

2. Dipankar Gupta, 'Tricolour Over Kashmir-Territory , People and the Nation State,' *The Times of India*, 16 September 1999.
3. *Ibid.*
4. *Jawaharlal Nehru's Speeches, September 1946– May 1949*, Vol. I (New Delhi: Publication Division, 1949), p. 176.
5. *Ibid., Jawaharlal Nehru's Speeches August 1949– February 1953*, Vol. II (New Delhi : 1953), p. 112.
6. Kuldip Nayar, 'Deadlock on Kashmir,' *The Hindustan Times*, 11 April 1998.
7. *Jawaharlal Nehru's Speeches, September 1946-May 1949*, pp. 174-85.
8. Dr Akhileshwar Singh; *Political Leadership of Jawaharlal Nehru* (New Delhi: 1986), pp. 230-31.
9. *Jawaharlal Nehru to Chief Ministers*, 20 February 1948.
10. S.L. Poplai, Talbot Phillips (eds.), *India and America* (New Delhi), pp. 74-75.
11. *Jawaharlal Nehru's Speeches, September 1946-May 1949*, pp. 107-08.
12. Gwynne Dyer, 'The Slow Decline of Terror,' *The Hindustan Times*, 24 August 1998.
13. Ashok K. Mehta, 'The Truth About the Proxy War,' in *Ibid*, 11 August 1998.
14. *The Hindu*, 15 May 1990.
15. *Ibid.*
16. Ved Marwah, 'Hostage to Misrule,' *The Hindustan Times*, 16 July 1998.
17. S.K. Ghosh, *Muslim Politics in India* (New Delhi: 1987), pp. 113-17.
18. As quoted in Chandrika Bandaranaike Kumaratunga, 'Original Sins,' *The Hindustan Times*, 29 April 2002.
19. Bharat Bhushan, 'Match Fixing Won't Help in Kashmir,' in *Ibid.*, 21 April 2000.
20. R.K Jain (ed.), *Soviet – South Asian Relations – 1947- 1978*, Vol. I (Atlantic Highlands: 1979), pp. 3-4.
21. Shrikant Paranjpe, 'Dangers of Indo – Pak Confrontation on Kashmir,' *The Times of India*, 21 February 1990.
22. *The Tribune*, 17 April 1990.
23. *The Indian Express*, 26 July 1990.
24. Pramit Pal Chaudhuri, 'The Return of the Great Game,' *The Hindustan Times*, 14 October 2001.
25. Michael Krepon, 'Forbearance is the Key Word,' in *Ibid.*, 14 October 2001.
26. Sumantra Bose, *The Challenges in Kashmir, Democracy, Self – Determination and a Just Peace* (New Delhi: Sage Publications, 1997), pp. 125-126.

27. *Ibid.*, p. 94.
28. As quoted in Victoria Schofield, *Kashmir in Conflict* (London: 1996), p. 231.
29. *The Indian Express,* 23 February 1997.
30. *Indian Recorders*, April 9-15 1997, Vol. IV, No. 15 (New Delhi: 1997), p. 2726.
31. Rajkumar Singh, *Indo – Pak Nuclear Tension 1974-1998* (New Delhi: Samiksha Prakashan, 2001), pp. 103-104.
32. *Ibid.*, p. 126.
33. *The Hindustan Times*, 3 July 2000.
34. Brahma Chellaney, 'Pakistan as Problemistan,' in *Ibid.*, 8 July 2002.
35. Manoj Joshi, 'The Marathon Begins,' *Ibid.*, 30 June 2004.
36. J.N. Dixit, 'Clarity on Kashmir,' *Ibid*, 23 July 1998.
37. A.G. Noorani, 'Find a Happy Medium,' *Ibid.*, 20 April 2004.
38. Rajkumar Singh, *India – South Asia Minus Congress Regimes* (Patna: Novelty Prakashan, 2000), p. 68.
39. Kuldip Nayar, 'Deadlock on Kashmir,' *The Hindustan Times*, 11 April 1998.
40. Sahil Showkat, 'Normalcy in Kashmir: Myth or Reality,' *South Asia Politics*, Vol.11, No. 5, September 2012 (New Delhi: 2012), p. 47.
41. Happymon Jacob, 'Kashmir Insurgency, 20 Years After,' *The Hindu*, 25 December 2009.
42. J.N. Mohanty, S.K. Mohanty, 'Pakistan's Kashmir Policy,' 'The Smoke Screen of Fundamentalist Agenda?,' *The Indian Journal of Political Science*, Vol. LXV III, No.1, January – March 2007 (Meerut: 2007), p.141.
43. Ashutosh Misra, 'The Problems of Kashmir and the Problem in Kashmir: Divergence Demands Convergence,' *Strategic Analysis*, Vol. 29, No. 1, January – March 2005, pp. 16-43.
44. Rizwan Zeb, 'Pakistan and Jihadi Groups in the Kashmir Conflict,' in Waheguru Pal Sindhu, Bushra Asif and Cyrus Samii (eds.), *Kashmir: New Voices, New Approaches* (London: Lynne Rienner Publishers, 2006), pp. 65-95.
45. Masood Haider and Anwer Iqbal, 'Kashmir a Threat to the Peace, Warns Musharraf: World Help Sought for Indo–Pak Talks', *The Dawn*, 13 September 2002.
46. Text of President General Pervez Musharraf's Speech at SAARC Summit, *The News*, 6 January 2002.
47. Pratapbhanu Mehta, 'Turning a Corner,' *The Telegraph* (Calcutta), 21 April 2005.
48. *Text of President's address to the nation*, 13 January 2002.
49. *Ibid.*

50. Irfan Husain, 'Giving Peace a Chance,' *The Dawn*, 1 June 2002.
51. Happymon Jacob, 'Kashmir Insurgency, 20 Years After.'
52. *Ibid.*
53. Adfer Rashid Shah, 'The Uncertain Kashmir,' *South Asia Politics*, Vol. 12, No.10, February 2014 (New Delhi: 2014), p. 28.
54. Sanjeeb Kumar Mohanty, 'Indo-Pak Peace Process: Impact of Post – 9/11 Factors,' *The Indian Journal of Political Science*, Vol. LXIX, No. 2, April-June 2008 (Meerut : 2008), p. 396.
55. *Ibid.*
56. *The Dawn* (Karachi), 7 January 2004.
57. Sanjeeb Kumar Mohanty, 'Indo-Pak Peace Process: Impact of post – 9/11 Factors,' pp. 401-2.
58. *The Times of India*, 9 September 2005.
59. *The Daily Times*, 5 October 2005.
60. Praveen Swami, 'Kashmir : Pessimism May Be Good News,' *The Hindu*, 8 June 2010.
61. Sahil Showkat, 'Kashmir Imbroglio,' *South Asia Politics*, Vol. II, No. 10, February 2013 (New Delhi: 2013), p. 31.
62. Dexter Filkins, 'Kashmiri Militants Angry at Being Blocked from India,' *The Newyork Times*, June 2002, as quoted in J.N. Mohanty and S.K. Mohanty, 'Pakistan's Kashmir policy: The Smoke – Screen of Fundamentalist Agenda?,' p. 142.
63. Rajkumar Singh, *Relations of NDA and UPA with Neighbours* (New Delhi: Gyan Publishing House, 2010), p. 144.
64. Rajkumar Singh, *Myth and Reality of Terrorism in South Asia* (New Delhi: Kalpaz Publications, 2013), p. 140.
65. D.C. Pathak, 'India's Role in the War on Terror,' *South Asia Politics*, Vol. 9, No.10, February 2011 (New Delhi:2011), p. 4.
66. Dr Shaheen Akhtar, 'Kashmir : Pakistan's Unfinished Agenda,' *Aljazeera* (English), 21 August 2011.
67. B. Krishnamurthy, 'Kashmir Imbroglio – No To Third Party Involvement,' *South Asia Politics*, Vol. 7, No. 11, March 2009 (New Delhi : 2009), pp. 6-7.
68. *The Indus Equation Report, Strategic Foresight Group*, 2011.
69. *BBC News*, 5 December 2006.
70. *International Herald Tribune*, 30 December 2008.
71. Nirupam Hazra, 'The Kashmir Crisis-Time Has Come to Address The Real Issues,' *South Asia Politics*, Vol. 9, No. 9, January 2011 (New Delhi:2011), p. 52.
72. Praveen Swami, 'Kashmir : Pessimism May Be Good News.'

73. *The Washington Times*, 28 March 2008.
74. Praveen Swami, 'Kashmir : Pessimism May Be Good News.'
75. Vijay K. Sazawal, 'American Policy and Kashmir Dispute,' *The Rising Kashmir*, 27 July 2012.
76. *Ibid.*
77. *The Washington Times*, 6 January 2009.
78. *The Australian*, 4 December 2008.
79. *Forbes*, 1 December 2008.
80. *Financial Times*, 3 February 2009.
81. *CNN News*, 15 October 2009; also visit CNN.com/asia.
82. *The Dawn*, 12 April 2006.
83. Geelani Rejects Indian Quiet Diplomacy Initiative at www.freshinitiative.net/ kashmir.../2571.
84. Madanjeet Singh, 'South Asian Agenda for Jammu and Kashmir,' *The Hindu*, 29 December 2009.
85. *Ibid.*
86. Praveen Swami, 'A Decade After 9/11 , Indian Jihad Still Thrives,' in *Ibid.*, 10 September 2011.
87. B.B. Dutta, '2014: The End of Nehruvian Republic,' *South Asia Politics*, Vol.13, No. 3, July 2014 (New Delhi: 2014), p. 13.
88. *The Indian Express*, 18 May 2014.
89. *Ibid.*
90. *The Rising Kashmir*, 28 August 2014.

Chapter V

Terrorism in Jammu & Kashmir : An Overview

5.1 Background of the Problem

Amid fear and suspicion the accession of the princely State of Jammu and Kashmir with the Union of India was completed in October 1947 after the signing of an Instrument of Accession between the then Maharaja of State and the Government of India. In initial years India got support of its main political party the National Conference and its leader Sheikh Abdullah who, at the time wanted to join India. An overriding factor in the situation is that Kashmir has over the years become a symbol as well as a test of India's secularism. If in 1947 Kashmir had acceded to Pakistan, Indians would have accepted the fact without being upset. But after the invasion of Kashmir by Pathan tribesmen and Pakistani troops and the persuasion of its leader Sheikh Abdullah, the situation became different and it all these put Abdullah in a privileged position. On the one hand he was a man of remarkable courage and integrity having mass appeal but on the other an autocrat, wayward and arbitrary.[1]

Even at that time as today the State of Jammu and Kashmir was inhabited by pro-India and pro-Pakistan elements. These communal forces had given an upper hand to Sheikh Abdullah in his dealings with the government over the future of territory in which the secular weakness of India also remained a factor. Once Abdullah's position in state's politics became a certain he began to talk about the limited character of the accession in the Indian union and full autonomy for the state. Initially he praised India's secular democracy which is based on justice, freedom and equality for all without distinction and hoped these all to be realised while deciding the future of the state.[2] In his speeches Abdullah considered the provisions of Article 370 as secondary and laid emphasis on the identity of democratic and secular aspirations,[3] he however, also liked to add a note of caution and a thinly veiled warning, 'I would like to make it clear that any suggestion of arbitrarily altering this basis of our relationship with India would not only constitute a breach of the spirit and letter of the Constitution but might invite serious consequences for a harmonious association of our State with India.'[4]

Sheikh Abdullah not only took undue advantage from the Indian government but also tried to put the latter in perennial pressure tactics first in the name of State's autonomy and later hinted independence to be achieved with the help of the US and other foreign powers. From the start in Indian opinion the alternative to mollifying Kashmiris in the eyes of Nehru, in particular, was to hold up Abdullah as the most accredited and popular leader of the state and appease him to remain steadfast in keeping Kashmir with India. Even at the juncture Nehru pleaded with him for sanity and restraint but with little effect. His utterances before the public that Kashmir should become independent annoyed several of his colleagues and displeasure at the level of central leadership. Ultimately he was dismissed from his post in July 1953 and immediately thereafter put under arrest on charges of corruption, malpractices, disruption and dangerous foreign contacts. In his place Bakshi Ghulam Mohammad was installed as Prime Minister. Personally Nehru was not happy with the turn of events but did not interfere with the state government.

Integrating Measures

With the Sheikh Abdullah out of the way, it became easier for the Central Government to work with Bakshi. The old suspicions had disappeared and the Kashmir Governments were by then convinced that the main aim of Delhi Operation was to prevent subversion, terrorisation, sabotage and conspiracy by Pakistani agents. Bakshi was a liberal-minded and large-hearted person with his feet planted strongly amongst the masses. He tried to do much for improving the material conditions of the people of Kashmir and achieved a great deal. But above all he was completely loyal to Jawaharlal Nehru and considered himself an Indian out and out. Bakshi's Government lasted till 1963 and eventually G.M. Sadiq was installed in his place.

Article 370 of the Indian Constitution stands for the special care taken and many due and undue favours shown to win the goodwill of the Kashmiris. But the arrest of Abdullah and installation of Bakshi compelled New Delhi to have a second thought on its Kashmir policy. From here and now a systematic erosion of the autonomy of Kashmir started and this was the beginning of the end of Article 370. In 1954, a constitutional order was promulgated by the President of India, which empowered the Indian Government to legislate on all matters on the Union List, not just defense, foreign affairs and communications. This order came into force on 14th May 1954 and superseded both the constitutional application order of 1950 and Delhi Agreement of 1952. The order also put a drastic curbs on fundamental liberties, freedom of speech, assembly and association in the state could now be suspended at any time on grounds of security. No judicial review was allowed as one author puts ably, "what we in India experienced for a brief period after 26th June 1975 during emergency of Indira Gandhi, Jammu and Kashmir has suffered for...years...We cannot deny a people rights that flow out of citizenship and expect their allegiance."[5]

Other integrating measures followed further. In 1958, a constitutional amendment was effected, whereby Jammu and Kashmir was brought under the purview of central services resulting in the destruction of representative democracy, outside domination in its day-to-day administration which had no mass root. However, the peak of the process reached under Sadiq during 1964-65. Articles 356 and 357 of the Indian Constitution which respectively empower central government to dismiss elected provincial governments and to assume all the legislative functions of the state, were made applicable to Jammu and Kashmir. Article 249, which empowers the central government to legislate even on subjects on the provincial list was similarly made applicable to Jammu and Kashmir. Some twenty pieces of central economic legislation were extended to Jammu and Kashmir, and the designations of head of state and premier were formally changed to governor and chief minister as in any Indian state. Further the governor was to be appointee of Delhi, rather than a nominee of the (elected) Kashmir legislature. By mid 1960s there was hardly any trace of substantive autonomy in Jammu and Kashmir.[6]

Closely related to it is the aspect of free and fair elections in Jammu and Kashmir. The people of the state had never seen genuine elections except in 1977, 1983 and now in 2002. All other elections in J&K witnessed a meaningless rituals. A democratic polity is supposed to be one in which the government and the people together create an open and civil society an integrated whole that is brought and kept together by virtue of its being open, one in which the people participate not just in things like elections and development projects, but together in creating a common future.[7]

Erosion of representative democracy continued in Jammu and Kashmir. In the assembly elections of 1957 and 1962, the official National Conference, headed by Bakshi, won between 95 and 97 per cent of seats. The ruling party's candidates were returned unopposed in almost all seats in the valley where virtually there was no contest at all in 43 and 34 seats. The recurrent unopposed elections were earning a bad reputation. Riled by adverse reports in the international press, Nehru even wrote to Bakshi after the 1962 polls, advising him to lose a few seats in the future, so that the image of the world's largest democracy would not be unnecessarily tarnished. Further in 1967, 39 out of 75 seats were uncontested in the Valley. Congress candidates were elected unopposed in 22 out of 42 seats.

In 1977, the first reasonably democratic election was held. The Plebiscite Front, revived under the aegis of the National Conference, obtained a decisive majority in the Valley where Congress was wiped out. In post-Independence Kashmir, a new generation has arisen which is more educated, more politically conscious and self-assertive; it is in search of human and democratic rights denied to the people for three decades. The educated Muslim youth whose number multiplied several times since independence realised by 1977 that Abdullah's inconsistent behaviour had thwarted the progress of the state people in every sphere of social life. While free elections were common in all other states, Jammu and Kashmir alone suffered from gerrymandering and rigging every time elections to parliament or State Assembly. Kashmir, although disappointed with Abdullah's capitulation, obviously preferred him to the alternatives available.

Death of Sheikh Abdullah in 1982 followed a reasonably free and fair election in 1983. His party National Conference, now led by Farooq Abdullah, his eldest son, won a solid majority 47 of 76 assembly seats. This was a major achievement, since the election had been fiercely contested against the Congress (I), the party ruling Delhi. In both the above, the National Conference faced a well entrenched Congress with genuine Kashmiri support, and trounced it badly. Given a genuine contest and a Kashmiri ethno-nationalist alternative to the Congress, the Kashmiris of the valley came out to vote in droves. Seventy-four per cent cast their vote in 1977 and 73 per cent in 1983.

As a result of the assembly elections held in 2002, a new coalition government of Congress and People's Democratic party, headed by Mufti Mohammad Sayeed has taken over the reign in Jammu and Kashmir. The new dispensation had announced a Common Minimum Programme which among other things, noted that, 'the goal of the coalition government is to heal the physical, psychological and emotional wounds inflicted by fourteen years of militancy, to restore the rule of law in Jammu and Kashmir state, to complete the revival of the political process which was begun by the recently concluded elections, and to request the Government of India to initiate and held, sincerely and seriously, wide ranging consultations and dialogue, without conditions, with the members of the legislative and other segments of public opinion in all the three regions of the state, to evolve a broad-based consensus in restoration of peace with honour in the state.[8]

Negative Effects

Despite governments attempt to put democracy back on the rails in Kashmir, and thereby end the prevailing acute dissatisfaction in the state, is on the verge of failure. It has neither been able to convince the Kashmiris that the elections would be truly free and fair, nor create the conditions in which the various Kashmiri nationalist groups can agree to fight the election and thereby turn it into a genuine contest for power among the Kashmiri themselves.[9] What distinguishes democratic rulers from non-democratic ones are the norms that condition how the former came to power and the practices that hold them accountable for their actions. For democracy specific procedural norms must be followed and civil rights respected. Any polity that fails to follow the 'rule of law' with regard to its own procedures should not be considered democratic. The political history of Indian administered Jammu and Kashmir clearly does not satisfy these minimal conditions and requirements of democratic governance. Other basic indispensable component of a democratic framework, for example, a functioning political opposition, has not been permitted in the state. Democratic system rely on institutionalised oppositions and it is doubtful that any regime could long survive as minimally democratic without them.

Frustration and anger of the new generation accumulated and events began to take a new turn from mid-eighties. In late 1986 Farooq Abdullah committed a disastrous blunder and concluded a rapprochement with the centre, where upon he was reinstalled as chief minister pending fresh elections in March 1987. In exchange he agreed to contest the elections in partnership with Rajiv Gandhi's Congress (I). Although Farooq justified his decision in terms of a hard political reality he had come to accept, the arrangement met with widespread public hostility and contempt because it was an alliance with those who had disrespected and denied Kashmiriyat for forty years. The development was followed by formation of a coalition in the valley called Muslim United Front (MUF) to fight the NC-Congress alliance at the polls. In an anti-climax MUF eventually won just four seats with the NC-Congress combine taking almost all the rest with the help of rigging and strong arm tactics, booth capturing, not being allowed to vote and balantant working of administration in favour of the establishment. Mass arrests of MUF activist had immediately followed the spurious election and in fact it was in prison during 1987 that the five young men formed the Jammu and Kashmir Liberation Front (JKLF). On their release they took a collective decision to go to Pakistan-controlled Kashmir in search of military training and weapons. Yasin Mallik currently chairman of the JKLF is one of them.

Specially after 1987 all institutional channels of protest and dissent effectively blocked and even perfectly peaceful agitations were suppressed with lethal force. The first JKLF bombing in Srinagar in late July 1988 signalled the arrival of insurgency. According to

Newberg, 'Kashmiris come to insurgency when all politics seemed to fail, the politics of Kashmir's traditional politicians, politics between Srinagar and Delhi, and politics between India and Pakistan. They view themselves as victims of profound corruptions that sully the meaning of politics.[10] Indeed, most Kashmiris who developed a renewed commitment to the idea of self-determination by the late 1980 sincerely believe that they have given India's democracy more than its fair share of chances. The vast majority of Kashmiris are apparently prepared to make considerable sacrifices in order to resist this oppression. And the reason why they seem so insistent on "Freedom" which means freedom from Indian rule, is the conviction, born of their experiences, that their collective will for democratic responsible and accountable government is incompatible with their presently coerced status as 'an integral part of India.'

Two factors are mainly responsible for changing the social psychology in Kashmir. One, the growing perception and public resentment that proliferation and availability of small arms and ammunition and its use by individuals and groups with impunity is a sham democracy is a better alternative to anarchy, and a bad government is still a better option to chaos. It is a healthy development if there is an urge in initiating measures to bring an improvement in the governance of the state.[11] Good governance, as some analyst viewed it, is the way out. To some in India better governance in Kashmir means handing the state or the valley, to army rule. Others see it in terms of a clean development-oriented administration, with or without 'autonomy'. In their view, all that people in Kashmir want like people everywhere in India, is a minimum of roads, schools, dispensaries and electricity and an attentive administration. Provide these things back them up with firm security measures and the militants would be isolated.

It is true that due to over a decade of militancy, religious identities have become more pronounced and imposition of a unitary form of constitution on the state has suppressed all forms of identities except those based on religion, the distance between Kashmiri Muslims and Hindus has increased, they share a common language, culture and heritage. Militancy might have bruised Kashmiriyat, but it never succeeded in diluting it. However, it needs conducive social and political conditions to make this culture thrive again. Kashmir, apart from political problem, represents a human tragedy of epic proportions. This task of reconciliation and healing is not one that the government alone can do. Civil society as a whole in the state as well as in the rest of India, and especially organisations working in the field of inter-faith harmony would have to get involved in this process which would necessarily take many years to complete. However, a "beginning" must be made without delay.

Expansion of Insurgency in Kashmir

Factors responsible for the birth and proliferation of insurgency in the Indian State of Jammu and Kashmir were many. Having permitted conditions within Kashmir to deteriorate to the level that they had reached in 1989, the Indian state had little option but to fight hard to break the insurgency in Jammu and Kashmir and the external support it was receiving. In fact, the democratic ideals of the freedom movement in India and its support to the struggle of the people of the princely states for a responsible government inspired and influenced the people in the valley. However, these very ideals remained elusive after the State acceded to the Indian Union. The alienation of the people of Kashmir made considerable headway due to the sequence of events that took place in coming decades. Kashmir policy of the Government of India has been marked mainly by what may be called the carrot and stick approach. But neither stick nor carrot helped win favour of the Kashmiri people. Force and aid were used as instruments to win the loyalty of the people not for the nation but for the Government and the Party in power.

Terrorism in Kashmir, or for that matter anywhere else, can not be ascribed to administrative or economic reasons alone. The main cause of it is the deprivation of political power due to which the community believes that its dignity and identity are threatened. In general a secessionist-terrorist movement often seek outlets if the political system does not have adequate provision for its expression.[12] This is what actually happened in Jammu and Kashmir after 1987. All institutional channels of protest and dissent which are essential to generating both democratic values among the citizenry and their allegiance to the established framework of authority were effectively blocked.[13]

Frustration and anger of the new generation accumulated and events began to take a new turn at the close of the Eighties.

Before 1989, India and Pakistan fought over Kashmir. Since late 1989, it is Kashmiris who have done the fighting and most of the dying.[14] In early 1990, a group of young men in the Kashmir valley launched a guerilla revolt against Indian rule under the banner of a movement calling itself the Jammu and Kashmir Liberation Front (JKLF). The new organisation had received weapons and training from its part located across the border in Azad Jammu and Kashmir (AJK) as well as from Pakistani military agencies. The JKLF's stated objective was to liberate and reunite the whole of state held by India and Pakistan into a single independent state. It received mass support for freedom of Jammu and Kashmir and huge pro-independence demonstrations were organised in the valley during 1990.

Expansion of insurgency in the State has an international aspect too. The Soviet intervention that took place in December 1979 and lasted about for a decade, had several far-reaching implications. It not only made available additional armaments to the insurgents but also changed the very nature of Pak society. Social disintegration appeared to escalate in the 1980s and 1990s. As both cultivation and drug smuggling escalated, Pakistan emerged as a frontline heroin production point and transit route for the international drug trade.[15] According to a report about 5,000 Kashmiri youth were taken into Pakistan in the summer of 1988 for training and sent back in the spring of the following year. During 1988-94, over 50,000 Kashmiri youth are estimated to have been trained in Pakistan. Mujahideen, freed from the Afghan conflict, were sent to Kashmir and their numbers peaked at about 1600 in 1994.[16]

The struggle in the State of Jammu and Kashmir continued to evolve. The guerilla war rapidly intensified, to a significant degree because of an Indian response of repression and reprisal targeted not just against armed militants but frequently also against 'disloyal' civilian communities that aided and sheltered the rebels.[17] Gradually, militancy entered a new phase. It was no longer a fight between the militants and the security forces. In fact, it assumed the form of a total insurgency of the entire population and was marked by demoralisation within the political system, followed by the collapse of the administration.[18]

Though the mid of 1990s witnessed a wane to the local support for insurgency, in the second half of the decade Pan-Islamist fighters, primarily from Pakistan, infiltrated into Indian Jammu and Kashmir in significant numbers, adding a supra-local, strongly Islamist flavour to the conflict. The protracted 'low-intensity' warfare in the interior of the State between thousands of guerillas and hundreds of thousands of Indian security forces signalled a great transformation in the military and political character of the Kashmir conflict.[19]

Thus, the political history of India-administered Jammu and Kashmir clearly does not satisfy the minimal conditions and requirements of democratic governance. No Kashmir policy can succeed without taking into account the political and psychological urge of the people. The controversy over whether the policy should be tough or soft, whether it should be based on nationalist or moral appeal, on realpolitic or idealpolitik is unreal and irrelevant. What the question needs is a correct assessment, a correct diagnosis, a correct strategy. The government, despite its attempt to put democracy on the rails in Kashmir has neither been able to convince the Kashmiris that the elections would be truly free and fair, nor create the conditions in which the various Kashmiri nationalist groups can agree to fight the election and thereby turn it into a genuine contest for power among the Kashmiris themselves. What Kashmir badly needs and sadly lacks is a "healing touch" policy - a step towards a serious, sustained and multidimensional peace process. A beginning must be made without delay.

5.2 Terrorism : Perception and Proliferation

Meaning with Explanation

The famous English poet John Milton once wrote 'The mind is its own place, it can make heaven of hell and hell of heaven'. The term 'Terrorism' has recently been defined by Paul J. Smith, a security expert at the Asia- Pacific Center for Security Studies, as a form of psychological warfare that is used to create extensive fear through the use of extensive force against non-combatant civilian military targets. It thrives in a milieu characterised by some festering and unresolved issue in an atmosphere of financial crisis and in situation where unlawful trade in narcotics and small arms.[20] The possibility of proliferation of Weapons of Mass Destruction (WMD) through the innovation of modern technology is more real today than it has ever been in human history. Weapons of Mass Destruction terrorism involves the most modern and the most extreme form of random violence. Nuclear, chemical and biological weapons are inherently terrifying; in most cases of their being used, the fear they would cause would dwarf the injury and death. Its dreadful nature creates its own dangers; of victims panic and try to flee, they spread contamination and disease still further. The effects of these weapons are also inherently random. The radius of injury depends on conditions that are impossible to control or predict with certainty.[21] The use of these innovations for terrorist activities is limited only by the imagination of the terrorist. Every one is a potential target and this creates a climate of fear and suspicion within a society.

Different scholars have tried to come to terms with terrorism depending upon their ideological moorings. Today terrorism is the new form of warfare then it is evident that politics for some states has become an offshoot of this deadly virus and has acquired its own autonomy.[22] For example, Yonah Alexander, links terrorism with national security. To him, 'terrorism is the use or threat of violence against random or civilian threats in order to intimidate or create generalised pervasive fear for the purpose of achieving political goals'. But Paul Wilkinson makes a difference between political terrorism and other forms of violence. He defined political violence as "the systematic use of murder and destruction, and the threat of murder and destruction in order to terrorise individuals, groups, communities or governments into conceding to the terrorists' political demands."[23] While the United States' Department of State defined it as a, "pre-meditated, politically motivated violence penetrated against non-combatant targets by sub-national groups or clandestine State Agents, usually intended to influence an audience." In the state of terrorism, nation found itself in a condition in which it is very difficult to provide security and the environment of development to its citizens in terrorist affected areas. In so many cases terrorists also run their parallel government in specific part of territory, in this situation governments face so many challenges for safeguarding territorial integrity and preserving sovereignty of the nation state.

On the other hand, terrorism has been analysed by several social science disciplines, intelligence agencies, militaries, law enforcement agencies, IGOs and NGOs and legislatives and judicial bodies. They all use different type of framework, institutional perspectives, requirements and dimensions. According to them terrorism seems to possess four key elements – (i) cause (generally political), (ii) non-state entities with group dynamics, (iii) chosen place and (iv) indiscriminate use of violence.[24] When all these four key elements combine together they create an environment of psychological fear and terror, all these combined are known as terrorism.

In a nutshell, despite lack of consensus on what terrorism actually encompasses, there are, however, certain features common to all forms of terrorism. For instance, terrorism, in all forms, is aimed to generate fear, panic and terror in the minds of the general public. It may be politically motivated or may emerge because of obscure ideologies or beliefs, the acts of terror may be perpetrated for political ends or for changing the cultural norms or religious ethos of a targeted country or a segment of population. Further, terrorism, unlike ordinary violence, employs inordinate lethal force against civilian targets to erode the political will of the targeted country, undermine the morale of the people, spread despondency and panic through catastrophic terrorist attacks.[25] Moreover, terrorism is arbitrary and unpredictable as far as its effects are concerned. And it does not recognise any rules and conventions of war and geographical limitations.

Thus, a 'terrorist' is a person who indulges in criminal acts with manifestly political motive without exhausting legitimate remedies at his disposal for the redressal of his grievances. His acts may be organised or unorganised, sporadic or widespread, commanding public support or hatred. The decisive element is that he indulges in criminal acts without invoking legitimate remedies for his alleged grievance or suffering.[26] The terrorist hypothesis is that the system itself suicides in response to the multiple challenges of death and suicide. Neither the system, nor power, themselves escape symbolic obligation and in this trap resides the only chance of their demise (catastrophe). In this vertiginous cycle of the impossible exchange of death, the terrorist death is an infinitesimal point that provokes a gigantic aspiration, void and convection. Around this minute point, the whole system of the real and power gains in density, freezes, compresses, and sinks in its own super – efficacy. The tactics of terrorism are to provoke an excess of reality and to make the system collapse under the weight of this excess. It indicates that terrorist actions are both the magnifying mirror of the system's violence and the model of a symbolic violence that it cannot access.[27] By using violence and terror, terrorists disturb communal harmony in society, create fear and suspicion between communities. That is why they pose and direct threat to maintaining domestic peace.

In its latest manifestations, terrorism is violence for a cause and terrorists always want the world to know about their existence, their causes and the power they wield.[28] From the ongoing discussions the theories of terrorism have been derived as the following:

- Terrorists are not born but created by particular sociological, economic and political conditioning processes.
- Terrorism is not based on reason and is nothing but a series of senseless and mindless actions to create fear.
- It is deliberate and systematic assault on civilians to inspire fear for political ends.
- It is a method whereby an organised group or party seeks to achieve its avowed aims, chiefly through the systematic use of violence.
- It is a weapon of the weak employed against powerful opponent not with the aim to defeat but as an attempt to show itself as all powerful and a good force with a view to change the balance of power.[29]

To conclude terrorism is not an act, but, it is a thinking in which some people think that political objectives could be achieved by illegitimate use of violence. Its motivations are also changing. A new breeds of terrorist including ad hoc groups motivated by religious convictions or revenge, right-wing extremists and apocalyptic and millenarian cults, appear more likely than terrorist of the past to commit acts of extreme violence. Religious groups are becoming more common and are more violent than secular groups.

Basically, the concept of 'Terrorism' is as old as the civilisation of mankind itself and has existed in all ages in some form or other which might be known anarchists, revolutionaries, fundamentalists or dissents against the established authority or even ruling tyrants having no tolerance or dissent. However, terrorism was not as widespread phenomenon as it is today in contemporary political system of the world. Terrorism has, in fact, become a global phenomenon with increasing and rather well identifiable links between different terrorist group and organisation. They use each other's areas for recruitment and training, exchange of illegal weapons, engage in joint planning and ventures and also provide administrative and other logistic support. This type of terrorist activities show a new dimension due to circumstances characterised by the advancement of science, technology and diverse social, economic, political and historical reasons conditioning it. It will remain a menace as long as there are people who are driven by fanaticism, paranoia and extremism. So long as there exists in the world poverty, strife, injustice and oppression, conditions will exist which terrorists can turn to their advantage.

The term terrorism comes from the French word *terrorisme*, which is based on the Latin verb *terrere* (to cause to tremble). It dates back to 1795 when it was used to describe the actions of the Jacobin Club in their rule of post-Revolutionary France, the so-called 'Reign of Terror'. Jacobins are rumored to have coined the term 'terrorists' to refer to themselves. Terrorism refers to a strategy of using violence, social threats, coordinated attacks, in order to generate fear, cause disruption, and ultimately, brings about compliance with specified political, religious, or ideological demands. Traditionally, terrorism is a highly organised enterprise that fits into a clear political strategy. It has been filling the news for most of our lives and will doubtless go on demanding the attention of our children and grand-children as well.[30] What is new is how it achieves its goals these days.

Until today the world under UN has failed to come to an agreement about what is an acceptable definition for terrorism. It is still under debate despite attempts made by many experts. The effort to approach terrorism from a definitional perspective has thus become a never-ending effort. 'Terrorism is a term used to describe the method or the theory behind the method whereby an organised group or party seeks to achieve its avowed aims chiefly through the systematic use of violence. Terroristic acts are directed against persons who as individuals, agents or representatives of authority interfere with the consummation of the objectives of such a group.[31] In the sense it differs in several important aspects from such phenomena as mob violence, mass insurrection and governmental terror. Terror practised by a government in office appears as law enforcement and is directed against the opposition, while terrorism in its proper sense implies upon defiance of law and is the means whereby an opposition aims to demoralise a governmental authority, to undermine its power and to initiate a revolution or counter-revolution.[32]

Terrorism as a revolutionary technique was for many years an accepted tenet of anarchism. The writings of Bakunin with their emphasis upon violence as a method of achieving social change were the inspiration, if not the actual source of this doctrine. The idea of the propaganda of the deed was developed in the years following Bakunin's death by Kropotkin, Brousse and others, who stressed the failure of generally accepted methods and the educative and publicity value of acts of terrorism. This theory was translated into action principally in the last two decades of the nineteenth century. It was almost always part of the strategy of an armed national liberation movement, and in the colonial context it usually worked in the end. The reason terrorism worked so well in anti-colonial struggles was that you did not have to defeat the imperial powers superior military forces in order to win. They were a long way from home and there was a limit to how many lives and how much money the imperial government would spend to hang into its possessions. But the early, easy successes of terror tactics in the anti-imperial context left everybody with a greatly inflated notion of what the technique could achieve against an established national government with local roots.

With its initial success in several spheres, the concept of terrorism also gained other valuable characters such as mass realisation and publicity. Even today terrorism as a method is always characterised by the fact that it seeks to arouse not only the ringing government or the nation in control but also the mass of the people to a realisation that constituted authority is no longer safely intrenched and unchallenged. The publicity of the terroristic act is a cardinal point in the strategy of terrorism. If terror fails to elicit a wide response in circles outside of those at whom it is directly aimed, it is futile as a weapon in a social conflict. In this phase and type of terrorism violence and death are not intended to produce revenue or to terrorise the persons attacked but to cause society or government to take notice of the imminence of large scale struggles. The terroristic act committed in secrecy by one person or several is conceived as the advance notice of what may be expected from mass action.

The fullest expression of the theory and practice of this terrorism is to be found in the functioning of the famous Russian revolutionary organisation Narodnaya Volya, formed in 1879. In the same year it made an unsuccessful attempt to shoot the Czar and in the following year a revolutionary workman, Khalturin, succeeded in dynamiting the Czar's dinning room at the Winter Palace, where the royal family was to entertain a large official assemblage. But in 1881, Alexander II was killed by a bomb. Such an effective start encouraged the Narodnaya Volya and its activity spread despite the efforts of the government to exterminate the organisation at all costs. The newly formed Party explained its method of action in paragraph 2, section D, of its programme, which defined destructive and terroristic activity as follows: 'Terroristic activity, consisting in destroying the most harmful person in government, in defending the party against espionage, in punishing the perpetrators of the notable cases of violence and arbitrariness on the part of the government and the administration, aims to undermine the prestige of the government's power, to demonstrate steadily the possibility of struggle against the government, to arouse in this manner the revolutionary spirit of the people and their confidence in the success of the cause, and finally, to give shape and direction to the forces fit and trained to carry on the fight.'[33]

Apart from this terroristic commitment, the organisation was crystal clear in matters of motivation and end. The motivation of the party was frequently stated in paragraph 1, section V, of the same programme which reads, 'By this overturn, in the first place, the development of the people will be to proceed independently and in line with its disposition, and, in the second place, many purely socialist principles common to us and the people will gain recognition and be supported in our Russian life. It also stressed that the use of terror was not an end in itself but only a means to effect the transference of power from the government to the people; that the party proposed to seize and retain power only until a form of popular government could be determined upon by a Constituent Assembly; and that it would not decree revolutionary reforms and impose its desires upon the people but on the contrary would aid the latter to express its own will, to which the party would submit. In later years, although it was revived in 1901 when the Socialist Revolutionary Party came into existence and in 1917, upon the cessation of the temporary political alliance of the Socialist Revolutionary Party with the Bolsheviks, it however, never attained real success as a method of revolution.

The Present Dimension and Devastations

Current day terrorism has many faces. Its objectives are multifaceted and operations multi-pronged. The entire world is its stage, which has made it a prime concern for governments and societies around the world. No society is safe from its impact. It ranges from individuals to groups to international networks and thus poses a challenge to internal intelligence system of nationstates round the world.[34] In the opinion of some analysts it is indeed a world war, not the third one, but the fourth and the truly world war. The first two world wars were traditional wars were classical wars. The first ended European supremacy and the colonial era. The Second ended Nazism. The third, which did not happen, as a dissuasive cold war, ended communism. From one war to the other, one went further each time toward a unique world order. But the fourth world war is elsewhere. It is that which haunts every global order and every hegemonic domination. Terrorism, like virus, is everywhere. Immersed globally, terrorism, like the shadow of any system of domination is ready everywhere to emerge as a double agent. There is no boundary to define it; it is in the very core of this culture that fights it.

The root cause of present, devastating terrorism is religious fundamentalism. Every religion comes into existence in given society with its values, its ethos, customs and traditions. A religion tries to reform a society by providing certain ideals and values. But the human behaviour is never determined simply by the religion one follows. It is determined by several factors – personal or group interest and inspiration, social mores and traditions and tribal or national expectation.[35] Thus, understanding religion varies according to tribal, national and ethnic considerations and one always finds a tension between the theological and the sociological. This tension could be creative or destructive, depending on the situation or approach of the people concerned. In fact, any religion, particulary those that have existed over long periods of time and continue to be practised – speak to us in many voices. Their multivocality, which expresses the diversity of historical experience, allows for a degree of internal and external critique. Extremism in any religion propagates intolerance and hatred for other communities and that generally leads to violence that may take form of terrorism. Religious extremism driven by political motives invariably leads to terrorism, as the aim of the extremist groups is to capture or retain power. A fundamentalist sect or group may also want to isolate other sects or religious factions from national mainstream so that they are unable to compete with it politically or gain equal status.

The fundamentalists look upon scriptures as the word of God. Fundamentalist traits have uniformally appeared in all the major religions of the world in recent years. In the USA, there are the Operation Rescue Protesters. In Israel, there is the Gush Emunium, who claim that God has given the Land of Israel, with precise boundaries, to his children. In Sri Lanka, there are militant Buddhists. However, it is Islamic fundamentalism which has the broadest global sweep, stretching from the Mediterranean through the Balkans, the Black Sea, across the Caucasus and Southern Russia, through Western China enveloping Pakistan and Bangladesh, affecting India moving on to Southern Thailand, Malaysia, Indonesia and Philippines. It is, in fact the best organised fundamentalist force with a worldwide network.[36] It is however, of an entirely different variety, it emanates from extreme rigidity of beliefs and disdain for other religions though it is against the true tenets of Islam.

Originally, the term Islam means submission to God, and as such, designates a religion, preached by the Prophet Muhammad at the beginning of the seventh century A.D. It believes that in obedience of God, lies peace, prosperity, happiness and the salvation of man. According to Islam, the other prophets who preceded Muhammad were all true prophets, and Islam is nothing but a confirmation of the true faith taught by previous religions and teachers. Religion is certainly a vital force in every society and Muhammad made Islam a permanent force vitally by giving it a natural and rational basis.[37] It spread from Arabia to different countries of Asia, Africa and Europe. Thus, Islam could embrace diverse social and ethnic countries and it emerged as a universal religion from the very beginning.

The Quran is the scripture of Islam and the authentic source of its teachings. Its emphasis on the need for tolerance of diversity and the sanctity of life is worth nothing. God in the Quran requires the believers to show tolerance and respect to those who differ in their ways. It says: 'to every people we have appointed a way of worship, which they have followed. So let them not wrangle with you over the matter.[38] It emphasised the universal concept of religion such as the unity of God and the unity of human race. As regards the sanctity of human life, the Quran says : 'anyone who kills a human being if not in retaliation for a murder, nor for causing corruption in the land – must be accounted to have killed all mankind, and who ever saves a life it will be as if he had saved the life of all mankind.[39] Islam's concept of the unity of man had very deep and far-reaching effects on the social, political, economic and moral way of life of the Muslims.

Islam started as a great revolutionary movement based on equality, human dignity and justice. These ideals were partly acceptable to the tribal society of Mecca. Equality and human dignity was acceptable in a limited way within tribal social boundaries. Members of a tribe could be accepted as equals, but not those of other tribes. Members of other tribes could be accepted only as a client, not as an equals. Radical Islam is what Prophet Muhammad is believed to have given to the citizens of Medina after his fight from Mecca. He outlined an ideology, couched in religious terms, from which an escape was next to impossible. The ideology offered no accommodation except on its terms, ruled out all compromises, and demanded an allegiance any violation of which was declared blasphemous, inviting instantaneous annihilation.[40] As radical Islam spread far and wide beyond Mecca and Medina, often in the shadow of the sword, it did encounter powerful ideas which sometimes mellowed it and some-times led to the emergence of new sprouts. In the circumstances, the concept of universal brotherhood and inter-tribal equality created social tension throughout the Islamic history. Even within Arab society these became explosive after the death of the prophet. By the time the prophet died, different tribes of Arabia had embraced Islam.

Thus, the ideas of radical Islam are in contrast to the message of Quran that the mystery of divine mercy is also being experienced in other traditions. Prophet Muhammad accorded the world-view and encouraged the Muslims to approach non-Muslims with respect and know how the mystery of God found expression in older traditions. With their internationalist attitude and travelling to foreign countries either in connection with their overseas and overland trade or in search of knowledge, the Muslims became the pioneers in starting inter-religious dialogue. In fact, the desire on their part to understand what other cultures might have to offer enriched their cultural heritage. However, the lofty ideals of Islam received a setback when the tribe of Quraysh claimed the Caliphate quoting a 'hadith and superiority over other tribes.'

Islamic society soon transformed into a feudal society. The reasons for embracing a religion could be quite varied. Some embrace it collectively along with other members of the caste or tribe or nation; some embrace it for political or economic advantages; and some after studying the religion. In its historical march to its present expanse, Islam has destroyed empires, countries, religions, cultures and people. In the process it even opposed the Sufi Islam which toned down the hard features of the original and introduced new concepts. Sufi Islam conditioned the Islamic mindset to acceptance of co-existence with other cultures and religions. Islamic extremism is invariably been politically driven and seldom a purely religious movement. It has no sanction either in Quran or in the practices of the holy Prophet of Islam. Distorted interpretation of various historical events by some Islamic clerics led to violence against non-Muslims in the past. The creed of tolerance compassion, charity and civilised behaviour preached and practised by Prophet Muhammad were forgotten soon after his departure from the scene. The stern commands in the Holy Quran pertained to particular situations such as murderous attacks on Muhammad and his followers by the pagan tribesman. These were later misinterpreted or used by vested interests to wage wars against political opponents. The terrible massacre of Karbala, in a battle for political supremacy and power illustrated for ruthlessness of the tribal customs to achieve political ends.

In course of its spread far and wide Islam came to India with Arab invasions, Sultan Mahmud, of Ghazni, in particular. Initially the Islam that settled down in India was not so radical. Its core got impacted by Hindu philosophy, bhakti movements which provided Islam a broad based co-existence with all religions of India. For over 300 years, Islam remained peacefully as a religion and taken its place among the many religions of India without trouble or conflict. Before Islam, Jainism and Buddhism had been absorbed by Hinduism. Also there were Christianity and the Hebrew religion which had reached India probably during the first century after Christ, had found a place in the country. Historically, Hindu society had shown a peculiar ability to absorb and culturally assimilate groups which entered its fold from outside, even with military power.[41] But Islam was the first exception. Islamic groups had much greater cultural self-confidence, and clearer self-recognition in terms of doctrines and observances. This prevented an absorption into Hindu society in the treacherously insidious way that had been the common fate of earlier intruders. The new approach produced powerful psychological reactions among the people and filled them with bitterness. There was no objection to a new religion but there was a strong objection to anything which forcibly interfered with and upset their way of life.

As a result of the industrial revolution more or less world over, large sections of the population from their original surroundings, resulting in a deep sense of dislocation and alienation. At the same time it fails to provide an alternative set of values and along with it, a sense of belonging to these people. To offset this deficiency they try to reclaim and assert their traditional identities more stridently. The alienation generated in the process of modernisation provided the material for the growth of orthodox religious forms.[42] It is said that this modern phenomenon of terrorist movement is born out of frustration and despair. Despair caused by social marginalisation, economic decline and political defeat. Leon Trotsky once described the two emotions central to terrorism as being despair and vengeance. The betrayed hopes, one talks of are, as we are aware, the hopes of diverse communities to obtain their fair share of the cake.[43] In a nutshell, the Islamic fundamentalism or pristine puritan Islam had lost its original dynamism and failed to meet the challenges of the time.

The continuous enjoyment of political power for over 1,000 years had given the Muslims a self-confidence which was based on a faith in Islam, which they believed would never let them down. But as a result of the renaissance in Europe, with the age of reason, the invention of gun powder, the geographical explorations, the industrial revolution and the colonial expansion of the European powers, Islamic glory became a thing of the past. The mainstream of the intellectual and creative section of the society fell into the grip of traditionalists who valued piety more than progress. Islamic decline became more apparent from the eighteenth century, when the French Revolution gave new concepts of democracy and nationalism to Europe and the Muslims were left far behind in every sector of human life. With them declined a civilisation which had consistently flourished in the major areas of three continents, Asia, Europe and Africa. Even their political authority was seriously challenged by the British in India, the Dutch in Indonesia, the French in Western Africa and the Russian in Central Asia.[44] The question before Islam was not how to find few channels for its expansion, not even to retain the superiority they had enjoyed, but to survive and escape total annihilation and humiliation.

In the circumstances fundamentalist revival sought to strip modern, innovative and foreign influence from the Islamic faith. Earlier when Muslims were unable to meet the challenge posed by Western countries, the situation created fundamental doubts among the educated Muslims in Islamic values and ideas, and they were inclined more and more towards an appreciation of Western culture and outlook. The matter became much worse when not only the Westerners but also the Western-educated Muslims began to think the same way. Hence, Islam came under fire both from within and without. But this does not mean that the Muslims did not resist the European onslaught. They fought every battle in India, including the one in 1857. Apart from this several movements were started to revise the tenets of Islam, each in their own way.

The quest for such an identity can be identified with the efforts of Syed Ahmed Khan and Amir Ali, for calling upon Muslims to strengthen the bonds of community. These efforts were akin to that of Shah Waliullah who urged the glorification of Islam in the wake of the disintegration of the empire under Aurangzeb. Shah Waliullah (1703-62) who was celebrated in history as a Muslim reformer or a hardliner was of the view that the essence of the scriptures i.e. Quran, Sunnah and Hadith could not be diluted and the purpose of Islam must remain synchronous with the Prophet's vision. Two generations later, Waliullah's followers founded the Deoband seminary of theology. The seminary was not just a Madrassah for religious teachings. Its instructions were inspired by one larger purpose of avenging the 1857 defeat by the British of the Muslim Empire.[45] The Indian Muslims under the impact of the Wahabi movement preached the slogan 'Back to the Koran and sought to restore *Jihad* (holy war) for an Islamic ideal state. There had been the movements of the Mujahideen, dedicated to the establishment of an ideal Muslim state in the North-West Frontier. Thus, Islam became politically useful after the revolt of 1857 as aptly remarked by Abbas Rashid that the elite managed to foster a degree of general Muslim identification with issues like lack of education, discrimination in employment, inadequate political representation etc. He maintained that while their use of Islam may have been subjectively opportunistic, it was nevertheless effective given the context.[46] Later on, of course, the British policy of divide and rule widened the cleavages of Hindu-Muslim differences, encouraged the Muslim Leaguers and used them to counter the Congress to strengthen their rule.

However, within the Muslim community, in contrast to the Westernised elite, the orthodox religious leaders or traditionalists who struggled to attain a position of leadership, regarded the credentials of the former to lead the Muslim Ulama with contempt. They considered the Muslim League a bunch of loyalist toadies and accused them of cooperating with the Satans of Europe against the Islamist Caliphate and Pan-Islamism. However, the foremost of the causes that ultimately led the Muslims to take to the gun was the betrayal by the imperialist powers of the West of the Arabs after the first World War (1914-18). As a result of this French domination was established over Syria and Lebanon while Palestine was excluded from all obligations to the Arabs. In contrast to Palestine, the Jewish immigrants from the Eastern European countries and Russia were out of harmony with the local environment but went on turning it into their homeland on European pattern and at the cost of Arabs.[47] Further the creation of Israel and its recognition by the United Nations Organisation (UNO) shook the confidence of the Islamic world in this international organisation.

In post-World War II phase radical Islam's opposition to the West in general and the USA in particular continued unabated. No doubt the West has given the world science and technology and also introduced the concept of democracy and human rights. But it has also rubbished India, China and the Muslim world. They have imposed on these civilisations. Missionaries have been sent with foreign funds to subvert the religion and culture of those people. Muslims resent it more because they have recent memories of their power. Many Muslim countries were occupied. Even after independence their government were either toppled or turned into puppets. Their oil wealth still goes to enrich the West. Their oil revenues are diverted to arms purchases. Neighbouring countries are encouraged and armed to fight each other.[48] The recent militant image of Islam has come basically from the use of religion to generate political consciousness in the Middle East where external involvement, on account of oil and Israel, has not permitted democracy to take root. The fear of confrontationist Islam became a burning issue in the West with the rise to power of militant Islam in Iran and the resilience it has displayed in several countries including Egypt, Algeria, Sudan, Pakistan, Libya, Lebanon and Afghanistan.[49]

The end of second world war witnessed the beginning of Cold War between the two superpowers of world politic – the USA and USSR. Initially the USSR was a territorial power against the nuclear dominance of the United States. At the height of Cold War for supremacy in world politics the USA blocked the USSR in Europe through the North Atlantic Treaty Organisation (NATO), and both the USSR and China in East Asia through alliances with Japan, South Korea and Taiwan. In early years with a view to pursue its policy of containing communism, it placed higher priorities on West Asia, where a Soviet military threat was perceived, and to Southeast Asia where the Chinese were suspected of long-term expansionist ambitions. In response the USSR contained the vision of changing the world in direction of a particular ideology.[50] However, they both emerged comfortably dominant in its respective sphere.

Major Terror Attacks in India

Security and independence for the nation-state have become a complex mosaic in the uneasy post-cold war years. In this phase the ability to inflict mass destruction is no longer the sole purview of the state and the non-state actor and fringe group zealot has emerged as a new challenge to state security and stability. The insidious proxy war, often supported and abetted by external agencies has the potential to pose a strategic challenge not merely to India but to the region and globe as well.[51] A heady infusion of religious fervour and the proliferation of lethal small arms–the prefix being a complete contrast to the massive destruction possible have enhanced the profile of the practitioners of this proxy war. It is not uncommon to find terrorist/ militant /proxy war waging groups on the Indian periphery now having at their disposal fire power capability including artillery pieces and anticraft missiles that would normally be associated with a regular army brigade.[52] For India stakes are high since what is threatened by this proxy war is not mere territoriality but a concerted attempt to hack at the roots of the often taken-for-granted Indian independence and nationhood based on democratic principles and abiding secularism.

In this context India, even today, continues to look at the military dimension of the security aspect long after the rest of the world has understood it to include other important elements. The use of the state's armed apparatus to maintain order, without regard to the political and socio-economic factors of dissent, has been the basic approach of successive Indian governments. The militarisation of political and social discourse by the use of arms in urban and rural areas has grown over the years.[53] This has happened as a consequence of an armed response by the government. Ever more frequently, and in the states, the normal response to an outbreak of violence is of rushing to raise more battalions of armed police and other paramilitary forces. Hardly any effort goes into addressing the political and other non-military issues which are at the root of the problem. National security has therefore been given a distorted perspective over the years. The roles of the citizen and the state have also been wrongly viewed in regard to the security.

In reality India has been at the receiving end of cross-border terrorism in Kashmir and surrounded areas. With the Soviet withdrawal from Afghanistan in the year 1989, the US interests in Afghan affairs declined and the pro-American elements in Kabul suffered a set-back on account of Gulf crisis that prevented them to be famous internationally. At the juncture the Government of Pakistan exploited the changing situation in its favour to a large extent and tactfully turned the face of Afghan rebels and others towards Kashmir.[54] According to an estimate during 1988-94, over 50,000 Kashmiri youth have been trained in Pakistan. Terrorist incidents went up from 400 in 1988 to 5,000 in 1993, and deaths from 30 to 2,600. Mujahideens freed from Afghan conflict were sent to Kashmir and their numbers peaked at about 1,600 in 1994.[55] Gradually and knowingly the entire social spectrum was converted to the point where violence and terror began to be considered a justified means of communication.[55] The overall environment and even state institutions sustained terror in which collection of funds, settings up of training camps, free movement of arms and drug trafficking was not uncommon. The entire Kashmir problem as it exists now is because of Pakistan's extraordinary interest in our internal affairs and also due to the fact that most militants operating in India enjoy support from the ISI as well as the Jihadi groups based in Pakistan and Afghanistan.

In the decade nineties and thereafter it has been clearly established that riding the wave of success in Afghanistan, the Pak-Army-ISI combined had decided to replicate the Jihad in Kashmir by diverting the surplus of the Mujahideen on the Valley. With its new-found leverage with the Americans, Pakistan had in fact launched a new proxy war against India using the groups like HuM and Lashkar-e-Toiba that were totally under the thumb of its Army and extended the scope of its attacks beyond Jammu and Kashmir to targets in the rest of India.[56] This is how foreign Mujahideen started making their appearance in Kashmir for the first time in the early nineties and terrorist attacks also started occurring in Delhi, Mumbai and other centres. These Pak-sponsored outfits had no quarrel with the West–historically, politically and ideologically, which made it easier for Pakistan to get the US to easily accept its denial in the acts of cross-border terrorism.[57] The other notable groups participating in the terrorist attacks on India were Jaish-e-Mohammad and the Harkat-ul-Jehad Islami (HuJI) and these two were under the clutches of the ISI.

As a result, scores of innocent civilians continued to be gunned down at all with almost frequent intervals, and bomb explosions kill and maim hapless victims in buses and trains as well as in the market place. From the arms captured from terrorists and from the statements of those apprehended, it has been abundantly clear that the ISI, Pakistan's intelligence wing, has its fingerprints all over the terrorist intrusions into Kashmir.[58] The bomb blasts have outraged every patriotic Indian. No civilised nation can allow this kind of barbaric inhumanity to be partly or fully supported or sponsored by any neighbour or domestic insurgents. The only way we can combat it is to minimise, if not eliminate such occurrences.

In an important development of Indian politics the Babri Masjid was demolished on 7th December 1992. It hurt the religious sentiments largely in India and all Muslim countries of the world, the Pakistan in particular. Although the destruction of Babri Masjid was condemned by virtually all segments of opinion in the country, it raised the communal temperature and gave comfort to all the forces of intolerance and irrationality. In reaction the extremists in Pakistan had a field day, arousing the emotions of religious bigotry and fanaticism, much to the delight of their Indian counterparts, some of whom had gleefully participated in the destruction of the Mosque's structure.[59] Its net result was the Bombay blast of 1993 in which more than 300 lives were lost with the niddle of suspicion pointing to Pakistan's involvement. Although this was a serial blast of 13-bombs across the city which was hotly denied by Pakistan but in time Indian suspicions were confirmed. India believed that the prime suspects had fled to Dubai and from there to Karachi. India warned Pakistan of "serious consequences" if Islamabad did not hand over to the Indian authorities six members of the Menon family who were the main suspects in the explosions.[60] Another disturbing fact about the blast was that in this incident many of the new terrorists were from the middle-class, well educated, not terribly religious with no previous criminal records.[61] This means more and more middle class Muslims will be subjected to surveillance, search and interrogation.

To probe the overall issue of communal riots in Mumbai during December 1992-January 1993 and March 1993 serial blast the government appointed justice B.N. Srikrishna Commission.

The Commission in its report attributed the immediate causes to: (i) the demolition of the Babri masjid, (ii) the aggravation of Muslim sentiments by the Hindus with their celebration rallies and (iii) the insensitive and harsh approach of the police while handling the protesting mobs which initially were not violent.[62] On the serial bomb blasts, the Commission says, "There was a large amorphous body of angry frustrated and desperate Muslims keen to seek revenge for the perceived injustice done to and atrocities perpetrated on them or to others of their community and it is this sense of revenge which spawned the conspiracy of the serial blast."[63] Whenever blasts occur, we blame the police and the Intelligence Bureau (IB). Instead of indulging in blame game which will lead us nowhere, we should try to cleanse the socio-cultural ambience from which this cold-blooded inhumanity spawns.

In its 18-page fifth chapter report the Commission strongly recommended strict action against the police personnel who were found actively participating in riots, communal incidents and incidents of looting, arson and so on. The recommendations of the Commission aim at strengthening the secular fabric of our society. It says that religious observances in open public places must be strictly discouraged. The Commission hoped that the calamitous events of December 1992, January 1993 and March 1993 would serve as eye-openers and lead to introspection and that all concerned attain the maturity to accept constructive criticism and mend their ways.[64] However, it was frank enough to add that the deep-rooted polarisation that took place in our country after the Babri Masjid demolition in 1992 is growing at the vitals of the nation. We should find sincere ways to stop it. At the moment, if we stand together as Indians, irrespective of our religions, blasts and attacks will cease to occur in our cities.

Attacks, both major and minor, and other related terrorist activities continued unabated in different parts of the country and in line the Indian Airlines IC-814 was hijacked in December 1999 by Pakistan-based elements and took it to Kandahar (Afghanistan) via Kathmandu from where they put their initial demands through the Taliban.[65] Simultaneously, the incident also questioned the security lapses at Kathmandu airport where the hijackers were able to board the aircraft with weapons and grenades. For most of this decade, Indian security agencies have been warning that Kathmandu has become the terror capital of South Asia. Virtually every militant group from the LTTE to the Taliban is allowed free access through Nepal.[66] After the hijacking the Government of India, initially seemed unable to make up its mind about the necessary steps. In fact, considerable risk is involved in dealing with the kind of terrorists who have taken over the Indian Airlines plane. Driven by religious frenzy, they were seemingly capable of any desperate action that may be justified by their fanatical adherence to their faith.[67] As such any move to approach them had to be undertaken with great care.

Right from the time when the news of hijacking became known, both the government and the airline authorities had given the impression of being overwhelmed by the event. Attacking the citizen is the means by which the population is terrorised. This makes the government look helpless and incompetent. The citizens' pressure builds up in due course the government capitulates and seeks to come to terms with the terrorists. The legitimacy of the government is then questioned by the citizens. The political cost of not being able to protect the citizens on the one hand, and the failure to tackle the terrorist threat on the other, is quite heavy.[68] In response to hijackers' demand the Government of India, ultimately agreed to release their terrorist colleagues from Indian jails and in this way the mighty authority of the state was undermined. The three terrorists who were released in exchange, were hardcore militants of the outfit. After the release Masood Azhar became a public figure in Pakistan and Omar Sheikh later kidnapped journalist Daniel Pearl. The hijackers numbering half a dozen, wielding knives and pistols, obtained what they wanted and got away. More than the release of their colleagues, the terrorists showed up the security vulnerabilities of the Indian state. Through one incident they lowered the confidence of the citizens in the government's ability to protect lives.[69] The hijackers had energised others who had sought ways of making the Indian state respond to their perceived grievances. Now it became a hot issue of debate whose security matters more–the state's or the citizen's.

In continuation two devastating attacks were made in the year 2001. On 1 October 2001 a brutal suicide squad of JeM was made on the Kashmir Assembly complex followed by a terrorist attack on the Indian

Parliament, located at the heart of the capital's high security zone on 13th December, the same year. The car bomb explosion at the State Assembly building in Srinagar that killed many innocent bystanders came just three weeks after the appalling attacks on the twin towers of the World Trade Centre. Complicitly with the insertion of militants who carry out any heinous act means complicity with the act itself. Much was riding on the understanding of this linkage by Pakistan's new military hierarchy.[70] This attack had a direct linkage with Pakistan's volatile situation emanating from Jihadi violent demonstrations against Pakistan's decision to make common cause with US against the Taliban. Having joined the US in its fight against terrorism, General Musharraf needed as rarely before to pacify the Jihadis and demonstrate its commitment to Kashmir.[71] Terrorism has several consequences that have to be faced in the context of a growing threat to the country.

The Jammu and Kashmir Chief Minister broke down in public the daring terrorist attack on State Assembly complex in Srinagar and the gruesome deaths that ensued on that fateful day. The Indian official reaction to this attack was terse-it noted that, 'there is a limit to India's patience'. On the other hand, the global community had reacted cautiously to Srinagar since the focus of this constituency was on September 11 and the possibility of an imminent military strike by the US-led coalition against the Taliban regime. In addition the event of 1st October 2001 symbolised the significance of the target-the seat of democratic rule in the state and not just any government building.[72] The timing of the attack was no less relevant. It occurred on the eve of Gandhi jayanti and the tenets of non-violence were placed in the sharp contrast to the blood and gore that was strewn in Srinagar.

On 13th December 2001 the JeM made a well-planned, carefully crafted attack on the Indian Parliament which was timed with precise intelligence inputs. The Indian Prime Minister Atal Bihari Vajpayee, promptly laid the blame for this "stab at the heart of Indian democracy" on two Kashmiri militant groups, Lashkar-e-Toiba (the Army of the Pure) and Jaish-e-Muhammad (the Army of Muhammad).[73] He said that the terrorist attack on Indian Parliament had shown beyond a shadow of doubt that the anti-India forces in Pakistan are prepared to wreak any havoc on our soil. It was an attack on our sovereignty, on our national self-respect, and it was a challenge to our democratic system. He took the opportunity to reiterate that India has been a victim of cross-border terrorism for the past decades and has lost tens of thousands of innocent men and women and security forces.[74] Pakistan would be solely responsible for the consequences of encouraging terrorism against India and when expedient, turning a blind eye to terrorist groups with trans-national linkages operating from its soil.

The terrorist attack on Indian Parliament was aimed, on the part of Pakistan, to convey two strident messages. The first was that despite the success of the United States-led coalition in the Afghan war, terrorism is alive and well. It had become imperative to send it to raise the morale of terrorists in India and Pakistan which had sunk to their boots following the collapse of the Taliban regime. Secondly, the attack was a proof of the fact that the Musharraf had not sold out to the US, and its alliance with the latter was meant to safeguard Pakistan's nuclear arsenal and prevent the US from including its cross-border terrorism against India in its anti-terrorist agenda.[75] At the juncture, quite clearly, there was a crying need to fight the menace of terrorism unitedly. Partisanship of any sort in dealing with the ISI-sponsored terror attacks in India should be abandoned forthwith. Today terrorism has reached the heart of India in New Delhi's Parliament House. And to suggest that preventive detention laws without any safeguards whatsoever against their misuse were required in the seventies and eighties but are not required now.

In the post-Taliban scenario General Musharraf had only the Kashmir issue to build domestic support in his favour and divert attention from the failure of the foreign policy. In the situation one easily finds the evidence of Pakistan's close ties with the Taliban, Osama bin Laden and the Al-Qaeda, and these three had with terrorist militias like the LeT, JeM and HuM directly and through Pakistan's ISI. Its genesis lies in post-9/11 predicament of the Inter-Services Intelligence (ISI) when the agency realised that in the changed global environment it needed a tactical shift in its strategy of using terrorism as an instrument of State policy.[76] The run up to 9/11 was laid in Afghanistan after the US took a leading hand in ousting the Taliban that had assumed power there in 1996. Left to itself Pakistan had no problems with the Taliban; it was Benazir Bhutto who had dispatched the Taliban to that country in 1993 to clear the mess created by the tribal war lords in the post-Soviet scenario and established a friendly rule in Afghanistan to give 'strategic depth' to Pakistan against India.

In continuation Indian big cities/places remained number one target of the Pakistani terrorists. However, terror's first preference was Mumbai in Maharashtra where they exploded bombs on short intervals. On 6th December 2002, 27 January, 23 March and 28 July 2003, 11 July 2006, several serial blasts were undertaken by the terrorists of LeT, JeM and HuM in which hundreds were killed and thousands injured. The bomb blasts on local trains at various places killed 209 and injured over 700 innocent people. The number of blasts in Mumbai since 1983 is more than sufficient for anyone intending to do an analysis to get the root of the problem. It just can not happen that the few individuals who placed the blast devices did so without support or assistance from the local population.[77] It becomes all the more pronounced as Mumbai has a total floating population which surpasses the resident population of the city. If only our local police are a little more alert, the chances of such schemes getting leaked can not be ruled out. At least, the previous incident that happened must have alerted us to get ourselves ready for any eventuality.

In the ever-worst terror attack in India, a devastating event took place on 26th November 2008 in which Mumbai, the financial capital of India, was the target. On this saddest day Mumbai faced a terror attack by ten professionally trained men of Pakistani origin which represented the gravest provocation to the Indian states in decades. The terror attack was made at Hotel Taj, Nariman House, Hotel Trident Oberoi and other places in the city. It took about two hundred precious lives, and left over 300 people severally injured. The casualties included Indians, foreigners, police personnel, NSGs and others. It lasted for about 60 hours in which nine terrorists were gunned down and one was caught alive. In the operation against the terrorists 20 policemen and 2 NSG Commandos were killed. Among the dead 23 were of foreign nationals.[78] The 26/11 attack on Mumbai was in several respects very different from those in the past. It was a bold, brave frontal, ferocious attack in which terrorists were well prepared. Once again the attack demonstrated how incapable India is as a nation to prepare itself to fight against terrorism. It not only shocked the nation, but also gave us an impression that we can only boast of preparedness, but the reality is all together different.[79] Our intelligence agencies are not as alert and fast as the terrorists are. Now after six decades, the state can not even perform its basic function of protecting its citizens, never mind giving them a better life.

The terror attack in Mumbai at different places in the city had furthered India-Pakistan relations in all spheres near collapse and created a war-like situation between the two countries. For a long Islamabad refused the truth that the attackers were Pakistani nationals, it however, lastly accepted the fact that they were our citizens and attack's plan was prepared on Pakistani soil. But to India's dismay, the US establishment–obviously driven by its own national interests, refused to see the Pakistani's hand in 26/11. The US policy-makers desperately wanted to bail out Pak army from the well founded charge of complicity in the Mumbai terrorist attack. Their primary concern was somehow not to let this grave provocation cause an escalation of Indo-Pak tension that would give Pakistan a ruse for not concentrating on its task on the western front.[80] US responses might have been guided by the American national interests but they were unhelpful for India never-the-less.

About the sametime several attacks were made by the terror groups at different places in New Delhi, the capital of India. Earlier the repeal of POTA in 2002 had embolded the Students Islamic Movement of India (SIMI) and put the law enforcing agencies on the backfoot. Especially after the 9/11 the SIMI and the Indian Mujahideen have been a frontal to mislead the security agencies and simultaneously organising themselves aggressively. In a meeting after the 13th September 2008 attacks in Delhi, the SIMI leadership decided that the organisation should take advantage of the favourable environment to recruit for Jihad. They also decided to refrain from sporadic acts of terror till they strengthened themselves enough to make big strikes.[81] While they strengthened their relations with Pakistan through the LeT and the underworld, their role was by and large confined to assisting the Pakistan-based terrorists.

The SIMI/IM is only a motley growth of youth recruited and motivated by Pakistan for indigenisation of terror in India. It has negligible support among the Indian Muslims and all Muslim outfits have denounced their ideology and activities. In post-9/11 the big and famous terror outfits along with the ISI made SIMI their front organisation. Using Dawood Ibrahim, CAM Bashir, a SIMI leader from Mumbai was called to Dubai in 2001 and the process of converting a radical Islamic youth organisation into Pakistan-controlled terrorist outfit started. With re-organisation of the outfit, its mentors hoped to use the groups for direct actions rather than the support role they were playing. The Students Islamic Movement of India (SIMI) is being accessed, financed and controlled through locations in West Asia and the underworld is being primed to enhance its striking capabilities. The group is also emerging as a coverging point for the ISI, crime syndicates, radicalised local youth to bleed India. If Pakistan and the radical forces supported by it succeed in their nefarious designs of indigenising terror, it could lead to violent communal conflict, a long cherished objective of Pakistan.[82] The new strength of SIMI and IM, good ground knowledge and local contacts are worrying. India's inadequate laws, ill-equipped police force and the absence of political will to deal with the threat have only increased the problem.

Even in the years 2010 and 2011 several terror attacks were made in different parts of the country- at New Delhi and Mumbai in particular. In 2010 the Jama Masjid firing on 19 September and the Sheetla Ghat bomb blast on 6 December took place in which many precious lives lost and hundreds injured. Later it became clear that the rabid-e-mails sent by the terrorist group Indian Mujahideen after the Jama Masjid and Sheetla Ghat incidents were uploaded from Mumbai through the Opera Mini platform using servers in Norway. The recent bomb blast before the Delhi High Court is also in line. The chain of events poses serious questions about our capability to root out terror in the country. The answer, perhaps, lies in radically over-hauling our counter–terror strategy. Broadly speaking, enhancement of our capabilities to neutralise terror threats outside our land and sea borders should be our first priority.

Another and the latest terror attack took place in Mumbai on 13th July 2011. On that day the terrorists exploded three blasts at Opera House, Zaveri Bazar and Dadar West in which 26 persons were killed and over 130 injured. As a custom the incident will be remembered again, when the next blasts occur, to compare statistics on the number of persons killed and injured and the names of the groups responsible for the ghastly attacks. The chain of terror incidents with links to Mumbai indicate that terror modules in Maharashtra have regrouped and they have dedicated-and-tested lines of communication and logistics.[83] For any counter-terror strategy to succeed, these lines need to be disrupted on a regular basis. The investigations in the Mumbai 13/7 bombings are stuck partly because we do not have information to either dismiss or confirm theories about the involvement of the ISI or any terror outfit. The line of defence should be to unearth and uproot terror modules within our country so that terrorist's don't get time to regroup and launch attack. This is the task of the local police and dedicated anti-terror squads as the logic is that a terrorist on the run can't plan and, thus, can't strike.

In fact, we follow a hit-and-miss strategy to tackle terrorism. The last firewall in our fight against terrorism should be a proper and scientific investigation after the strike. It's a matter of concern that important clues at terror spots get trampled upon by an intrusive media and curious onlookers or they get hosted out by over-eager civic agencies. The next set of problems emanate from the fact that our counter-terrorist-doctrines, structures and systems have evolved around the threats from foreign terrorists. Apprehending domestic problems, the government has always denied that there could be local participation. But this reality should be accepted so that the intelligence agencies can include domestic players in their coverage. This acceptance will also increase the role and responsibility of the district and local-level intelligence units of the states that are in the state of neglect.

In the emerging scenario, the government must increase their contacts with the religious, social and civil society, Muslim leaders and deny any space to foreign-inspired subversive elements. It is important that while taking firm actions against anti-national elements, the innocents are protected and collateral damages are avoided. The same logic applies to living in cities. There is no fun blaming every person on this earth but we can start our own surveillance and protection wings in each area. There is need for the police to conduct area-wise, local get-togethers and attend to problems. We have many things in our favour and the nation is capable of meeting the threats. But to do this, the political parties must start looking at the problem from a national–and not an electoral perspective.

5.3 Globalisation and Terrorism

In today's world globalisation, liberalisation and privatisation is gaining growing attention as a strategy for survival, competition and growth. True economic globalisation involves a qualitative shift towards a system based on a consolidated global market place for production, distribution and consumption rather than on autonomous national economies.[84] It is an inexorable technology-driven process, which is bringing about an economic impact. The ship, the steam engine, the railroad, civil aviation and the Internet have reduced geographical distances and inspired global economic integration as never before.[85] The compression of time and space triggered by the Third Industrial Revolution–roughly, since 1980–has changed our interactions with the international environment. For many, globalisation–the intensified cross-border exchange of goods, services, capital, technology, ideas, information, legal systems, and people is both desirable and irreversible. In this age of increasing globalisation and interdependence, the national and international dimension of terrorism in fact, constitutes two facets of the same social phenomenon which infringes upon the interest of all states, not only as an assault against their public order and institutions that protect the liberty and security of their citizens but, also at the same time as a serious danger to peaceful international relations and cooperation, which is clearly understood as encompassing human rights and values as well as the principles of equal rights and self-determination of people. It is, therefore, that the transnational character of contemporary terrorist events has prompted international efforts to suppress them at the global, regional and bilateral levels.

However, the concept and phenomenon of globalisation, in its first phase, dated back between 1840 and 1914 when it reached its height and ended shortly before the World War I. During the height of globalisation, tariff barriers were reduced and prices of goods travelling between continents came down because with bigger ships being used to carry goods, transportation costs were lowered. There was also the huge migration of Europeans, about 60 million, for various destinations across the Atlantic. It swelled America's labour force and reduced

Ireland's working population leading to a convergence of wage levels across the Atlantic. There was a greater volatility of funds travelling across the continents and those losing out from globalisation triggered a political backlash against it.[86] American wheat imports for instance hurt the interests of European farmers who protested and continental Europe closed its agricultural markets and imposed high import tariffs. The United States too raised tariffs to protect its infant manufacturing industry and migration was clamped because it threatened American workers, living standards. Other rich countries followed in becoming protectionist and the stage of globalisation came to an end.

In between the years the world in general made achievements in all the spheres of human life and in the sixties the concept of global village was given by Marshall Mcluhan which is realising in the current phase of globalisation. There are several things in the concept of global village–an ideal, a destination to be reached and a conceptualisation of the ongoing transformation in the community. The earth in which we live is an integrated, interpenetrated and interconnected unit. The advances of communications and information technology have made the global village a virtual reality and this has paved the way for evolving frameworks of global governance. A major impact of the globalising world is that security can no longer be compartmentalised regionally or nationally and any analysis of the security environment of a region or area has to take into consideration global issues that have a direct or indirect impact on the region.[87] In broader context, the genesis of terrorism can be attributed to the development of exclusive instead of inclusive societies. Terrorism draws its strength from one of the three sources: militant religious fundamentalism, ethnic intolerance or deprivation. Religion sans frontiers, therefore religious militancy, has to be addressed globally. Ethnic intolerance and deprivation are region specific, with the common thread of economies running through them, and are best dealt with regionally or nationally.

The current position and dark side of globalisation has reminded us the capitalist mode of production which always maintained a global reach whether in the form of colonies or as trading partners across the continents. The inherent logic of capitalist economic system pushes it towards borderless economic transactions and is characterised as 'centralisation-cum-globalisation of finance capital.' This is the epoch of finance capital and of monopolies and we are in a phase of imperialism-led-globalisation. The finance capital operates in the context of unity among the finance exporting leading capitalist countries in which every recipient country of this finance capital operates under a common sword of democles wherein foreign investments can be withdrawn without a moment notice to the recipient of such a finance.[88] It proves the volatility of movement of finance capital and its most disastrous implication is that capital market of any country of the South can be destabilised by the investors who want quick and immediate profits and returns on investments. Joseph Stiglitz, an insider of the World Bank, published a seminal work on Globalisation and its Discontents (2002) in which he warned about the disastrous consequences of the present stage of capitalist globalisation. His brief description clearly indicated that national economy which is controlled and guided by a national state has been replaced and displaced by united globalisation capitalism.[89] Even in normal circumstances state systems of the peripheral developing countries are weak while dealing with the centre of capitalism, in the new context of highly mobile and volatile operations of finance capital the nation states have been completely marginalised under the impact of these new trends in global capitalist system. Marginalisation of the state and unity of the capitalist bloc is the reality of present phase of global capitalism.

Under globalisation the movement of people remains tightly restricted. The flow of capital is highly asymmetrical. Over the last two decades, overseas development assistance from the rich to poor countries has totalled $ 50-80 billion per year. In the same period, every year, $ 500-800 billion of illegal funds have been sent from the poor to rich countries. That is, for every one dollar of aid money over the table the West gets back $ 10 under the table.[90] The benefits and costs of linking and delinking are unequally distributed. Industrialised countries are mutually interdependent; developing countries are largely independent in economic relations with one another; and developing countries are highly dependent on industrialised countries. In addition there is also a growing divergence in income levels between countries and peoples, with widening inequality among and within nations. Assets and incomes are more concentrated. Wage shares have fallen. Profit shares have risen. Capital mobility alongside labour immobility has reduced the bargaining power of organised labour.[91] Professor Paul Krugman has admitted in his book *The Return of Depression Economics* that technical change and globalisation have increased the demand for highly skilled workers in the US while reducing the demand for the less skilled.[92] He said that inequality of both wealth and income has increased to levels not seen before since real wages actually declined for many workers.

The emerging implications of the liberalisation process which had begun in the early 1990s, are far more evident in terms of the resultant of new economic policy and change in the historical–ideological orientation of our political economy. Though considerable progress has been achieved in terms of higher growth rate and GDP, the basic needs and the crucial concerns of the core sectors of Indian economy such as agriculture and textiles affected millions of people pose a challenge to the successive governments.[93] Developed countries erect obstacles to trade in particular, barriers to trade in agricultural products and textiles. The West, under the guise of globalisation, pushes the developing countries to open their markets. But they raise barriers of entry into their markets. Globalisation, the way it is practised, encourages an unequal distribution of power and wealth among the countries of the world.[94] The rich agricultural countries fear that agricultural trade liberalisation will be harmful to their highly protected agriculture and the European Union and Japan are reluctant to open up their markets for agricultural products. The US has also retained a protectionist stance regarding its textile industry and has readily used anti-dumping laws. Even the South East Asian countries which became prosperous through globalisation have also witnessed a strong backlash against the trans-nationalisation and internationalisation of capital because trillions of dollars travel across the globe in seconds.

Like India in many traditional societies agriculture is not considered merely as an occupation but a major source of livelihood and for the vast majority a way of life. The traditional relationship between the people, land and agriculture has emotive overtones and any careless tampering with this delicate subject could unleash waves of violence and social disruption. Its direct result is the increase of insecurity of individuals, groups and nations in various domains-economic, financial, culture, employment, legal, social, healthcare, ecological, political and personal. And this is why the concept of globalisation is encountering resistance from various interest groups– environmentalists, labour leaders, cultural traditionalists, religious leaders of different persuasions and non-government officers.[95] This apart, the influential international NGOs have been against multinationals and the fast pace of globalisation that they have triggered. They have also come to form an international civil society because national governments no longer have a monopoly on information and because civil society now has access to data on the workings of multinationals and governments around the world.

The new system of capital finance and the ideology of 'roll-back the state' which allows market forces and private domestic and global operators to manage the economy in society has a definite impact on social life of the country. Since, every capitalist society is class–divided, a socially disastrous impact of such social divisions is felt very acutely on the majority of peasant and working classes in poor developing countries especially if economy in such societies is handed over to domestic and external private capitalists. The scholars– James K. Galbraith and John Williamson have also criticised the new global economic policy. Galbraith observed that 'rising inequality after 1980 is the rule' and stated, 'The patterns strongly suggest that forces of globalisation, including high global interest rates, debt crisis, and shock liberalisation are associated with rising inequality in pay structures. John Williamson has also lamented that the 'Washington Consensus' as a policy manifesto of the New Age 'omitted a concern for income distribution.'[96] In the circumstances so long as there exists in the world poverty, strife, injustice and oppression, conditions will exist which terrorists can turn to their advantage. No doubt that the campaign against terrorism is one that must be mounted at various levels, including political, economic and humanitarian.

Even before the Global Financial Crisis (GFC), many developing countries were worried that globalisation would impinge adversely on economic sovereignty, cultural integrity and social stability. "Interdependence" among unequals translates into the dependence of some on international markets that function under the dominance of others. The deepening of poverty and inequality–prosperity for a few countries and people, marginalisation and exclusion for the many–has implications for social and political stability among and within states. The rapid growth of global markets has not seen the parallel development of social and economic institutions to ensure balanced, inclusive and sustainable growth. Labour rights have been less sedulously protected than capital and property rights, and global rules on trade and finance are inequitable. This has asymmetric effects on rich and poor countries.

Recently, globalisation has also let loose the forces of uncivil society and accelerated the transnational flows of terrorism, human and drug trafficking, organised crime, piracy, and pandemic diseases. Terrorism continues to be generated by recurrent social crises, arising from the increasing fear of marginalisation of some sections of society caused by the indiscriminate spread of capitalism and the free economy, through much publicised globalisation which may be perceived another dimension of religious fanaticism. Despair caused by social marginalisation, economic deprivation, and political defeat is another cause of this modern phenomenon.[97] When the situation is thus monopolises by global power, when one deals with this formidable condensation of all functions through technocratic machinery and absolute ideological hegemony, what other way is there than a terrorist reversal of the situation. It is the system itself that has created the objective conditions for this brutal distortion. By taking all the cards to itself it forces the other to change the rules of the game. And the new rules are ferocious, because the stakes are ferocious. The terrorist groups are not ordinary civilians or some misguided youth but the paramilitary organs of militant extremism such as LeT, Naxalites, and the like who believe in the culture of extreme violence and whose objective is destruction of the established social system and structures, that is, the whole way of life of free societies. This virus does not take long to infect home-grown products and soon enough local criminal gangs get drawn into the terrorist's web.

Globalisation also cast a dark shadow on the governing pattern and civil society of the nation-state system. The growth in transnational flows has not been matched by an equivalent growth in global governance mechanisms to regulate them. And yet the very nature of the structure of globalised network, which intertwine global actors and interests, ensures that no single power is able to maintain its position within the newly emerging global disorder without making compromises with other global players. The transfer of state functions to supranational forms of regional governance could enhance the capacity of individual states to combat uncivil society. The sharing of expertise, institutions, policy tools, personnel and other resources can go a long way in stemming the tide of unwanted activities. In this context justice is one of the strongest pillars for the Parliamentary democracy. Justice is truth in practice. Rule of law provides citizens a sense of protection and self-confidence. We should not forget that denial of justice breeds terrorism.[98] It is not terrorist or terrorism who divided Ireland nor caused Israel-Palestinian problem. Terrorists did not separate India and Pakistan neither they carved out Bangladesh. As a result of the injustices and inequalities, a different kind of challenge is faced by countries of the world in general especially the developing and underdeveloped.

In the circumstances, the outright rejection of globalisation and a retreat into autarky is neither practical nor desirable. Opposing globalisation is like opposing the sun coming up every morning and about as fruitful. A country cannot ignore an absolute majority of its population which is poor and dissatisfied. A society cannot be peaceful if the majority of its poor population is socially alienated. Even a highly developed modern coercive apparatus of the state will not be able to deal with popular anger and the ruling classes will have to find some answers to meet the challenge of angry and alienated mass of society.[99] Jurgen Habermas, the German Philosopher, clearly brings out the 'Real Assumptions Underlying Globalisation' by mentioning: (i) that social inequality is a fate; or (ii) a necessary market outcome; that (iiii) the state is no more than a corporation providing services; and (iv) citizens are primarily entrepreneurs and customers. Thus, the message of globalisation is loud and clear that the poor should not expect anything from their society and state because market would create its own equilibrium.[100] The Indian Prime Minister Atal Bihari Vajpayee also acknowledged that the experiment that began in 1991 has increased inequalities and his government has decided to give a new pro-poor, pro-village, and pro-employment orientation to the Indian economy.

The big gap which appeared due to globalisation and its offshoot social inequality turned the poor masses look toward the pre-capitalist system of the past for some security and succour. Tribal or caste or religious solidarities of the past attract the vulnerable and helpless poor of the present. In other words the Western capitalist mode of production has not been able to shake the Asiatic social system based on caste or tribe, or religious loyalties and belief system. Religion is a common binding factor for the whole society in Hindu India, or Buddhist East Asia or Islam in the Arab world and other Muslim majority countries. Since religion exercises great influence over the whole societies of Asian countries, it plays significant role in the present crisis-ridden social order of these societies. However, at large, terrorism is motivated by a variety of inner drives ranging from financial gains to revenge, from fundamentalism to deprivation, political frustration, regional disparities, marginalisation of subnational groups, extremism, despair, injustice, discrimination, resentment against the existing regime, feeling of insignificance, intervention into personal freedom, weak government, separatism and oppression and inequality.

References

1. Bipin Chandra, Mridula Mukherjee and Aditya Mukherjee, eds., India After Independence 1947-2000 (New Delhi: Penguin Books, 2002), p. 320.
2. Sumantra Bose, *Kashmir; Roots of Conflict, Paths to Peace* (New Delhi : 2003), p. 45.
3. Saifuddin Soz, *Why Autonomy for Kashmir* (New Delhi: 1995), pp. 121-39.
4. A. G. Noorani, *The Kashmir Question* (Bombay: 1964), p. 101.
5. Sumantra Bose, *Kashmir: Roots of Conblict, Paths to Peace*, p. 33.
6. *Ibid.*, pp. 34-35.
7. Rajni Kothari, 'Interpreting Indian Politics : A personal Statement, in Upendra Baxi and Bhikhu Parekh, eds., *Crisis and Change in Contemporary India* (New Delhi: 1995), p. 165.
8. Karan Singh, 'Peace with Honour', *The Hindustan Times*, November 2, 2002.
9. Prem Shankar Jha, 'Farce Sighted', *Ibid.*, August 19, 2002.
10. R. Paula Newberg, *Double Betrayal: Repression and Insurgency in Kashmir* (Washington: 1995), p. 73.
11. Riyaz Punjabi, 'Resurrect Kashmiriyat', *The Hindustan Times*, July 18, 2002.
12. Balraj Puri, *Kashmir Towards Insurgency* (New Delhi: 1995), p. 84.

13. Jung Courtney and Ian Shapiro, 'South Africa's Negotiated Transition : Democracy, Opposition and the New Constitutional Order', *Politics and Society*, September 1995, pp. 271-73.
14. Paula R. Newberg, *Double Betrayal: Repression and Insurgency in Kashmir*, p. 74.
15. Selig S. Harrison, Paul H. Kreisberg and Deunis Kux (eds.), *India and Pakistan-The First Fifty Year* (United Kingdom: Cambridge University Press, 1999), pp. 149-50.
16. Verghese Koithara, *Society, State and Security: The Indian Experience* (New Delhi: Sage Publications, 1999), p. 113.
17. Sumantra Bose, *Kashmir: Roots of Conflict Paths to Peace* p. 3.
18. *Ibid.*, p. 4.
19. D.R. Goyal, 'International Terrorism: Challenge and Response', in Mahavir Singh (ed.), *International Terrorism and Religious Extremism–Challenges to Central and South Asia* (New Delhi : Anamika Publishers, 2004), p.1.
20. Jessica Stern, *The Ultimate Terrorist* (Massachusetts: Harvard University Press, 1999) pp. 11-12.
21. C. Uday Bhaskar, 'New Rules for the New War', *The Hindustan Times*, 7 October 2001.
22. Suman Singh, 'Terrorism in South Asia', *South Asia Politics*, Vol. 9, No. 2, June 2010 (New Delhi), p. 50.
23. Jagdish Prasad Verma, 'If You Wish for Peace, Understand Terrorism', in *Ibid.*, Vol. 9, No. 7, November 2010 (New Delhi : 2010), p. 49.
24. Suman Singh, 'Terrorism in South Asia'.
25. Jagdish Prasad Verma, 'If You Wish for Peace, Understand Terrorism'.
26. Jean Baudrillard, 'The Spirit of Terrorism', 2 November 2001.
27. Ajit Doval, 'Outsourcing Terror,' *The Times of India*, 18 July 2011.
28. Jagdish Prasad Verma, 'If You Wish for Peace, Understand Terrorism.'
29. Gwynne Dyer, 'The Slow Decline of Terror', *The Hindustan Times*, 24 August 1998.
30. R.A. Seligman (ed.), *Encyclopaedia of the Social Sciences*, Vols. 13-14 (Newyork : The Macmillan Company, 1954), p. 575.
31. *Ibid.*, p. 576.
32. *Ibid.*, p. 578.
33. Jagdish Prasad Verma, 'If You Wish for Peace, Understand Terrorism', p. 49.
34. Rajkumar Singh, *Past, Present and Future of Kashmir* (New Delhi: Gyan Publishing House, 2008), p. 47.
35. Prakash Singh, 'Militancy from Kashmir to Coimbatore,' *The Hindustan Times*, 23 February 1998.
36. B. Sheik Ali, *Islam: A Cultural Orientation* (Delhi: 1981), p. 14.

37. *The Quran*, English Translation, Abdullah Yusuf Ali (Leicester), 5:35.
38. *Ibid.*
39. Afsir Karim, 'Challenges of Terrorism and Religious Extremism in Central and South Asia' in Mahavir Singh (ed.), *International Terrorism and Religious Extremism-Challenges to Central and South Asia*, pp. 69-70.
40. Rajkumar Singh, *Past, Present and Future of Kashmir*, pp. 51-52.
41. Nandy, 'The Sociology of Sati', *The Indian Express*, 5 October 1989.
42. Chandrika Bandaranaike Kumaratunga, 'Original Sins', *The Hindustan Times*, 29 April 2002.
43. B. Sheik Ali, *Islam: A Cultural Orientation*, pp. 137-38.
44. A.K. Verma, 'Radical Islam and Terror', *South Asia Politics*, Vol. 7, No. 8, December 2008 (New Delhi : 2008), p. 16.
45. Abbas Rashid, 'Pakistan : The Ideological Dimensions in Mohammad Asghar Khan (ed.), *Islam, Politics and the State: The Pakistan Experience* (London: Zed Press, 1985), p. 75.
46. K.R. Malkani, 'Inside the Muslim Mind', *The Hindustan Times*, 13 October 2001.
47. Paul Kennedy, *Preparing for the Twenty-first Century*, p. 224.
48. Samuel Huntington, 'The Clash of Civilisations', *Foreign Affairs* (Summer, 1993), pp. 22-49.
49. John Mueller, 'Nine Propositions About the Historical Impact of Nuclear Weapons', in Jorn Gjelstad and Olav Njolstad (eds.), *Nuclear Rivalry and International Order* (London: 1996), pp. 56-57.
50. C. Uday Bhaskar, 'Strategic Implications of the Proxy War', *The Hindustan Times*, 18 August 1998.
51. *Ibid.*
52. V.R. Raghvan, 'Response to Terror,' in *Ibid.*, 6 January 1999.
53. Rajkumar Singh, *Contemporary India with Controversial Neighbours* (New Delhi:Gyan Publishing House, 2011), pp. 128-29.
54. Verghese Koithara, *Society, State and Security : The Indian Experience*, p. 113.
55. Manvendra Singh, 'Threshold of Patience,' *The Hindustan Times*, 15 January 2002.
56. D.C. Pathak, 'India's Role in the War on Terror,' *South Asia Politics*, Vol. 9, No.10, February 2011 (New Delhi : 2011), p. 4.
57. *Ibid.*
58. N.C. Menon, 'Terrorism as an Epidemic,' *The Hindustan Times*, 18 August 1998.
59. V.P. Dutt, *India's Foreign Policy in a Changing World* (New Delhi: Vikas Publishing House, 1999), pp.121-22.

60. *The Indian Express*, 25 March 1993.
61. Prem Shankar Jha, 'Sowing Dragon Seed,' *The Hindustan Times*, 13 September 2003.
62. C.V. Sukumaran, 'Let's Stop the Blame Game and Start Addressing the Grievances,' *The Hindu*, 7 August 2011.
63. *Ibid.*
64. *Ibid.*
65. Rajkumar Singh, *Relations of NDA & UPA with Neighbours* (New Delhi: Gyan Publishing House, 2010), p. 94.
66. *The Hindustan Times*, editorial, 29 December 1999.
67. *Ibid.*
68. V.R. Raghvan, 'Response to Terror'.
69. *Ibid.*
70. Michael Krepon, 'Forbearance is the Key Word', *The Hindustan Times*, 14 October 2001.
71. Veena Kukreja, '*Contemporary Pakistan: Political Processes, Conflicts and Crises* (New Delhi: Sage Publications, 2008), p. 288.
72. C. Uday Bhaskar, 'New Rules for the New War', in *Ibid.*, 7 October 2001.
73. Dilara Chowdhury, 'Toying with Weapons of Mass Destruction: What are India and Pakistan Up To?,' *The Daily Star*, 14 March 2002.
74. Atal Bihari Vajpayee, 'We Shall Triumph Against Terrorism', *The Hindustan Times*, 1 January 2002.
75. Veena Kukreja, *Contemporary Pakistan: Political Processes, Conflicts and Crises*, p. 290.
76. Ajit Doval, 'Outsourcing Terror,' *The Times of India*, 18 July 2011.
77. R.V.S. Mani, 'We Can Tackle Terror and Save Mumbai,' *The Hindu*, 7 August 2011.
78. *Ibid.*, editorial, 27 December 2008.
79. Rajkumar Singh, *Relations of NDA & UPA with Neighbours*, p.144.
80. D.C. Pathak, 'India's Role in the War on Terror,' p. 4.
81. Ajit Doval, 'Outsourcing Terror.'
82. *Ibid.*
83. Shishir Gupta, 'Target for Terror,' *The Hindustan Times*, 7 September 2011.
84. J.C. Mohanty, 'WTO and Implications for Indian Agriculture', in Ramesh K. Arora (ed.), *Administrative Change*, Vol. XXX, No. 1 and Vol. XXXI, No. 2, January – December 2002 (Jaipur : 2002), p. 67.
85. Rahul Mukherji, 'Noose Tightens Over Global Order', *The Hindustan Times*, 30 June 2003.
86. B. Ramesh Babu, 'The Liberal Capitalist West as the New Global State', *International Studies*, Vol. 43, No. 3, July–September 2006 (New Delhi: Sage Publications, 2006), p. 291.

87. A.S. Kalkat, 'Ensuring Security in the Age of Global Terror', *The Hindu*, 13 September 2006.
88. Prabhat Patnaik (Introduction), V.I. Lenin, *Imperialism: The Highest Stage of Capitalism* (New Delhi: Leftword, 2000), p. 24.
89. C.P. Bhambhri, 'Globalisation and Neo-Primordialism', in Mahavir Singh (ed.), *International Terrorism and Religious Extremism–Challenges to Central and South Asia*, pp. 11-14.
90. Jorge Heine and Ramesh Thakur, 'The Dark Side of Globalisation', *The Hindu*, 10 January 2011.
91. *Ibid.*
92. Jayshree Sengupta, 'Threats to Globalisation', *The Hindustan Times*, 4 February 2000.
93. Rajkumar Singh, *Contemporary India with Controversial Neighbours*, p. 76.
94. C. Sheela Reddy, 'Globalisation'–A Human Rights Perspective *South Asia Politics*, Vol. 5, No. 2, March 2007 (New Delhi: 2007), pp. 39-40.
95. James K. Galbraith, 'Rising Inequality After 1980 is the Rule', *Foreign Affairs*, July–August 2002 (Newyork: 2002), p. 179.
96. John Williamson, 'The Washington Consensus and Beyond', *Economic and Political Weekly*, Vol. XXXVIII, No. 15, 12-18 April 2003 (Mumbai: 2003), pp. 1475-1481.
97. Sheikh Saleem Ahmed, 'Dimensions of Terrorism and Religious Extremism: Two Sides of the Same Coin', in Mahavir Singh (ed.), *International Terrorism and Religious Extremism–Challenges to Central and South Asia*, p. 38.
98. *Ibid.*, pp. 38-39.
99. C.P. Bhambhri, 'Globalisation and Neo-Primordialism', p. 22.
100. As quoted in *Ibid.*

Appendices on People's Republic of China

Agreement on the Maintenance of Peace and Tranquility along the Line of Actual Control in the India-China Border Areas

September 7, 1993

The Government of the Republic of India and the Government of the People's Republic of China (hereinafter referred to as the two sides), have entered into the present Agreement in accordance with the Five Principles of mutual respect for sovereignty and territorial integrity, mutual non-aggression, noninterference in each other's internal affairs, equality and mutual benefit and peaceful coexistence and with a view to maintaining peace and tranquility in areas along the line of actual control in the India-China border areas.

1. The two sides are of the view that the India-China boundary question shall be resolved through peaceful and friendly consultations. Neither side shall use or threaten to use force against the other by any means. Pending an ultimate solution to the boundary question between the two countries, the two sides shall strictly respect and observe the line of actual control between the two sides. No activities of either side shall overstep the line of actual control. In case personnel of one side cross the line of actual control, upon being cautioned by the other side, they shall immediately pull back to their own side of the line of actual control. When necessary, the two sides shall jointly check and determine the segments of the line of actual control where they have different views as to its alignment.

2. Each side will keep its military forces in the areas along the line of actual control to a minimum level compatible with the friendly and good neighbourly relations between the two countries. The two

sides agree to reduce their military forces along the line of actual control in conformity with the requirements of the principle of mutual and equal security to ceilings to be mutually agreed. The extent, depth, timing, and nature of reduction of military forces along the line of actual control shall be determined through mutual consultations between the two countries. The reduction of military forces shall be carried out by stages in mutually agreed geographical locations sector-wise within the areas along the line of actual control.

3. Both sides shall work out through consultations effective confidence building measures in the areas along the line of actual control. Neither side will undertake specified levels of military exercises in mutually identified zones. Each side shall give the other prior notification of military exercises of specified levels near the line of actual control permitted under this Agreement.

4. In case of contingencies or other problems arising in the areas along the line of actual control, the two sides shall deal with them through meetings and friendly consultations between border personnel of the two countries. The form of such meetings and channels of communications between the border personnel shall be mutually agreed upon by the two sides.

5. The two sides agree to take adequate measures to ensure that air intrusions across the line of actual control do not take place and shall undertake mutual consultations should intrusions occur. Both sides shall also consult on possible restrictions on air exercises in areas to be mutually agreed near the line of actual control.

6. The two sides agree that references to the line of actual control in this Agreement do not prejudice their respective positions on the boundary question.

7. The two sides shall agree through consultations on the form, method, scale and content of effective verification measures and supervision required for the reduction of military forces and the maintenance of peace and tranquility in the areas along the line of actual control under this Agreement.

8. Each side of the India-China Joint Working Group on the boundary question shall appoint diplomatic and military experts to

formulate, through mutual consultations, implementation measures for the present Agreement. The experts shall advise the Joint Working Group on the resolution of differences between the two sides on the alignment of the line of actual control and address issues relating to redeployment with a view to reduction of military forces in the areas along the line of actual control. The experts shall also assist the Joint Working Group in supervision of the implementation of the Agreement, and settlement of differences that may arise in that process, based on the principle of good faith and mutual confidence.

9. The present Agreement shall come into effect as of the date of signature and is subject to amendment and addition by agreement of the two sides.

Signed in duplicate at Beijing on the Seventh day of September 1993 in the Hindi, Chinese and English languages, all three texts having equal validity.

[Signed:]
R. L. Bhatia Minister of State for External Affairs Republic of India
Tang Jiaxuan Vice-Foreign Minister People's Republic of China.

Agreement between the Government of the Republic of India and the Government of the People's Republic of China on Confidence-Building Measures in the Military Field Along the Line of Actual Control in the India-China Border Areas

November 29, 1996.

The Government of the Republic of India and the Government of the People's Republic of China (hereinafter referred to as the two sides), Believing that it serves the fundamental interests of the peoples of India and China to foster a long-term good-neighbourly relationship in accordance with the 'five principles of mutual respect for sovereignty and territorial integrity, mutual non-aggression, non-interference in each other's internal affairs, equality and mutual benefit and peaceful co-existence, Convinced that the maintenance of peace and tranquility along the line of actual control in the India-China border areas accords with the fundamental interests of the two peoples and will also contribute to the ultimate resolution of the boundary question, Reaffirming that neither side shall use or threaten to use force against the other by any means or seek unilateral military superiority, Pursuant to the Agreement between the Government of the Republic of India and the Government of the People's Republic of China on the Maintenance of Peace and Tranquility along the Line of Actual Control in the India-China Border Areas, signed on 7 September, 1993, Recognizing the need for effective confidence building measures in the military field along the line of actual control in the border areas between the two sides, Noting the utility of confidence building measures already in place along the line of actual control in the India-China border areas, Committed to enhancing mutual confidence and transparency in the military field, Have agreed as follows:

Article I

Neither side shall use its military capability against the other side. No armed forces deployed by either side in the border areas along the line of actual control as part of their respective military strength shall be used to attack the other side, or engage in military activities that threaten the other side or undermine peace, tranquility and stability in the India-China border areas.

Article II

The two sides reiterate their determination to seek a fair, reasonable and mutually acceptable settlement of the boundary question. Pending an ultimate solution to the boundary question, the two sides reaffirm their commitment to strictly respect and observe the line of actual control in the India-China border areas. No activities of either side shall overstep the line of actual control.

Article III

The two sides agree to take the following measures to reduce or limit their respective military forces within mutually agreed geographical zones along the line of actual control in the India-China border areas:

(1) The two sides reaffirm that they shall reduce or limit their respective military forces within mutually agreed geographical zones along the line of actual control in the India-China border areas to minimum levels compatible with the friendly and good neighbourly relations between the two countries and consistent with the principle of mutual and equal security.

(2) The two sides shall reduce or limit the number of field army, border defence forces, paramilitary forces and any other mutually agreed category of armed force deployed in mutually agreed geographical zones along the line of actual control to ceilings to be mutually agreed upon. The major categories of armaments to be reduced, or limited are as follows: combat tanks, infantry combat vehicles, guns (including howitzers) with 75 mm or bigger calibre, mortars with 120 mm or bigger calibre, surface-to-surface missiles, surface-to-air missiles and any other weapon system mutually agreed upon.

(3) The two sides shall exchange data on the military forces and armaments to be reduced or limited and decide on ceilings on military forces and armaments to be kept by each side within mutually agreed geographical zones along the line of actual control in the India-China border areas. The ceilings shall be determined in conformity with the requirement of the principle of mutual and equal security, with due consideration being given to parameters such as the nature of terrain, road communication and other infrastructure and time taken to induct/ deinduct troops and armaments.

Article IV

In order to maintain peace and tranquility along the line of actual control in the India-China border areas and to prevent any tension in the border areas due to misreading by either side of the other side's intentions:

(1) Both sides shall avoid holding large scale military exercises involving more than one Division (approximately 15,000 troops) in close proximity of the line of actual control in the India-China border areas. However, if such exercises are to be conducted, the strategic direction of the main force involved shall not be towards the other side.

(2) If either side conducts a major military exercise involving more than one Brigade Group (approximately 5,000 troops) in close proximity of the line of actual control in the India-China border areas, it shall give the other side prior notification with regard to type, level, planned duration and area of exercise as well as the number and type of units or formations participating in the exercise.

(3) The date of completion of the exercise and de-induction of troops from the area of exercise shall be intimated to the other side within five days of completion or de-induction.

(4) Each side shall be entitled to obtain timely clarification from the side undertaking the exercise in respect of data specified in Paragraph 2 of the present Article.

Article V

With a view to preventing air intrusions across the line of actual control in the India-China border areas and facilitating overflights and landings by military aircraft:

(1) Both sides shall take adequate measures to ensure that air intrusions across the line of actual control do not take place. However, if an intrusion does take place, it should cease as soon as detected and the incident shall be promptly investigated by the side operating the aircraft. The results of the investigation shall be immediately communicated, through diplomatic channels or at border personnel meetings, to the other side.

(2) Subject to Paragraphs 3 and 5 of this Article, combat aircraft (to include fighter, bomber, reconnaissance, military trainer, armed helicopter and other armed aircraft) shall not fly within ten kilometers of the line of actual control.

(3) If either side is required to undertake flights of combat aircraft within ten kilometers from the line of actual control, it shall give the following information in advance to the other side, through diplomatic channels:

(a) Type and number of combat aircraft;

(b) Height of the proposed flight (in meters);

(c) Proposed duration of flights (normally not to exceed ten days);

(d) Proposed timing of flights; and

(e) Area of operations, defined in latitude and longitude.

(4) Unarmed transport aircraft, survey aircraft and helicopters shall be permitted to fly up to the line of actual control.

(5) No military aircraft of either side shall fly across the line of actual control, except by prior permission. Military aircraft of either side may fly across the line of actual control or overfly the other side's airspace or land on the other side only after obtaining the latter's prior permission after providing the latter with detailed information on the flight in accordance with the international practice in this regard. Notwithstanding the above stipulation, each side has the sovereign right to specify additional conditions, including at short notice, for flights or landings of military aircraft of the other side on its side of the line of actual control or through its airspace.

(6) In order to ensure flight safety in emergency situations, the authorities designated by the two sides may contact each other by the quickest means of communications available.

Article VI

With a view to preventing dangerous military activities along the line of actual control in the India-China border areas, the two sides agree as follows:

(1) Neither side shall open fire, cause bio-degradation, use hazardous chemicals, conduct blast operations or hunt with guns or explosives within two kilometers from the line of actual control. This prohibition shall not apply to routine firing activities in small arms firing ranges.

(2) If there is a need to conduct blast operations within two kilometers of the line of actual control as part of developmental activities, the other side shall be informed through diplomatic channels or by convening a border personnel meeting, preferably five days in advance.

(3) While conducting exercises with live ammunition in areas close to the line of actual control, precaution shall be taken to ensure that a bullet or a missile does not accidentally fall on the other side across the line of actual control and causes harm to the personnel or property of the other side.

(4) If the border personnel of the two sides come in a face-to-face situation due to differences on the alignment of the line of actual control

on any other reason, they shall exercise self-restraint and take all necessary steps to avoid an escalation of the situation. Both sides shall also enter into immediate consultations through diplomatic and/or other available channels to review the situation and prevent any escalation of tension.

Article VII

In order to strengthen exchanges and cooperation between the military personnel and establishments in the border areas along the line of actual control, the two sides agree:

(1) To maintain and expand the regime of scheduled and flag meetings between their border representatives at designated places along the line of actual control;

(2) To maintain and expand telecommunication links between the border meeting points at designated places along the line of actual control;

(3) To establish step-by-step medium and high-level contacts between the border authorities of the two sides.

Article VIII

(1) Should the personnel of one side cross the line of actual control and enter the other side because of unavoidable circumstances like natural disasters, the other side shall extend all possible assistance to them and inform their side, as soon as possible regarding the forced or inadvertent entry across the line of actual control. The modalities of return of the concerned personnel to their own side shall be settled through mutual consultations.

(2) The two sides shall provide each other, at the earliest possible, with information pertaining to natural disasters and epidemic diseases in contiguous border areas which might affect the other side. The exchange of information shall take place either through diplomatic channels or at border personnel meetings.

Article IX

In case a doubtful situation develops in the border region, or in case one of the sides has some questions or doubts regarding the manner in which the other side is observing this Agreement, either side has the right to seek a clarification from the other side. The clarifications sought and replies to them shall be conveyed through diplomatic channels.

Article X

(1) Recognising that the full implementation of some of the provisions of the present Agreement will depend on the two sides arriving at a common understanding of the alignment of the line of actual control in the India-China border areas, the two sides agree to speed up the process clarification and confirmation of the line of actual control. As an initial step in this process, they are clarifying the alignment of the line of actual control in those segments where they have different perceptions. They also agree to exchange maps indicating their respective perceptions of the entire alignment of the line of actual control as soon as possible.

(2) Pending the completion of the process of clarification and confirmation of the line of actual control, the two sides shall work out modalities for implementing confidence building measures envisaged under this Agreement on an interim basis, without prejudice to their respective positions on the alignment of the line of actual control as well as on the boundary question.

Article XI

Detailed implementation measures required under Article I to Article X of this Agreement shall be decided through mutual consultations in the India-China Joint Working Group on the Boundary Question. The India-China Diplomatic and Military Expert Group shall assist the India-China Joint.

Article XII

This Agreement is subject to ratification and shall enter into force on the date of exchange of instruments of ratification. It shall remain in effect until either side decides to terminate it after giving six months' notice in writing. It shall become invalid six months after the notification. This Agreement is subject to amendment and addition by mutual agreement in writing between the two sides. Signed in duplicate in New Delhi on 29 November, 1996 in the Hindi, Chinese and English languages, all three texts being equally authentic. In case of divergence, the English text shall prevail.

Agreement between the Government of the Republic of India and the Government of the People's Republic of China on the Political Parameters and Guiding Principles for the Settlement of the India-China Boundary Question

April 11, 2005

The Government of the Republic of India and the Government of the People's Republic of China (hereinafter referred to as the two sides) Believing that it serves the fundamental interests of the peoples of India and China to foster a long-term constructive and cooperative partnership on the basis of the Five Principles of Peaceful Co-existence, mutual respect and sensitivity for each other's concerns and aspirations, and equality, Desirous of qualitatively upgrading the bilateral relationship at all levels and in all areas while addressing differences through peaceful means in a fair, reasonable and mutually acceptable manner, Reiterating their commitment to abide by and implement the Agreement on the Maintenance of Peace and Tranquillity along the Line of Actual Control in the India-China Border Areas, signed on 7 September 1993, and the Agreement on Confidence Building Measures in the Military Field along the Line of Actual Control in the India-China Border Areas, signed on 29 November 1996, Reaffirming the Declaration on Principles for Relations and Comprehensive Cooperation between India and China, signed on 23 June 2003, Recalling that the two sides have appointed Special Representatives to explore the framework of settlement of the India-China boundary question and the two Special Representatives have been engaged in consultations in a friendly, cooperative and constructive atmosphere, Noting that the two sides are seeking a political settlement of the boundary question in the context of their overall and long-term interests, Convinced that an early settlement of the boundary question will advance the basic interests of the two countries and should therefore be pursued as a strategic objective, Have agreed on the following political parameters and guiding principles for a boundary settlement:

Article I

The differences on the boundary question should not be allowed to affect the overall development of bilateral relations. The two sides will resolve the boundary question through peaceful and friendly consultations. Neither side shall use or threaten to use force against the other by any means. The final solution of the boundary question will significantly promote good neighbourly and friendly relations between India and China.

Article II

The two sides should, in accordance with the Five Principles of Peaceful Coexistence, seek a fair, reasonable and mutually acceptable solution to the boundary question through consultations on an equal footing, proceeding from the political perspective of overall bilateral relations.

Article III

Both sides should, in the spirit of mutual respect and mutual understanding, make meaningful and mutually acceptable adjustments to their respective positions on the boundary question, so as to arrive at a package settlement to the boundary question. The boundary settlement must be final, covering all sectors of the India-China boundary.

Article IV

The two sides will give due consideration to each other's strategic and reasonable interests, and the principle of mutual and equal security.

Article V

The two sides will take into account, inter alia, historical evidence, national sentiments, practical difficulties and reasonable concerns and sensitivities of both sides, and the actual state of border areas.

Article VI

The boundary should be along well-defined and easily identifiable natural geographical features to be mutually agreed upon between the two sides.

Article VII

In reaching a boundary settlement, the two sides shall safeguard due interests of their settled populations in the border areas.

Article VIII

Within the agreed framework of the final boundary settlement, the delineation of the boundary will be carried out utilising means such as modern cartographic and surveying practices and joint surveys.

Article IX

Pending an ultimate settlement of the boundary question, the two sides should strictly respect and observe the line of actual control and work together to maintain peace and tranquility in the border areas. The India-China Joint Working Group and the India-China Diplomatic and Military Expert Group shall continue their work under the Agreements of 7 September 1993 and 29 November 1996, including the clarification of the line of actual control and the implementation of confidence building measures.

Article X

The Special Representatives on the boundary question shall continue their consultations in an earnest manner with the objective of arriving at an agreed framework for a boundary settlement, which will provide the basis for the delineation and demarcation of the India-China boundary to be subsequently undertaken by civil and military officials and surveyors of the two sides.

Article XI

This Agreement shall come into force as of the date of signature and is subject to amendment and addition by mutual agreement in writing between the two sides.

Signed in duplicate in New Delhi on 11 April, 2005, in the Hindi, Chinese and English languages, all three texts being equally authentic. In case of divergence, the English text shall prevail.

For the Government of the Republic of India, For the Government of the People's Republic of China, New Delhi, April 11, 2005.

Agreement between The Government of the Republic of India and The Government of the People's Republic of China on the Establishment of a Working Mechanism for Consultation and Coordination on India-China Border Affairs

January 17, 2012

The Government of the Republic of India and the Government of the People's Republic of China (hereinafter referred to as the "two sides"); Firmly believing that respecting and abiding by the Line of Actual Control pending a resolution of the Boundary Question between the two countries as well as maintaining and strengthening peace and tranquility in the India-China border areas is very significant for enhancing mutual trust and security between the two countries, for resolving the Boundary Question at an early date and for building the India-China Strategic and Cooperative Partnership for Peace and Prosperity;

Desiring to materialise the spirit of the Agreement between the Government of the Republic of India and the Government of the People's Republic of China on the Maintenance of Peace and Tranquility Along the Line of Actual Control in the India-China Border Areas signed on 7th September 1993, the Agreement between the Government of the Republic of India and the Government of the People's Republic of China on Confidence Building Measures in the Military Field Along the Line of Actual Control in the India-China Border Areas signed on 29th November 1996 and the Protocol between the Government of the Republic of India and the Government of the People's Republic of China on Modalities for the Implementation of Confidence Building Measures in the Military Field Along the Line of Actual Control in the India-China Border Areas signed on 11th April 2005; Aiming for timely communication of information on the border situation, for appropriately handling border incidents, for earnestly undertaking other cooperation activities in the India-China border areas, have agreed as follows:

Article I

The two sides agree to establish a Working Mechanism for Consultation and Coordination on India-China Border Affairs (hereinafter referred to as "the Working Mechanism") to deal with important border affairs related to maintaining peace and tranquility in the India-China border areas.

Article II

The Working Mechanism will be headed by a Joint Secretary level official from the Ministry of External Affairs of the Republic of India and a Director General level official from the Ministry of Foreign Affairs of the People's Republic of China and will be composed of diplomatic and military officials of the two sides.

Article III

The Working Mechanism will study ways and means to conduct and strengthen exchanges and cooperation between military personnel and establishments of the two sides in the border areas.

Article IV

The Working Mechanism will explore the possibility of cooperation in the border areas that are agreed upon by the two sides.

Article V

The Working Mechanism will undertake other tasks that are mutually agreed upon by the two sides but will not discuss resolution of the Boundary Question or affect the Special Representatives Mechanism.

Article VI

The Working Mechanism will address issues and situations that may arise in the border areas that affect the maintenance of peace and tranquility and will work actively towards maintaining the friendly atmosphere between the two countries.

Article VII

The Working Mechanism will hold consultations once or twice every year alternately in India and China. Emergency consultations, if required, may be convened after mutual agreement.

Article VIII

This Agreement shall come into force on the date of its signature. It may be revised, amended, or terminated with the consent of the two sides. Any revision or amendment, mutually agreed by the two sides, shall form an integral part of this Agreement.

Signed in duplicate in Hindi, Chinese and English languages at New Delhi, on 17th January 2012, all three versions being equally authentic. In case of divergence the English text shall prevail.

Agreement between the Government of the Republic of India and the Government of the People's Republic of China on Border Defence Cooperation

October 23, 2013

The Government of the Republic of India and the Government of the People's Republic of China (hereinafter referred to as the 'two sides'), Firmly believing that the India-China Strategic and Cooperative Partnership for Peace and Prosperity serves the fundamental interests of the people of the two countries, Reiterating that neither side shall use its military capability against the other side and that their respective military strengths shall not be used to attack the other side, Reaffirming that neither side shall use or threaten to use force against the other side by any means nor seek unilateral superiority, Having accepted the principle of mutual and equal security, Acknowledging the need to continue to maintain peace, stability and tranquility along the line of actual control in the India-China border areas and to continue implementing confidence building measures in the military field along the line of actual control, Recognising the importance of materialising the spirit of the Agreement between the Government of the Republic of India and Government of the People's Republic of China on the Maintenance of Peace and Tranquility Along the Line of Actual Control in the India-China Border Areas signed on 7th September 1993, the Agreement between the Government of the Republic of India and the Government of the People's Republic of China on Confidence Building Measures in the Military Field Along the Line of Actual Control in the India-China Border Areas signed on 29th November 1996, the Protocol between the Government of the Republic of India and the Government of the People's Republic of China on Modalities for the Implementation of Confidence Building Measures in the Military Field Along the Line of Actual Control in India-China Border Areas signed on 11th April 2005 and the Agreement between the Government of the Republic of India and the Government of the People's Republic of China on the Establishment of a Working Mechanism for Consultation and Coordination on India-China Border Affairs signed on 17th January 2012.

Have agreed as follows:

Article I

The two sides shall carry out border defence cooperation on the basis of their respective laws and relevant bilateral agreements.

Article II

The two sides shall implement border defence cooperation in the following ways:

- Exchange information-including information about military exercises, aircrafts, demolition operations and unmarked mines-and take consequent measures conducive to the maintenance of peace, stability and tranquility along the line of actual control in the India-China border areas,
- Jointly combat smuggling of arms, wildlife, wildlife articles and other contrabands,
- Assist the other side in locating personnel, livestock, means of transport and aerial vehicles that may have crossed or are possibly in the process of crossing the line of actual control in the India-China border areas,
- Work with the other side in combating natural disasters or infectious diseases that may affect or spread to the other side,
- Any other way mutually agreed upon by the two sides.

Article III

Border deference cooperation visualised in this agreement shall be implemented through the following mechanisms:

- Flag meetings or border personnel meetings at designated places along the line of actual control in the India-China border areas.

- Periodic meetings between officers of the relevant Military Regions of China and Army Commands of India and between departments responsible for military operations.
- Periodic meetings of the representatives of the Ministry of Defence of the Government of India and the Ministry of National Defence of the People's Republic of China.
- Meetings of the Working Mechanism for Consultation and Coordination on India-China Border Affairs.
- Meetings of the India-China Annual Defence Dialogue.

Article IV

In implementing border defence cooperation and to facilitate contacts and meetings between relevant organisations, the two sides may establish Border Personnel Meeting sites in all sectors, as well as telephone contacts and telecommunication links at mutually agreed locations along the line of actual control. The two sides may also consider establishing a Hotline between the military headquarters of the two countries. Specific arrangements shall be decided upon through mutual consultations between the two sides.

Article V

In order to enhance understanding and cooperation between the border defence forces of the two sides, each side may invite the other side for joint celebrations on major national or military days or festivals and organise cultural activities, non-contact sports events and small scale tactical exercises along the line of actual control in the India-China border areas. In addition, the two sides may also conduct joint military training exercises, at Army level, in each other's country on a regular basis. The theme of such joint exercises will be decided through mutual consultations.

Article VI

The two sides agree that they shall not follow or tail patrols of the other side in areas where there is no common understanding of the line of actual control in the India-China border areas.

Article VII

In case a doubtful situation arises with reference to any activity by either side in border areas where there is no common understanding of the line of actual control, either side has the right to seek a clarification from the other side. In such cases, the clarification shall be sought and replies to them shall be conveyed through any of the mechanisms established under Article III of this Agreement.

Article VIII

The two sides agree that if the border defence forces of the two sides come to a face-to-face situation in areas where there is no common understanding of the line of actual control, both sides shall exercise maximum self-restraint, refrain from any provocative actions, not use force or threaten to use force against the other side, treat each other with courtesy and prevent exchange of fire or armed conflict.

Article IX

The two sides shall implement this Agreement without prejudice to their respective positions on the alignment of the line of actual control as well as on the boundary question.

Article X

This Agreement shall come into force on the date of its signature. It may be revised, amended or terminated with the consent of the two sides. Any revision or amendment, mutually agreed by the two sides, shall form an integral part of this Agreement.

Signed in duplicate in Hindi, Chinese and English languages at Beijing on 23rd day of October month of 2013, all three versions being equally authentic. In case of divergence, the English text shall prevail. For the Government of the Republic of India, For the Government of the People's Republic of China.

Appendices on Jammu and Kashmir

Maharaja's Accession Offer to India

Text of letter dated October 26, 1947 from Sri Hari Singh, the Maharaja of Jammu and Kashmir to Lord Mountbatten the Governor-General of India.

My dear Lord Mountbatten,

I have to inform your Excellency that a grave emergency has arisen in my State and request immediate assistance of your Government.

As your Excellency is aware the State of Jammu and Kashmir has not acceded to the Dominion of India or to Pakistan. Geographically my State is contiguous to both the Dominions. It has vital economical end cultural links with both of them. Besides my State has a common boundary with the Soviet Republic and China. In their external relations and Dominion of India and Pakistan cannot ignore this fact.

I wanted to take time to decide to which Dominion I should accede, or whether it is not in the best interests of both the Dominions and my State to stand independent, of course with friendly and cordial relations with both.

I accordingly approached the Dominions of India and Pakistan to enter into Standstill Agreement with my State. The Pakistan Government accepted this Agreement. The Dominion of India desired further discussions with representatives of my Government. I could not arrange this in view of the developments indicated below. In fact, the Pakistan Government are operating Post and Telegraph system inside the State.

Though we have got a Standstill Agreement with the Pakistan Government permitted steady and increasing strangulation of supplies like food, salt and petrol to my State.

Afridis, soldiers in plain clothes, and desperadoes with modern weapons have been allowed to infliter into the State at first in Poonch and then in Sialkot and finally in mass area adjoining Hazara District on the Ramkot side. The result has been that the limited number of troops at the disposal of the State had to be dispersed and thus had to face the enemy at the several points simultaneously, that it has become difficult to stop the wanton destruction of life and property and looting. The Mohara power-house which supplies the electric current to the whole of Srinagar has been burnt. The number of women who have been kidnapped and raped and makes my heart bleed. The wild forces thus let loose on the State are marching on with the aim of capturing Srinagar, the summer Capital of my Government, as first step to over running the whole State.

The mass infiltration tribesman drawn from the distant areas of the North-West Frontier coming regularly in motor trucks using Mansehra-Muzaffarabad Road and fully armed with up-to-date weapons cannot possibly be done without the knowing of the Provincial Government of the North-West Frontier Province and the Government of Pakistan. In spite of repeated requests made by my Government no attempt has been made to check these raiders or stop them from coming to my State. The Pakistan Radio even put out a story that a Provisional Government has been set up in Kashmir. The people of my State both the Muslims generally have taken no part at all.

With the conditions obtaining at present in my State and to great emergency of the situation as it exists, I have no option but to ask for help from the Indian Dominion. Naturally they cannot send the help asked for by me without my State acceding to the Domination of India. I have accordingly decided to do so and I attach the Instrument of Accession for; acceptance by your Government. The other alternative is to leave my State and my people to fee-booters. On this basis no civilised Government can exist or be maintained. The alternative I will never allow to happen as long as I am Ruler of the State and I have life to defend my country.

I may also inform your Excellency's Government that it is my intention at once to set up an interim Government and ask Shaikh Abdullah to carry the responsibilities in this emergency with my Prime Minister.

If my State has to be saved immediate assistance must be available at Srinagar. Mr Menon is fully aware of the situation and he will explain to you, if further explanation is needed.

In haste and with kindest regards.

Yours Sincerely
Hari Singh

The Palace, Jammu
26th October, 1947.

Instrument of Accession of Jammu and Kashmir State 26 October, 1947

Whereas the Indian Independence Act, 1947, provides that as from the fifteenth day of August, 1947, there shall be set up an independent Dominion known as INDIA, and that the Government of India Act 1935, shall with such omissions, additions, adaptations and modifications as the Governor General may by order specify, be applicable to the Dominion of India.

And whereas the Government of India Act, 1935, as so adapted by the Governor General, provides that an Indian State may accede to the Dominion of India by an Instrument of Accession executed by the Ruler thereof.

Now, therefore, I Shriman Inder Mahinder Rajrajeswar Maharajadhiraj Shri Hari Singhji, Jammu & Kashmir Naresh Tatha Tibbetadi Deshadhipati, Ruler of Jammu & Kashmir State, in the exercise of my Sovereignty in and over my said State do hereby execute this my Instrument of Accession and

- I hereby declare that I accede to the Dominion of India with the intent that the Governor General of India, the Dominion Legislature, the Federal Court and any other Dominion authority established for the purposes of the Dominion shall by virtue of this my Instrument of Accession but subject always to the terms thereof, and for the purposes only of the Dominion, exercise in relation to the State of Jammu & Kashmir (hereinafter referred to as "this State") such functions as may be vested in them by or under the Government of

India Act, 1935, as in force in the Dominion of India, on the 15th day of August 1947, (which Act as so in force is hereafter referred to as "the Act").

- I hereby assume the obligation of ensuring that due effect is given to provisions of the Act within this State so far as they are applicable therein by virtue of this my Instrument of Accession.
- I accept the matters specified in the schedule hereto as the matters with respect to which the Dominion Legislature may make law for this State.
- I hereby declare that I accede to the Dominion of India on the assurance that if an agreement is made between the Governor General and the Ruler of this State whereby any functions in relation to the administration in this State of any law of the Dominion Legislature shall be exercised by the Ruler of the State, then any such agreement shall be construed and have effect accordingly.
- The terms of this my Instrument of Accession shall not be varied by any amendment of the Act or the Indian Independence Act, 1947, unless such amendment is accepted by me by Instrument supplementary to this Instrument.
- Nothing in this Instrument shall empower the Dominion Legislature to make any law for this State authorising the compulsory acquisition of land for any purpose, but I hereby undertake that should the Dominion for the purpose of a Dominion law which applies in this State deem it necessary to acquire any land, I will at their request acquire the land at their expense, or, if the land belongs to me transfer it to them on such terms as may be agreed or, in default of agreement, determined by an arbitrator to be appointed by the Chief Justice of India.
- Nothing in this Instrument shall be deemed to commit in any way to acceptance of any future Constitution of India or to fetter my discretion to enter into agreement with the Government of India under any such future constitution.

- Nothing in this Instrument affects the continuance of my Sovereignty in and over this State, or, save as provided by or under this Instrument, the exercise of any powers, authority and rights now enjoyed by me as Ruler of this State or the validity of any law at present in force in this State.
- I hereby declare that I execute this Instrument on behalf of this State and that any reference in this Instrument to me or to the Ruler of the State is to be construed as including a reference to my heirs and successors.

Given under my hand this 26th day of October, nineteen hundred and forty seven.

Hari Singh
Maharajadhiraj of Jammu and Kashmir State.

Acceptance of Instrument of Accession of Jammu and Kashmir State

I do hereby accept this Instrument of Accession.
Dated this twenty seventh day of October, nineteen hundred and forty seven.

Mountbatten of Burma

Governor General of India.

Reply from Lord Mountbatten to Maharajah Sir Hari Singh 27 October 1947

My dear Maharajah Sahib,

Your Highness's letter, dated the 26th October has been delivered to me by Mr. V.P. Menon. In the special circumstances mentioned by Your Highness, my Government have decided to accept the accession of Kashmir State to the Dominion of India. Consistently with their policy that, in the case of any State where the issue of accession has been the subject of dispute, the question of accession should be decided in accordance with the wishes of the people of the State, it is my Government's wish that, as soon as law and order have been restored in Kashmir and her soil cleared of the invader, the question of the State's accession should be settled by a reference to the people. Meanwhile, in response to your Highness's appeal for military aid, action has been taken today to send troops of the Indian Army to

Kashmir to help your own forces to defend your territory and to protect the lives, property and honour of your people.

My Government and I note with satisfaction that your Highness has decided to invite Sheikh Abdullah to form an Interim Government to work with your Prime Minister.

Yours Sincerely,
(Sd/-) Mountbatten of Burma

Bibliography

Documents

Acceptance of Instrument of Accession of Jammu and Kashmir State, 27 October 1947.

All India Congress Committee, The *Background of India's Foreign Policy* (New Delhi, 1952).

Bhasin, A.S.(ed.), *Documents on Nepal's Relations with India and China 1949-1966* (Bombay, Academic Book,1970); *Nepal's Relations with India and China, Documents 1947-1992*, Vol.1 (Delhi, Siba Exim, 1994).

China Disregards the Colombo Proposals : Attempts to Regain Gains of Aggression against India (New Delhi, 1965).

Chou En-lai's Letter to Prime Minister Bandarnaike of Ceylon Giving Chinese Interpretation of the Colombo Conference Proposal, 19 January 1963.

Chou En-lai's Report on the Works of the Government the First Session of the Third National People's Congress, 21-22 December 1964, *Peking Review*, 1 January 1965.

Defence Minister Lin Piao's Report to the Ninth National Congress of the Communist Party of China, 1 April 1969, *Peking Review*, 10 April 1969.

Deng Xiaoping's interview with Krishna Kumar, 21 June 1980, *News from China*, 24 June 1980.

Documents on Sino-Indian Question (Peking, Foreign Language Press, 1960).

Foreign Affairs Record, Ministry of External Affairs, External Publicity Division, (New Delhi, Government of India).

Foreign Policy of India : Text of Documents 1947-58 (New Delhi, Lok Sabha Secretariat, 1958).

Government of India, Ministry of External Affairs, Kashmir : White Paper Meetings and Correspondence between Prime Ministers of India and Pakistan, July1953-October 1954 (Delhi, 1954).

India-China Conflict (New Delhi, 1964).

India, Military Alliances, 1947-1957 : Text of Documents (New Delhi, Lok Sabha Secretariat, 1957).

India, *Kashmir and the United Nations*, (New Delhi, External Publicity Division, 1948).

India, *Muslims in India*, Ministry of Information and Broadcasting (New Delhi, 1966).

Instrument of Accession of Jammu and Kashmir State, 26 October 1947.

Leading Events in Indo China Relations (New Delhi, 1962).

Letter from Governor General to Maharaja Gulab Singh, 7 January 1847.

Lok Sabha Debates (New Delhi).

Maharaja Hari Singh's Accession Offer to India, 26 October 1947.

Mao Tse-tung, Selected, Works, Vol. 1 (New York, International Publisher, 1954).

Ministry of External Affairs, *China Builds Strategic Road in Kashmir, Sinkiang and Tibet : A Threat to Peace in Asia* (New Delhi).

New Developments in Friendly Relations between China and Nepal, Chinese Peoples Institute of Foreign Affairs (Peking, Foreign Language Press, 1960).

Notes, Memoranda and Letters Exchanged and Agreements Signed between the Government of India and China : White Paper : 1954-1959 (New Delhi, 1959).

Premier Chou En-Lai on International Situation; *Peking Review,* Vol. 15, No. 28, 14 July 1972.

Premier Hua Guofeng's report at first session of the Fifth National Peoples Congress, 26 February 1978, *Peking Review*, 10 March 1978.

Prime Minister Rajiv Gandhi Statements of Foreign Policy (New Delhi).

Report of the Ministry of External Affairs, 1956-1959 (New Delhi, Government of India Publication).

Report, Ministry of External Affairs, Government of India Prime Minister's Statements and Foreign Ministers Statements (New Delhi, 1977-1979).

Report of the Officials of the Government of India and the People's Republic of China on the Boundary Questions (New Delhi, 1961).

Reply from Lord Mountbatten to Maharaja Sir Hari Singh, 27 October 1947.

Resolution, Ministry of External Affairs (New Delhi, 1970).

Resolution of National Conference, 1950.

Resolution of UN Security Council, 13 August 1948.

Selected Speeches of Indira Gandhi, January 1966-August 1969 (Delhi, 1971).

Selected Speeches of Indira Gandhi, August 1969-August 1972, Years of Endeavour (New Delhi, 1975).

Sino-Pakistan Agreement 2 March 1963 : Some Facts (New Delhi, 1963).

Speeches of Prime Minister Lal Bahadur Shastri : August 1965-September 1965 (New Delhi, 1965).

Statement of the Chinese Government Putting forward three-point proposal, 24 October 1962, *Peking Review*, 26 October 1962.

Statement by the Spokesman of the Chinese Ministry of Foreign Affairs, *Peking Review*, 20 August 1963.

Statement of the Chinese Government on the Sino-Indian Border Question, 9 October 1964, *Peking Review*, 16 October 1964.

Statement of the Ministry of Foreign Affairs of China on Sikkim, 11 September 1974, *Peking Review*, 20 September 1974.

Statement of the Spokesman of the Chinese Foreign Ministry on Border incident with India, 3 November 1975, *Peking Review*, 7 November 1975.

Statement of the Foreign Minister Hua at the banquet given in honour of Atal Bihari Vajpayee, *News from China*, 16 February 1979.

Suhrawardy, H.S; Statement on Foreign Relations and Defence (Karachi, Government of Pakistan, 1957).

Text of Joint Communiqués, Lok Sabha Secretariat, *Foreign Policy of India, Text of Documents 1947-1964* (New Delhi, 1966).

The Chinese Threat (Delhi, 1963).

The Question of Tibet (Peking, Foreign Language Press, 1969).

The Treaty of Amritsar, 16 March 1846.

US Central Intelligence Agency, Report on *Heroin in Pakistan : Sowing the Wind* (September 1992).

Vice-Premier China, Yells Statement on Sino-Indian Boundary Question, 21 January 1963, *Peking Review*, 25 January 1963.

World Armaments and Disarmaments SIPRI, Year Book (Oxford, 1974-2000).

Zhao Ziyang on Sino-Indian Relations, *Beijing Review*, 11 October 1982.

Books

Acimovic L. (ed.), *Non-alignment in the World of Today* (Belgrade Institute of International Politics and Economics, 1969).

Akbar, M.J., *India, The Siege Within : Challenges to a Nations Unity* (Penguin, 1985).

Nehru : *The Making of India* (Penguin, London, 1988).

Allen, Douglas (ed.), *Religion and Political Conflict in South Asia* (Oxford University Press, New Delhi, 1993).

Appadorai, A. (ed.), *Selected Documents on India's Foregn Policy and Relations 1947-1972* (Oxford University Press, New York, 1982).

Asghar, Ali Engineer (ed.), *Secular Crown on Fire : The Kashmir Problem* (Ajanta, New Delhi, 1991).

Bains J.S., *India's International Disputes. : A Legal Study* (Asia Publishing House, Bombay, 1962.

Bajpai, U.S.(ed.), *India's Security : The Politico-Strategic Environment* (Lancer, New Delhi, 1983).

Banerjee, D.K., *Sino-Indian Border Dispute* (Intellectual Publisher, New Delhi, 1985).

Bandyopadhyaya, J., *The Making of India's Foreign Policy : Determinant Institution, Processes and Personalities* (Allied Publishers, Bombay, 1979).

Bazaz, Premnath, *The History of Struggle for Freedom in Kashmir* (New Delhi, 1954).

_______*Inside Kashmir* (Murpur, 1987).

Bose, Sumantra, *Kashmir–Roots of Conflict and Paths to Peace* (Vistaar Publications, New Delhi, 2003).

Brecher, Michael, *The Struggle for Kashmir* (Oxford University Press, New York, 1953).

Buzan, B. and Rizvi, *South Asian Insecurity and the Great Powers* (Macmillan, London, 1986).

Chakravarty, P.C., *India's China Policy* (Indian University Press, Bloomington, 1962).

Cheema, P. I., *Pakistan's Defence Policy, 1947-58* (Macmillan, London, 1990).

Chiang Kai-shek, *China's Destiny* (Rov Publishers, New York, 1947).

Cohen, Stephen P., *The Pakistan Army* (Himalayan Books, New Delhi, 1964).

Dalvi, J.P., *Himalayan Blunder : The Curtain Raiser to the Sino-Indian War of 1962* (Thacker, Bombay, 1979).

_______, *India's Changing Villages – Human Factors in Community Development* (Routledge and Kegan Paul, London, 1958).

_______, Elliot, John, *India and China-Asia's New Giants* : *Stepping Stones to Prosperity* (New Delhi, 1995).

Dixit, J.N., *Anatomy of a Flawed Inheritance: Indo-Pakistan Relations: 1970-94* (Konark Publishers, New Delhi, 1995).

Esposito, John L. (ed.), *Islam in Asia: Religion Politics and Society* (Oxford University Press, Oxford, 1987).

Ganguli, Sumit, *The Origins of War in South Asia : Indo-Pakistan Conflicts Since 1947* (Westview Press, Boulder, 1986).

Ghurye, G.S., *Caste and Class in India* (Bombay, 1955).

Gupta, Sisir, *India and Regional Integration in Asia* (Asia Publishing House, Bombay, 1964).

_______, *India's Relations with Pakistan 1954-57* (Indian Council of World Affairs, New Delhi, 1961).

_______, *Kashmir-A Study in India – Pakistan Relations* (Asia Publishing House, Bombay, 1966).

Gupta, P.K., *Economic Development in India and China 1950-53* (New Delhi, 1977).

Hasan, K. Sarvar and Quresh, Khilida (eds.), *Pakistan : Documents on Foreign Relations of Pakistan* (Karachi, 1966).

Hayris, Lilliang Craig and Worden, Robert, L. (eds.), *China and the Third World: Champion or Challenger* (Arburn House, London, 1986).

Hussain, T. Karki, *Sino-Indian Conflict and International Politics in the Indian Sub-continent 1962-66* (Thompson Press, Faridabad).

Jackson, Robert, *South Asian Crisis: India, Pakistan, Bangladesh* (Chatto and Windus, London, 1975).

Jain, R.K. (ed.), *China-South Asian Relations 1947-1980,* Vol. 1 (Radiant, Delhi, 1981).

Jalal, Ayesha *Democracy and Authoritarianism in South Asia : A Comparative and Political Perspective* (Cambridge University Press, Cambridge, 1995).

Ayesha and Sugata Bose, *Modern South Asia-History, Culture, Political Economy* (Oxford University Press, New Delhi, 2005).

Jennings, Sir Ivor, *Some Characteristics of Indian Constitution* (Madras, 1953).

Jetly, Nancy, *India-China Relations 1947-1977* (Radiant, New Delhi, 1972).

Jha, D.C., *Indo-Pakistan Relations 1960-65* (Bharti Bhavan, Patna, 1972).

Johnson, Chalmers (ed.), *Ideology and Politics in Contemporary China* (Seattle and London, 1975).

Karkik, Sanjay and Taneja, Nisha, *India's Exports : The Challenge from China* (Indian Council for Research on International Economic Relations, New Delhi, 1985).

Kaul, B.M. *The Untold Story* (Allied Publishers, Bombay, 1967).

Kaul, T.N., India-China and Indo China (Allied Publishers, New Delhi, 1980).

Kavic, Lorne, J., *India's Quest for Security :Defence Policies 1947-1965* (University of California Press, Berkeley, 1967).

Khera, S.S., *India's Defence Problem* (Orient Longman, Delhi, 1968).

Kohli, Atul, *Democracy and Discontent* : *India's Growing Crisis of Governability* (Cambridge University Press, Cambridge, 1991).

Kukreja, Veena, *Military Intervention in Politics : A Case Study of Pakistan* (NBO, New Delhi, 1985).

Kumaraswamy, P.R. (ed.), *Security Beyond Survival* (Sage Publications, New Delhi, 2004).

Lall, Arthur, *How Communist China Negotiates* (Columbia University Press, New York, 1968).

Lamb, Alasteir, *The China-India Border : The Origin of the Disputed Boundaries* (Chatharo House Essay, Oxford University Press, London, 1964).

____________, *The Sino-Indian Border in Ladakh* (National University Press, Canberra, Australia, 1973).

Lawrance, Alan, *China's Foreign Relations Since 1949* (Routledge, London, 1975).

Laxmi, Y., *Trends in India's Defence Expenditure* (ABC, New Delhi, 1988).

Majumdar, Asis Kumar, *South East Asia in Indian Foreign Policy* (B. Mitra, Naya Prakash, Calcutta, 1982).

Mallik, Dev Narayan, *Postwar International Politics – A Quadripartite Survey* (Veena Mandir Publishers, Muzaffarpur, 1973).

Malviya, H.D., *Peking Leadership :Treachery and Betra*yal (Delhi, 1979).

Mankekar, D.R., *Guilty Men of 1962* (Tulsi Shah Enterprises, Bombay, 1968).

Maxwell Neville, *India's China War* (Jaico Publishing House, Bombay, 1970).

Mishra, Pramod K., *South Asia in International Politics* (Udh Publishers, Delhi, 1984).

Naik, J.A., *The Pak Bomb and Rajiv's India* (National Publishing House, New Delhi, 1986).

Nayak, Pandav (ed.), *Pakistan : Society and Politics* (South Asia Publishers, New Delhi, 1984).

Nettle, J.P., *Political Mobilisation : A Sociological Analysis of Methods and Concepts* (New York).

North, Robert C. *The Foreign Relations of China* (California, 1969).

Palit, D.K., *War in the High Himalayas: India in Crisis 1962* (Lancer International, New Delhi, 1991).

Pannikar, K.M., *India and China* (Asia Publishing House, Bombay, 1957).

Pye, Lucian W., *Asian Power and Politics : The Cultural Dimensions of Authority* (Harvard University, Cambridge, 1985).

Radhakrishnan, S., *India and China* (Bombay, 1944).

Ramakant, *Nepal, China and India* (Abhinav Publications, Delhi, 1976).

Rosen, Stephen Peter, *Societies and Military Power : India and Its Armies* (Oxford University Press, Delhi, 1996).

Rupesinghe, Kumar and Mumtaz, Khawar (eds.), *Internal Conflicts in South Asia* (Sage Publications, London, 1996).

Saijal J.R., *The Unfought War of 1962 : The NEFA Debacle* (Allied, Bombay, 1979).

Sanghvir, R., *India's Northern Frontier and China* (Contemporary Publishers, Bombay, 1962).

Sawney, Rathy, *China's Policy, Intentions and Capabilities* (Institute of Defence Studies and Analysis, New Delhi, 1968).

Singh, Jasjit (ed.), *Kargil 1999: Pakistan's Fourth War for Kashmir* (Knowledge World, New Delhi, 1999).

Singh, Maj. Gen. Sukhwant, *India's Wars Since Independence : General Trends* (Vikas Publishing House, New Delhi, 1982).

Singh, Mahavir (ed.), *International Terrorism and Religious Extremism–Challenges to Central and South Asia* (Anamica Publishers, New Delhi, 2004).

Singh, Rajkumar, *Less Tasty Indo-Nepal Political Relations 1947-1997* (Novelty, Patna, 1998).

__________, *India-South Asia Minus Congress Regimes* (Novelty, Patna, 2000).

__________, *Indo-Pak Nuclear Tension 1974-1998* (Samiksha Prakashan, New Delhi, 2001).

_________, *India's Foreign Policy- The First Study in Continuity and Change* (Samiksha Prakashan, New Delhi, 2001).

_________, *Past, Present and Future of Kashmir* (Gyan Publishing House, New Delhi, 2008).

_________, *India and Pakistan-Social Political and Military Perspectives* (Regal Publications, New Delhi, 2009).

_________, *Global Dimensions of Indo-Nepal Political Relations-Post Independence* (Gyan Publishing House, New Delhi, 2009).

________, *Relations of NDA and UPA with Neighbours* (Gyan Publishing House, New Delhi, 2011).

________, *Contemporary India with Controversial Neighbours* (Gyan Publishing House, New Delhi, 2011).

__________, *Myth and Reality of Terrorism in South Asia* (Kalpaz Publications, New Delhi, 2013).

_________, *Nuclear Power and Politics of South Asia–New Disclosures* (Kalpaz Publications, New Delhi, 2014).

Smith, Wilfred Cantwell, *Modern Islam in India : A Social Analysis* (Ripon Printing Press, Lahore, 1947).

Spear, Percival, *India, Pakistan and the West* (Oxford University Press, London, 1958).

Srinivas, M.N., *Caste in Modern India and other Essays* (Bombay, 1962).

Subrahmanyam, K., *Security in Changing World* (B.R. Publishing Company, Delhi, 1990).

Syed, Anwar, Hussain, *Pakistan : Islam, Politics and National Solidarity* (Praeger, New York, 1982).

Thomas, Raju G.C., *Indian Security Policy* (Princeton University Press, Princeton, 1986).

Trivedi, Ram Naresh, *Sino-Indian Border Dispute and Its Impact on Indo-Pakistan Relations* (Associated Publishing House, New Delhi, 1977).

Verghese Koithara, *Society, State and Security – The Indian Experience* (Sage Publications, New Delhi, 1999).

Verma, S.P., *Struggle for the Himalayas : A Study in Sino-Indian Relations* (Sterling Publishers, Delhi, 1971).

Victor, Cecil, *India : The Security Dilemma* (Patriot Publishers, New Delhi, 1990).

Waseem, Mohammad, *Politics and State in Pakistan* (National Institute of Historical and Cultural Research, Islamabad, 1994).

Wickert, Erwin, *The Middle Kingdom, Inside China Today* (Harwill Press, 1984).

Xinhua News Agency, *China's Foreign Relations : A Chronology of Events* (Foreign Languages Press, Beijing, 1989).

Zaidi, A.M., and Zaidi, S.G. (eds.), *The Encyclopaedia of Indian National Congress* (S. Chand and Company, New Delhi, 1981).

Zingel, Wolfgang Peter and Zingel, Stephanie Lallemant (eds.), *Pakistan in the 1980s: Ideology Regionalism, Economy, Foreign Policy* (Vanguard Books, Lahore, 1985).

Articles in Books, Periodicals and Newspapers

Abraham, A.S., 'China Look Anew at India : Changes in a Shifting Environment', *The Times of India*, 21 July 1985.

Ahmad, Aqueil, 'Science and Technology in Development Policy Opinion for India and China', *Economic and Political Weekly*, Vol.13, Nos. 51-52 December 1978.

Ahmar, Moonis, 'The Role of CBMs in the Post Cold War Era'. *ACDIS, Occasional Paper*, Department of International Relations.

Ahmed, Samina, 'The United States and Terrorism in South Asia: The Lessons of History', *International Security* (2002).

Anand, Vikas, 'China's Hostile Attitudes Towards India', *South Asia Politics*, February 2011.

Anderson Piers, India's Frontlines in the Himalayas', *Reporter*, 3-16 January 1964.

Appadorai, A., 'Where India Faces China', *Foreign Affairs*, 4 July 1959.

Arora, Gulji K., 'Economic Development in China: Some Lessons for India', in M. Rasgotra and V.D. Chopra (eds.), *India's Relations with Russia and China: A New Phase* (New Delhi, 1979).

Bains, J.S., 'India's International Disputes', *Indian Journal of Politics,* Vol. 2, No. 1 (Aligarh, January-June 1968).

Bandyopadhaya, Jayatanuja, 'India-China Relations : Outlook for the Nineteen eighties; *Foreign Affairs Report*, 8 (i), January 1979 (New Delhi, 1979).

Baudrillard, Jean, 'The Spirit of Terrorism,' 2 November 2001.

Bhadrakumar, M.K., 'Taliban's Return and India's Concerns,' *The Hindu,* 28 June 2011.

Bhambhari, C.P., 'The Chinese Aggression and India's Foreion Policy', *Political Science Review,* Vol. 2, No. 2, October 1963.

Bhaskar, Uday C., 'Strategic Implications of the Proxy War', *The Hindustan Times*, 18 August 1998.

Bhattacharjea, Mira Sinha, 'India – China : Into the 21st Century', *Key Issues*, Vol. 2, No. 3, September 1999.

Bhattacharjea, Debesh, 'India and China : Contract and Comparison, 1950-72', *Journal of Contemporary Asia*, Vol. 4, No. 4, 1974.

Bhushan, Bharat, 'Match Fixing Won't Help in Kashmir', *The Hindustan Times*, 21 April 2000.

Byres, T.J. and Peter Nolan, 'Inequality : India and China Compared 1950-70', (London, 1970).

Chai, Trong R., 'China's Policy Towards the Third World in the U.N. General Assembly', *IJPS*, 41 (2), June 1980.

Chellaney, Brahma, 'Hard Words Soft Actions,' *The Hindustan Times*, 29 February 2000.

_________, 'A Perilous Course,' in *Ibid.*, 11 January 2001.

_________, 'Jehad on Jehadi,' 20 September 2001.

_________, 'LoC Stock and Barrel', 31 August 2004.

_________, 'Fighting Terrorism in South Asia: The Lessons of History,' *International Security* (2002).

Chellaney, Brahma, 'An Act of War', *The Hindustan Times*, 18 December 2001.

________, 'Pakistan as Problemistan' *Ibid.*, 8 July 2002.

Dar, A.N. 'Solving the Kashmir Problem', in *Ibid.*, 23 March 1998.

Dar, A.N., 'Need for Cautious Approach in Kashmir,' *The Hindustan Times*, 27 August 1997.

Das, Sitanshu, 'An Overture to China', *The Tribune* (Chandigarh), 14 July 1980.

Das, Tapan, 'Chinese Interest in Kashmir Issue', *The Patriot*, 31 May 1982.

Diwan, Vivek M., 'Perspectives on India-China Relations,' *Third Concept*, Vol. 24, No. 288, February 2011 (New Delhi, 2011).

Dixit, Aabha, 'Developments in Pakistan', *Strategic Analysis*, Vol. XIX, No. 4, July 1996.

______, 'Narco-Power : Threatening the Very Roots of Pak Society', in *Ibid.*, Vol. XIII, No. 15, May 1991.

______, 'Focus on Pakistan's Army,' *The Times of India*, 24 April 1993.

______, Dixit, J.N., 'Clarity on Kashmir,' *The Hindustan Times*, 2 July 1986.

______, 'A Difficult Neighbour,' *Ibid.*, 27 October 1999.

______, 'In the General's Own Words,' *Ibid.*, 2 February 2000.

_______, Three is a Crowd Always,' *Ibid.*, 23 December 2001.

Dieter, Bram, 'Changes in South Asia Intra-regional and External Relationships', *The World Today*, Vol. 34 (London, October 1978).

Doval, Ajit, 'Islamic Terrorism in South Asia and India's Strategic Response' (Oxford University Press, New Delhi, 2007).

_________, 'Outsourcing Terror', *The Times of India*, 18 July 2011.

Dreze, Jean and Amartya Sen, 'India and China', in J. Dreze and A. Sen, *India: Economic Development and Social Opportunity* (Delhi, 1996).

Duara, Prasenjit, 'The Critique of Modernity in India and China', in Tan Chung (ed.), *Across the Himalyan Gap: An Indian Quest for Understanding China* (New Delhi, 1998).

Dutt, Vijay and Ninan Servanti, 'The Route of Discontent', *India Today*, 16-31 July 1978 (New Delhi, 1978).

Dyer, Gwynne, 'The Slow Decline of Terror,' *The Hindustan Times*, 24 August 1998.

Faleiro,Eduardo, 'Reflections on the Republic Day'. *South Asia Politics*, Vol. 10, No. 10, February 2013 (New Delhi, 2013).

Fisher, Margaret, W. and Bondurant Hoan V., 'The Impact of Communist China on Visitors from India, *The Far Eastern Quarterly*, February 1956.

Gandhi Kishore, 'Kashmir-A Holistic Approach', *The Hindustan Times*, 18 October 1994.

Ganguly Amulya, 'Image of Islam', *The Hindustan Times*, 1 October 2001.

Ganguly, Sumit, 'India-China Border Issues, Domestic Integration and International Security', in Frankel and Harding (eds.), *The India-China Relationships : Rivalry and Engagement*.

Ghosh, Ajay, 'Sojourn in China : Impressions of a Technologist', *Amrit Bazar Patrika*, 12 February 1979.

Ghose, S.K., 'Chinese Reactions to the Bangladesh Issue', *Foreign Affairs Report*, 21 (i), January 1972.

__________,'Indo-Soviet Treaty and China', *Journal of IDSA*, 5 (i) October 1972.

Gani, N.B., 'Flaws in India's Kashmir Policy', *The Hindustan Times*, 12 September 1998.

Gupta, Dipankar, 'Communalism and Fundamentalism – Some Notes on the Nature of Ethnic Politics in India', *Economic and Political Weekly*, Vol. XXXVI, No. 11-12, March 1991 (Mumbai, 1991).

_______, 'Tri-Colour Over Kashmir : Territory, People and the Nation State', *The Times of India*, 16 September 1999.

_________, 'Flagging India's Missing Freedom', *The Hindu*, 29 September 2009.

Gupta, Sisir K., 'Islam as a Factor in Pakistan's Foreign Relations,' *India Quarterly*, Vol. 18, No. 3, July-September 1962.

__________, 'Moslems in Indian Politics 1947 – 1960', in *Ibid*, Vol. 18, No. 4, December 1962.

Hah, Chong – do, 'The Dynamics of the Cultural Revolution', *World Politics*, Vol. 24, No. 2 (1972).

Harrison, Selig S., 'India, China and Tibet', *Economic and Political Weekly*, Bombay, 5 December 1964.

_________, 'Troubled India and Her Neighbours', *Foreign Affairs*, Vol. 43, (New York, 1964-65).

_________, 'India-China Relations : From Cold War to Détente', *China Report*, May-June 1976.

_________, 'India and China : A Limited Detente', *Radical, Humanist*, 40 (3), June 1976.

Hers, Peter, 'Nepal between India and China', *Swiss Review of World Affairs*, Vol. 17, No. 6 (September 1967).

Huria, Sonali, 'War on Terrorism in South Asia-Af-Pak and Beyond,' *Institute of Peace and Conflict Studies*, No. 108 (New Delhi, 2009).

Jagmohan, '50 Years of Kashmir's Accession to India.', *The Hindustan Times*, 27 October 1997.

Jain, Girilal, 'Peking and New Delhi: Towards Better Relations', *Ibid.*, 21 April 1976.

Jha, Prem Shankar, 'Subversions in Kashmir', *The Hindustan Times*, 17 July 1999.

_______, 'Where Next with Pakistan'. *Ibid.*, 11 February, 2000.

_______, 'Overcome by a Sense of Betrayal', *The Hindu*, 15 January 2013.

_________, 'That Other Neighbour,' in *Ibid.*, 13 August 2002.

_________, 'Fear and Loathing,' 27 September 2004.

_________, 'A Question of Trust,' 22 April 2005.

Kamath, M.V., 'China's Suggestions on Border Issue', *The Times of India*, 16 September, 1977.

Kao, Teh, 'A Chinese Views on the Mc Mahon Line,' *Eastern World*, 17(2), February 1973.

Kapur, Ashok, 'India and China : Adversaries or Political Partners', *World Today*, London, 39 (3), March 1973.

______, 'India-China Dialogue : Changing Perceptions', *China Report*, 11 (1), January-February 1975.

Kumar, Dilip, 'The Resurgence of the Taliban–Lessons Learned,' *South Asia Politics*, Vol. 6, No. 1 (New Delhi, 2007).

Kumar, Satish, 'Mistakes in Kashmir', *The Hindustan Times*, 24 September 1998.

Kumar, Sumit, 'Pakistan's Jehadi Apparatus : Goals and Methods', *Strategic Analysis*, Vol. XXIX, No. 12, March 2001.

Liu, Leo Y., 'Comparative Nuclear Policies : China and Other Developing Countries, India and Pakistan', *Asian Pacific* (Hongkong), February 1978.

Madhu, Limaya, 'India's China Policy', *The Illustrated Weekly of India*, Vol. XIIX, 12-18 November 1978 (The Times of India Press, Bombay, 1978).

Malhotra, Inder, 'China's Stance on Kashmir', *Ibid.*, 22 February 1990.

Malkani, K.R., 'Agra's Bitter Aftertaste', *The Hindustan Times*, 18 August 2001.

________, 'Inside the Muslim Mind,' *Ibid.*, 13 October 2001.

Marwah, Ved, 'Hostage to Misrule,' *Ibid.*, 16 July 1998.

Masud, Anwarul Kazi, 'Terrorism in South Asia and US Foreign Policy', Paper No. 3292, 5 July 2009 (South Asia Analysis Group, New Delhi, 2009).

Mehta, Ashok K., 'The Truth About the Proxy War,' *Ibid.*, 11 August 1998.

Menon, Madhava N.R., 'Combating Terrorism, and Some Management Issues,' *The Hindu*, 12 January 2009.

Mohanty, Manoranjan, 'China Commentary : Course of Sino-Indian Normalisation', *The Amrit Bazar Patrika*, 19 May 1978.

________, 'Development and Democracy : The Indian and Chinese Experience' in Tan Chung (ed.), *Across the Himalayan Gap* (New Delhi, 1998).

________, 'Chinese Revolution and the Indian Communist Movement', *China Report*, Vol.7, No. 1, January-March 1991.

Muni, S.D., 'Chinese Arms Pour into Nepal', *The Times of India*, 1 September 1998.

________, 'India and China's Global Strategy', *Nagpur Times*, 15 August, 1978.

Nandy, A., 'The Sociology of Sati', *The Indian Express*, 5 October 1989.

Nayar, Kuldip, 'Estranged Neighbour : The Arrogant India', in *Ibid.*, 12 December 1994.

________, 'Deadlock on Kashmir', *The Hindustan Times.*, April 1998.

Palmer, N.D., 'China's Relations with India and Pakistan', *Current History*, 61 (361), September 1971.

Paranjpe, Srikant, 'Dangers of Indo-Pak Confrontation on Kashmir', *The Times of India*, 21 February 1990.

Poole, Peter A., 'Communist China's Aid Diplomacy', *Asian Survey*, Vol. 17, No. 11, November 1966.

______, 'A Question of Semantics : Freedom vs. Independence in Kashmir', *The Times of India*, 25 November 2002.

Prabha, Kshitij, 'Terrorism Challenges Secular Fabric of South Asia,' in Mahavir Singh (ed.), *International Terrorism and Religious Extremism–Challenges to Central and South Asia* (Anamika Publishers, New Delhi, 2004).

Ramakant, 'Nepal's Foreign Policy and China', *India Quarterly*, Vol. XXVI, No. 3, July-September 1971.

Raghavan, V.R., 'Response to Terror,' *The Hindustan Times,* 6 January 1999.

_________'The Right Kind of War', *The Hindustan Times*, 22 March 2002.

Rajeshwar, T.V., 'LoC as the Border', in *Ibid.*, 18 July 1998.

Rashid, Ahmed, 'Taliban, Islam, Oil and the New Great Game in Central Asia' (London, 2000).

_________, 'The Taliban Exporting Extremism,' *Foreign Affairs*, Vol. LXXVIII, No. 6 (November–December, 1999).

Ray, Heman, 'Communist China's Strategy in the Himalayas-Nepal a Case Study', *Orbis*, Vol. 2, No. 3 (1967).

Reddy, Sheela C., 'Globalisation–A Human Rights Perspective,' *South Asia Politics*, Vol. 5, No. 2, March 2007 (New Delhi, 2007).

Rex, Hudson *A*., 'The Sociology and Psychology of Terrorism: Who Becomes a Terrorist and Why ?,' *Federal Research Division, Library of Congress*, September 1999.

Rimington, Stella, 'Terrorism Did Not Begin on 9/11,' *The Hindustan Times*, 8 September 2002.

Sathe, Vasant, 'Unwrapping Kashmir', *The Hindustan Times*, 7 July 2001.

______, 'The Pride of Kashmiriyat, *Ibid.*, 31 January 2002.

Sengupta, Bhabani, 'Waiting for India: India's Role as a Regional Power, *Journal of International Affairs*, Vol. 29, No. 2 (New York, 1975).

_________, 'A Deeply Divided Nation,' in Pran Chopra (ed.), *Contemporary Pakistan–New Aims and Images* (Vikas Publishing House, New Delhi, 1979).

_________, 'How to Avoid War with Pakistan,' *The National Herald*, 13 February 1990.

_________, 'Global Change Cripples Pakistan,' in *Ibid.*, 22 February 1990.

Sengupta, Jayshree, 'Threats to Globalisation,' *The Hindu,* 4 February 2000.

Sharma, Madan Lal, 'World After 9/11', *Third Concept*, September 2007 (New Delhi, 2007).

Sharma, Udayan, 'Kashmir's Anti-National Jammat-e-Islami', *The Sunday,* 2 December 1979.

Singh, L.P., 'The Line of Feud,' in *Ibid.*, 14 November 1998.

Singh, Prakash, 'Militancy from Kashmir to Coimbatore', in *Ibid.*, 23 February, 1998.

Singh, Suman, 'Terrorism in South Asia,' *South Asia Politics*, Vol. 9, No. 2, June 2010 (New Delhi.

Singh, S.K., 'Focus on Kashmir', *The Hindustan Times*, 18 July 1999.

Singh, S. Nihal, 'India-China : Time to Move Forward', *The Statesman*, 22 May 1979.

Steele, Jonathan, 'The Taliban's Wish List,' *The Hindu*, 22 January 2011.

Subrahmanyam, K., 'India's Relations with Her Neighbours', *Strategic Analysis*, Vol. 11, No. 12, March 1987.

Syed, Anwar, 'The Politics of Sino-Pakistan Agreements,' *Orbis* 1 (3), 1967.

Talbot, Phillips, 'Kashmir and Hyderabad,' *World Politics*, Vol. 1, April 1949.

Tan Chung, 'Ageless Neighbourliness between India and China,' *China Report*, 15 (2), March-April 1979.

Verghese, B.G., 'Mythology of Hate', *The Hindustan Times*, 6 June 2002.

Vohra, Pankaj, 'Prospects of a Full–scale Conflict in India's Backyard Are Real,' *The Hindustan Times*, 17 September 2001.

Verma, A. K., 'Radical Islam and Terror,' *South Asia Politics*, Vol. 7, No. 8 December 2008 (New Delhi, 2008).

Verma, Jagdish Prasad, 'If You Wish for Peace, Understand Terrorism,' *South Asia Politics*, Vol. 9, No. 7, November 2010 (New Delhi, 2010).

Victor, Cecil, 'Busting Terrorist Bases no Solution,' *The Patriot*, 18 May 1990.

Warty, B.M., 'The India-China Dialogue : Need to Define Limitations', *The Times of India*, 4 November 1985.

Waxman, Mathew C., 'The Structure of Terrorism Threats the Laws of War,' *Duke Journal of Comparative and International Law*, Vol. 20, May 2010.

Werake, Mahinda, 'China and South Asia in the Eighties' in Shelton U. Kodikara (ed.), *External Compulsions of South Asian Politics* (Sage, New Delhi, 1993).

Wriggins, Howard W., 'Pakistan's Search for a Foreign Policy After the Invasion of Afghanistan,' *Pacific Affairs*, Vol. 57, No, 2 (The University of British Columbia, 1984).

Yahuda, Michael, 'Perspectives on China's Foreign Policy,' *China Quarterly*, September 1983.

Yechury, Sitaram, 'Fundamentally Flawed', *The Hindustan Times*, 25 September 2003.

Zaidi, Mubashir, 'Jehad in Retreat,' *The Hindustan Times*, 20 January 2002.

Zaman Uz Rashed, 'WMD Terrorism in South Asia: Trends and Implications' (University of Bangladesh, Dhaka).

Zhurkin, V., 'India a Great Power', *New Times,* No. 5, 26 January 1956.

Newspapers

The Amrit Bazar Patrika (Calcutta).

The Dawn (Karachi).

The Financial Times (London).

The Hindu (Madras).

The Hindustan Times (New Delhi).

The Indian Express (Delhi).
The Indian Nation (Patna).
The Nagpur Times (Nagpur).
The National Herald (New Delhi).
The New York Times (New York).
The Patriot (New Delhi).
The Sunday Standard (New Delhi).
The Statesman (New Delhi).
The Times of India (New Delhi).
The Times (London).
The Tribune (Chandigarh).
The Xinhua (Beijing).

Periodicals

Administrative Change (Jaipur).
American Political Science Review (New York).
Eastern Economist (Bombay).
Economic and Political Weekly (Bombay).
Foreign Affairs (New York).
Foreign Policy Report (New Delhi).
Illustrated Weekly of India (Bombay).
India Today (New Delhi).
Indian Journal of Political Science (Hyderabad and Meerut).
International Affairs (Moscow).
International Studies (New Delhi).
Pacific Affairs (New York).
Political Science Quarterly (New York).
SAARC News (Calcutta).
South Asia Politics (New Delhi).
Third Concept (New Delhi).
Time (New York).
World Politics (Princeton).
World Today (London).

Index

A

Abdullah, Farooq, 165
  Image as CM, 165
  Election Rigging, 169
  Agreement with Centre
    -1987, 209
Abdullah, Sheikh, 199
  posture on J&K, 200 , 202
  removal, 200
  death, 203
Accession of J&K
  Acceptance , 269-70
  Validity, 158
  Instrument of, 267
  Text of Letter From Hari Singh
    to Mountbatten, 265
Afghanistan Rebels
  diversion to Kashmir, 224
Aksai - Chin
  India Claim on, 86
Article 249
  applicable to J&K, 201
Article 370(J&K), 201
Articles 356-357, 201
Arunachal Pradesh
  China claim on, 86
ASEAN Countries
  India's relations with, 144, 146
ASEAN
  India's Role, 147
    ...Levels, 147
Asia
  in World Politics, 33
Asia-USSR Relationship
  Post WW-II, 33
Assembly Elections
  J&K-2002, 203
Atomic Energy Council, 52

B

Babri Masjid
  Demolition,225
Bakshi Ghulam Mohammad
  (J&K), 200-201
  Govt role, 201
Bhutto, Benazir
  Govt Stance, 166
Bhutto,Z.A.,
  on Kashmir, 165
Bombay Blasts-1993, 225
Border Dispute
  Indo-China, 59
British India Policy
  on Tibet / Sinkiang, 61
British India Treaty
  with China, 60
Bus/Truck Services
  -Indo-Pak, 186

C

Chenab Formula
  Road Map, 188
China
  advantage in geopolitics, 33
  Communist Rule, 34
  adoption of new doctrine, 37
  attitude/image, 46

Military Policies, 137
territorial Limit, 63
- Tibet Treaty - 1951, 66
China (India Perceptions)
Military Doctrine, 127, 133
China
attack on India causes, 129
China
Nuclear Assistance
to Pakistan, 52-53
China Policy Shifts
1963-72, 48
China threat perception
(India), 136
China
Weapons Programmme
..Post Korean War, 47
..Soviet Assistance, 47
China/Pakistan
Aims against India, 137
China-Soviet Relations
post Stalin, 37-38
China-Soviet Union diffusion
- impact, 129
Chinese
Aims / Designs, 45
Communist Information Bureau
(COMINFORM), 31
Constitutional Order
/Amendment on J&K, 201
Conventional Weapons Programme
-Indo-China, 41
Cross :LOC Interactions
- Indo-Pakistan, 187
Cross Border Terrorism
Cross Border Terrorism, 162
Pakistan Role, 163
1988-89, 164
resistance, 179

D

Dalai Lama
- Political Asylum
- India on, 69
Declaration of Friendly
Relations, 29
Dept of Defence
Production, 43

E

European Economic Community
(EEC), 193
Expert Group (Indo - China)
.. meetings, 95
..Third Meeting
-achievement, 95

F

Forward Policy of Nehru
on Indo- China Border, 69
Fundamentalists,216

G

Gandhi Indira
govt relations with China, 77
meeting with
Hua Kuo - Feng, 77
assassination, 84
Gandhi, Rajiv
China Policy, 84
China Visit, 89
Global Village
Concept-Marshall Mcluhan, 235
Globalisation, 234-37
impact, 234-39
resistance to, 238-41
Gujral Doctrine, 175

H

Hexia Gongda Policy of
China in South Asia, 140-41
Huang Hua's India Visit
-1981, 77-78

I

India
Posture on Kashmir, 181
two pronged policy on China, 35
Global Image, 138
wars, 43-44
India/China
status, 136-38
Navy, 139
Military Balance, 140-41

role in Asia, 33
ideological gap, 34-35
diplomatic offensive, 35
Defence related steps, 35
Border Dispute /Talks, 59

India's China Policy, 131
- Suggestions, 141

India's
Defence Planning-1976-77
..thrust area, 44-45
Defence Policy, 41
Defence System
..breakthrough /policy/objectives, 43
..Plans, 44

India's
Negative Projection
by Media, 138
Perception
on neighbours, 125
on China, 129
Strategy elements, 162

Indo - China
Relations issues, 133
Talks
Beijing - 1981, 80
New Delhi -1982, 81
..proposals, 81
Beijing-1983, 82-83
New Delhi-1983, 83
Beijing-1984, 84
New Delhi-1985,85
Beijing-1986, 85-86
New Delhi-1987, 86
Agreement on CBMs, 132, 134
Armed Conflict-Possibilities, 139
Border Divisions, 59
Border talks, 71-72, 88
..background, 72
.. initiation (1981-82),79
..Package deal, 87
Perceptions
.. importance, 135
..negative views/ against China, 140

Indo-China War
-1962, 42 , 70-71
..India defeat causes, 43

Indo-Pak
Dialogue
..Suspension/Resumption, 185
..importance of, 173 .
CBMs, 185

Indo-Pak
War - 1947-48, 154
Relations, 155
Anti-Terrorism Mechanism, 181
Talks Revival-1996, 175

Insurgency
in J&K, 189

Insurgency/Terrorism
(J&K), 189
..Expansion, 206
..impact/aspects, 207

Internationalizing Kashmir
Issue
-Viewpoints, 190
..US on, 190

ISI
and Pakistan Army
Linkages, 172
role in J&K Terrorism, 168,170

Islam
belief, 216
movement, 217

J

J&K
Area, History, 153
Army Civilian Casualty
Figures 2007-2008, 189
Assembly Elections-2008, 186, 188
Elections, 202-203

Japanese Peace Treaty, 35
Policy on, 35

Jehad
and Terrorism, 176
Musharraf on, 172

JKLF, 204
Bombing, 205

Joint Declaration
(Indo - China)
on Principles for Relations
& Comprehensive
Cooperation-2003, 100
Three Phase Settlement, 100
Joint Working Group
-Indo-China
(1989-2003), 89
objectives, 90
Meeting/talks,90-93
Rounds 7/8 , 95
Rounds 9/10, 96-97
Round 11, 97
Rounds 12/13, 98

K

Kampuchean Issue
Indo/China Strategy, 77
Kandahar (Hijacking), 226-27
Karakoram Highway
construction, 130
Kargil War - 1999, 171
impact, 171
Kashmir
importance to India, 154
Problem – Solution
- Importance, 154-55
- views on, 158
Kashmir Assembly Attack
-2001, 223-=28
Kashmir Conflict
dimensions, 178
Khruschev era (USSR), 32
Korean War
Impact on China, 46-47

L

Lahore declaration, 177
Liberalisation
implications, 237
Lok Sabha Elections
-2014, 193
Look East Policy
- India, 142, 144, 147

M

Mao Zedong
on China Policy
towards India, 128
Mao-Tse-Tung
image of human race, 46
Marxist – Leninist
Ideology , 37, 45
McMahon Line, 60-61
Nehru on, 64-66
China on, 66-67
Modi, Narendra
China Visit-2015, 113-16
Image/approach
/vision, 193-94
China Visit-2015, 113-16
Mumbai Bomb Blasts
-2002,230
Mumbai Terror Attack
-2008-(26/11), 186,230-31
Musharraf Pervez
on Terrorism, 171
on Jehad, 172
Posture on Kashmir, 180-81
Muslim
rule and glory, 226
..decline-causes, 220
Muslim United Front, 204

N

Narasimha Rao
on India's Foreign
Relations, 148
Narodnya Volya
(Russian Revolutionary
Organisation), 214
National Security Concept, 40
Naval Exercises
(India) Port Blair, 147
Navy (India)
assistance in Tsunami/
Lebanon-2004-2006, 148
NDA Govt Policy
on neighbours, 145

Nehru,Jawaharlal
on China relations
/ strategy, 124, 127
role in Indo-China Friendship, 33-34
Non Aligned Movement
Chinese Response, 79
Nuclear Explosions
Indo/Pakistan
impact on Relations, 170
Nuclear Tests/Explosion
(India) impact, 177

O

Operation Topaz, 161

P

Pak Change of govts, 188
impact, 188
Pakistan
and Taliban, 229
Pakistan Arguments
on J&K Issue
..India Stance, 174
Pakistan
assessment of Terrorist
Situation, 168
Pakistan Dual Policy
on Terrorism, 180
Pakistan
external threat, 123
Foreign Policy, 159
Militants Objectives, 161
Nuclear Programme, 52
Posture on kashmir, 179
Support to Jehadi Elements, 187
terror outfits, 224
Pakistan Three Pronged
Strategy, 160
Panchsheel Principles, 29, 38
Acceptance/recognition, 29-30
Origin,30
Concept/dimension, 30
Signatories, 33
signing, 65
Post Phase, 65
Parliament Attack-2001, 228
Peace & Tranquillity Agreement
(Sino-Indian)-1993, 97
Peaceful Coexistence, 37, 39
People's Liberation Army
- China, 46
quality vis-à-vis India, 47
People's Republic of China
& India agreement on
..Border Defence Coopertion, 261
..CBM on Military Field
along LAC, 249-56
..Establishment of Working Mechanism
for Consultation & coordination
on India China Border Affairs, 259-61
..Maintenance of Peace on LAC
Indo-China Border, 247
..Political Parameters & Guiding
Principles for Settling Indo-China
Border Questions, 256-58
People's Republic of China, 62
emergence, 62-63
foundation/regime, 36, 45
US aggressive policies towards, 37
Technical Assistance to
Pakistan, 50
Plebiscite Front, 202
Post war Agreement
- Indo-Pakistan, 165
Proxy war - Pakistan, 153, 159

Q

Quiet Diplomacy Kashmir
(UPA Govts), 191
Quran, 217
Quranic Concept of War, 163-64

R

Radical Islam
vs Islam, 217-18
opposition to West, 222
Rao Narasimha (PM)
China Visit-1993, 93

S

Sept 11 2001 Bombings
  impact on Kashmir
    problem, 178, 182
  Indo-Pak relations, 183
Shastri Lal Bahadur
  on China motives, 126
SIMI (Students Islamic
  Movement of India), 231
  operation, 232
Simla Negotiations
  (on Tibet)-1913-14, 60
Sinkiang
  India Policy on, 61
  Chinese Control Over, 61
Sino-Indian Agreement
  - 1954, 29, 38
Sino-Indian
  Relations - 1954, 65-66
    ..Normalisation,74-75
    ..Hostility, 73
    ..Deadlock, 75
  incursions-1956, 66
    -1958, 67
  War- impact, 143
Sino-Pak
  Nexus, 48, 50-51
  Relations, 49-50
Sino-Soviet
  Rivalry, 129
South Asian Regions
  Posture on Kashmir, 192
Soviet Assistance to
  China Weapons
    Programme, 47
  Withdrawal, 48
Soviet Union
  stance Post World War, 31-32
Special Representative (SR)
  Level talks (1to 18)
    -Indo-China-2004, 100-113
SriKrishna Commission Report
  (Mumbai Riots), 225-26
Srinagar-Muzaffarabad
  Bus Service-2005, 186-187
Stalin
  era(USSR), 32
    death, 37
Superpowers
  relations, 31
  Perceptions, 31

T

Taliban, 229
Technical Cooperation
  Programme-India, 149
Territorial Issue
  (Indo China Approach), 67
Terror Attacks India
  - 2010-2011, 232
Terrorism, 163, 206, 212
  perception,proliferation, 208-211
  term, 212
  Causes of, 215
  Theories, 211
  Schools of Thought, 164
  Pakistan Policy-impact, 167
Terrorist , 211
  recruited by Pakistan
    -Nature, 169
  Network-Spread
    -role Players, 169
Terrorist Camps (Pakistan), 172-73
Terror Attacks, 187
The Lost Rebellion, 168-69
Tibet
  India Policy on, 132
  Independence
    - Supporters, 62
  Occupation by China, 64
  Autonomy, 64
  Treaty on British, 60
Training Camp
  of Insurgents,207

U

UN Security Council Resolution
  on Kashmir-1948, 157
    Nehru Role, 157

US on Kashmir Issue, 190
US Pakistan Policy, 157-58
..India attitude to, 158
USA stance
Post World War, 30-31

V

Vajpayee, A.B.,
China Visit - 2003, 100
Govt, 177
Indo-Pak relations
during, 177
Lahore Visit, 177
Vietnamese Intervention
in Cambodia, 76
Visuddhimago
(Buddhighosha), 30

W

War on Terror (US) , 182
Pak impact on, 179
Weapons of Mass destruction, 209
World Politics
India role,144
World War II (Post)
period, 214

X

Xi Jinping India visit
Sept 2014, 110-12